Architecture
Inside Out

Karen A. Franck and R. Bianca Lepori

WILEY-ACADEMY

We dedicate this book to students of architecture and design, past and present

Acknowledgements

Preparation of this book was generously supported by a grant from the Graham Foundation for Advanced Studies in the Fine Arts. Insightful letters of recommendation and ongoing encouragement were extended by our friends and colleagues Galen Cranz, Frank Lyons, and Lynda Schneekloth.

We would also like to thank Sherri Scribner for her detailed comments on draft chapters, Anthony Grimaldi for his patient bibliographical work, Peter Smith for his calm guidance on computers and computer programs, and Francesca Onorati for her thoughtful suggestions and drawings. We are very glad we could rely on Johanna Jacob for her excellent design recommendations and Tony Holmes for his fine photographs and joyful sense of humor. We are grateful to the architects, artists, and teachers who so willingly contributed their work to our effort and to friends who kindly contributed their photographs. Certainly without the warm hospitality and support of Teresa Howard and Shirley van Velden in London, this book would still be in the making.

Special thanks go to Maggie Toy and Mariangela Palazzi-Williams at Wiley-Academy who encouraged us in the best way possible – by almost always saying "yes."

Cover: "Wing Development" (monotype with hand coloring, Ellen Wiener)

First published in Great Britain in 2000 by
WILEY-ACADEMY

A division of
JOHN WILEY & SONS
Baffins Lane
Chichester
West Sussex PO19 1UD

ISBN: 0 471 98466 3

Other Wiley Editorial Offices
New York • Weinheim • Brisbane • Singapore • Toronto

Printed and bound in Italy

CONTENTS

Storefront for Art and Architecture, New York (Steven Holl with Vito Acconci). ABOVE: Street view; BELOW: Study

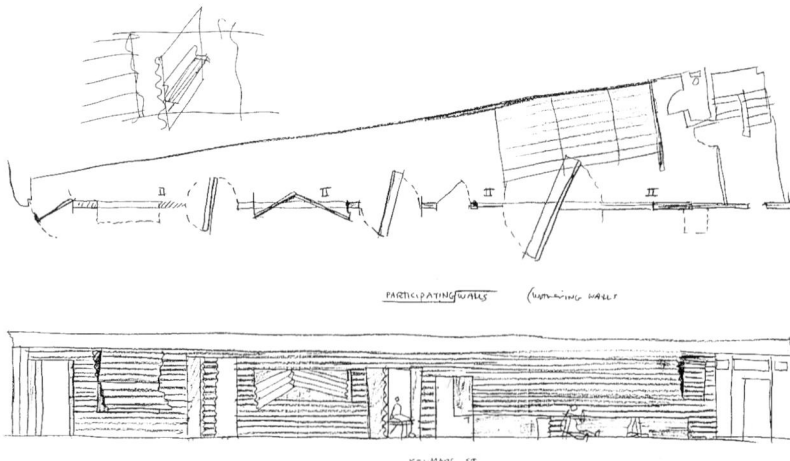

Preface

Karen: Ever since we started talking about this book, we've thought of it as a kind of manifesto, a gentle manifesto. It is a declaration of our views and it's also a way to make "manifest" what seems to be hidden or neglected in architecture.

R. Bianca: The book is our attempt to explain the process of creation that lies behind built form. It's also an attempt to convey the multidisciplinary aspect of architecture because architecture deals not only with materials and form but also with people, with emotion, and with context and the relationships between them. We are entering an era in which everyone has to be involved in what is going on. There is an inner beauty related to individual involvement in making. This beauty comes as a natural consequence of working from your own needs and those of others, with care and participation.

Karen: We describe an attitude to architecture that recognizes the value of people and matter not only as inspirations for design but as the very reasons for architecture to exist at all. The word attitude is very important to me. The first meaning of attitude listed in the dictionary is "the arrangement of the parts of a body or figure; a posture" and the last meaning listed is "a state of readiness of a living organism to respond in a characteristic way to a stimulus (e.g. an object, concept, or situation)." The combination of the two meanings suggests both a bodily position and a readiness to respond in a particular, repeated way. I would say the position we describe is one of openness and the readiness to respond in a receptive way.

R. Bianca: We suggest this openness as a way of approaching design and we recommend it to people who are going to design in the future and to the people they will design for. It is for them that we wrote this book, to make them aware of the complexity as well as the simplicity of the topic. There is something that has been forgotten and that is people and the possibility of transformation. In the making of buildings and goods there lies a great opportunity to reinvent ourselves as well as to shelter and support our activities.

Karen: Writing the book gave me the chance to explore circumstances that have troubled me for a long time. As a social scientist teaching in a school of architecture, I've been only too aware of how much architectural schools stress formal issues over human experience and activity. It is not only these aspects of life that are neglected but also materiality in the broadest sense, including furniture, lighting, materials. So much of the stuff of life, indeed the stuff of architecture, is given cursory attention while a more abstract approach to design is pursued and celebrated.

R. Bianca: Not only this. There is also something important about activity instead of passivity. I am not talking about the activity of producing but the activity of being in charge and acting upon circumstances that need to be faced and transformed. This book offers an opportunity for the kind of meditation that is needed before undertaking such action: it shows that it is possible to step out of assumptions and conventions and figure out what is breathing there, with you and around you. What we describe is a way of approaching design that gives importance to a process of discovery and growth as well as transformation. Maybe it is a feminine way, I don't know. It is a way of embracing circumstances and engaging with what is given, rather than simply projecting or just experimenting with new technologies.

Karen: In writing this book I found the opportunity to describe what I believe, what I consider to be important. I very rarely give lectures any more. I assign readings that I value, I pose questions and problems that I think are key, but I don't state the answer or the resolutions. I don't say directly what my own position is and yet I ask students in one way or another to state theirs. So now, to be fair, it is my turn. Students often ask me in some frustration, "What buildings *do* you like?" They're right. So often I've taken a purely critical stance, indicating in the readings or in the questions I pose what is missing, what is misguided. It was time to propose.

I come from a field – environmental design research – that is founded on the premise that architects, planners, interior designers, and policy-makers need more and better information to guide their decisions. I certainly agree that architects and designers need more information about people and their activities and experiences and how design may support and enhance them. However, even all the best information possible presented in ways architects can easily use will be useless unless architects want it. For that to happen, there needs to be a change in attitude.

R. Bianca: This I also believe. I didn't know I wanted to write this book until you asked me to. Then I felt a responsibility to point out the need for this change and also to say what is generally not said in architecture, to unveil its big myths and to confront its gods and fairies. I felt a sort of obligation to all those people who, like myself, do not feel at home in schools of architecture because there they have to follow somebody else's way which is not their own. This is an abstract way in which one feels incompetent and incomplete. Imagine what it's like when you have to design a museum, or a neighborhood for 750 families, as I had to in my thesis. How do you start out as a student, on your own? You go to the library and start to explore similar projects, trying to figure out what the building should look like. You design by tracking down similar designs. You don't have time to interview, to explore, to experiment with new behavioral patterns.

I know of many people who left architecture school because they found it too abstract and sort of old fashioned at the same time, because they couldn't find the engagement they wanted with reality. They often switch to social or artistic work but then they feel frustrated because in those fields they cannot fulfill their need to create and to transform at the same time.

I also wanted to leave architecture school many times because I couldn't grasp the reason for most of what I was studying. I remember a professor during a review who picked up the drawing of a building elevation and started criticizing it. When the student was able to get a word in, he said, "But you are holding it upside down." The professor said that it didn't matter if the design was good. So what was good design?

Once I started to work as an architect, there was the big shock of seeing how most architects were designing repetitive buildings for others and choosing something very special to live in themselves, often built one or more centuries earlier in the case of Italy. What was good design then?

I was still projecting into the future, playing with new materials and technologies, when I visited Ercolano, the ancient Roman city near Naples. There I felt that everything had been done already, that there wasn't anything to invent anymore in architecture. One could only relearn how to convey an atmosphere, how to play with spatial relationships. Caught by a sort of mutism I went into archeology, to learn from the past, to grasp what makes the difference. I also explored psychology and came to understand that maybe the difference was in the inner architecture of people.

I went to Cairo at that time to visit Hassan Fathy. I remember I was invited for supper one evening. Before sunset he took me to the terrace of his house, near the mosque, and, pointing to its dome, he said, "This is the architecture of the moon." Architecture of the moon? "Yes," he said, "there is a feminine architecture and a masculine architecture." He suggested that I read Swaller de Lubitch's book, *Le Temple de l'homme*, about the proportions of the Luxor temple and Olivier Marc's *Psychoanalise la maison*. Fathy introduced me to the poetics of architecture. I felt I was traveling the same path as he was then, and I feel that many are on that path now. I had to find my way without trying to be what I was expected to be as an architect. For me that was a big inside out indeed.

Karen: Inside out is such a powerful image, one that describes so many different situations. It conveys such a strong sense of movement, of revealing what is hidden. "Architecture inside out" means so many different things that perhaps we should explain what it doesn't mean for us. With respect to a building it could refer to indoor spaces that feel as if they are outdoors. With large expanses of glass, glass roofs and tensile structures, interior spaces can be exposed to light and sky and the distinction between being inside and being outside is lessened. One might also say that a space that is enclosed with walls but no roof, like a courtyard, is another kind of architecture inside out.

It could also mean that a building itself is turned inside out so that what is usually hidden is exposed, as for example, the Pompidou Centre in Paris where the ducts and building equipment are visible on the facade. That is a literal turning of inside out. Steven Holl and Vito Acconci created a curious inside out and outside in with their facade renovation for the Storefront for Art and Architecture in Lower Manhattan. Sections of the wall of the facade, of different size and shape, actually pivot on hinges so that when they are opened, some interior surfaces are outdoors and some exterior surfaces are indoors. The Storefront could be a spatial metaphor for what we mean. So could Eileen Gray's screen of lacquered blocks of wood.

Inside and outside are complementary; each exists by virtue of the other. For me it's important that inside and outside and what they stand for are not treated as oppositional, but as mutually defining. I tend to think of "architecture inside out" primarily as suggesting the process of growth you mentioned earlier, of letting what is there, within the needs of people and within the site, emerge and be transformed. It also gives importance to what too often is not given importance – to human experience and aspirations. And so architecture comes from the inside, from the needs and desires of people, from the site and context.

R. Bianca: We do need to be clear about what we want to convey. If "built form is an image of intention" (you remember this was the title of the conference where we met in Miami), then written form is the image of intention as well. What is our intention in using this title? For me it is to convey being-in-the-oneness, the impossibility of separating, not so much the outside of architecture from the inside, whatever that might be, but the impossibility of separating architecture from its reason to be. It is

Screen (lacquered wood on metal rods, Eileen Gray)

about the responsibility of architecture to aid our evolution and well being. Architecture is designed, built, created, not just given. It is designed, built, created by someone, for someone, each with their own inner architecture. There is no separation between architecture and life.

Karen: The examples we give come from different countries, different time periods, from both well-known and unknown architects, from teaching and practice and everyday life, from artists and writers and poets as well. We haven't separated the different kinds of examples, or the text that connects them, into distinct chapters, or even distinct sections. We've brought them together in a few pages, or even on the same page. This reminds me of the way architecture is experienced: the well-known and the anonymous buildings are side by side. We live at different scales, the scale of the door handle, the chair, the room, the building, and the city all at the same time. We are in a time called the present but we are deeply influenced by the past, and buildings from the past are all around us.

R. Bianca: We see architecture as something to experience, and also as an opportunity to reinvent, to help us avoid being stuck in old patterns hidden within new forms. As Galen Cranz teaches us, even chairs need to be reinvented to suit our bodies. And the reinvention of chairs doesn't lie in our minds or our imagination and fantasy but in the way people are built. Reinventing starts from ourselves, rather than from speculation on possibilities. This relates very much to the title of the book: the inside, our inside, has to come out and be an inspiration for design, rather than design imposing outsides that people have to fit into. "Architecture Inside Out" reminds me of the movie title *Back to the Future*. The future of architecture, and of ourselves, seems to be in finding out what we need and enjoy and who we are, rather than in making something that we have to adapt to and in being what we are forced to be.

Karen: Thinking about our own past, I remember how we started with so much energy and enthusiasm, generating lots of notes and lists of ideas and intentions, but it took a long time to transform this rich but schematic material into solid text and good examples. It's quite amazing how many of the basic themes and issues were there, in those very first lists and notes. And from the very beginning we wanted to speak in different voices, in a more measured descriptive one and in a more directly experiential one, without much of a break between the two.

I know I had difficulty getting inside the book; for a long time I was outside, talking about it, not inside making it. There were long periods of slack and uncertainty, of too many competing projects and being out of touch with each other and with the intentions we had. But we always rediscovered our energy and enthusiasm when we got together. Certainly the book was created from the inside out – from our own experiences and observations, from our collaboration.

We've written what we believe and what we feel. It's been difficult for me to do this because so much writing in academia today does not stem from personally held beliefs and individual experiences but from empirical or scholarly research or from theoretical explorations.

R. Bianca: As you well know, it has been very difficult for me to express myself in English. Italian and English represent two very different ways of thinking as well as speaking.

I have the freedom of not belonging to the academy and I also had the freedom to write long sentences that often did not lead to a conclusion but to assumptions and hypotheses. While writing this book I had to go through the process of cutting them into shorter sentences, of expressing the proper subject, of introducing the missing "transitions." At first I found this rather diminishing and frustrating because the original mood and dynamic of the sentence got lost. I had to learn to be essential, precise, without flights of any sort, and most of all, not to translate myself. Sometimes I found what I ended up writing too obvious, and, as you know, I lost patience. Sometimes simple concepts became complicated because of the process of expressing them in a simple way. I will never forget how you would tell me "Say it," almost as if I were a child unable to write down my thoughts. Then I would say it and everything became simple and clear.

Sometimes I found it contradictory to talk about something rather than doing and proving it. I felt that the slow pace of writing was taking time away from the fast way of producing, time I could not afford. However, this feeling vanished the moment I discussed topics with you and began writing. Then everything felt right.

Karen: Writing was difficult for each of us for different reasons and we didn't make it any easier by revising each other's text so that you could make my voice less academic and I could make yours more precise. We each wrote our own text in our own manner: me mostly in a more academic tone, reading and integrating the writings of others with our ideas, and you in a more intuitive way, often using metaphor and analogy as tools for analyzing and for explaining.

R. Bianca: There was a lot of laughter too – when you locked me in your room and forced me to write or when I pointed out that your sentences were too long and you had no transitions.

Karen: It seems extraordinary but I don't think we ever disagreed in any serious way. We may have had different opinions about the appropriateness of a particular quotation or image or something minor like that, but there was an amazing degree of shared understanding between us. Remember when we saw Ellen Wiener's print at the art show and each of us, independently of the other, thought it would make the perfect image for the cover?

Chapter 1

Inside, Outside, and Inside Out

We all began inside. In the womb, intimately embraced and nurtured by warm flesh, we were contained and held. We could hear, touch, and feel, but we could see only light and shadow. Sheltered closely, we grew. When birth brought us outside, we were still inside: inside the room where the birth took place, inside the building that held the room, in the city or village, in the region, in the country, in the world. From birth onwards, even though we are forever inside some spaces and outside others, the primary experience remains one of being inside.

> . . . the sensation of being surrounded is primary and universal: the maternal womb, the room, the house, the canyon of the street, the final enclosure of the horizon and the hemisphere of the sky – they all belong with us. The primary awareness of being inside is directly reflected in the house as a surrounding shelter and in the semi-spherical sky of the architectural vault or cupola. It is supplemented secondarily by the experience of being outside other things (Arnheim 1996, p46).

What is architecture most fundamentally but the physical demarcation of an inside from an outside? In the earliest times inside may have been within a circle of stones, still outdoors, or under a tent or thatched roof. The dim interior of a hut or a house made of adobe brought relief from sun and wind. Large stones, hewn from quarries and carried long distances, created the interiors of fortresses, castles, and walled cities where inside could be secured and protected from danger. And today with glass and steel or translucent plastic, the density and materiality of the walls between interior and exterior are lessened, the degree of separation between inside and outside reduced. An interior space may seem to be an exterior one, the inside becoming more like an outside.

Whatever the structure and whatever the material, an inside and an outside are created. Even without the presence of a physical boundary, the places we occupy with our bodies, particularly those that we imbue with memories and dreams, become another kind of inside, the *here* of human occupancy and aspiration. Even as we occupy a public place temporarily, possibly a seat on a bus or a train, the space immediately around us, our "personal space", is a kind of inside, an inside we carry with us, bounded invisibly but symbolically (Hall 1966).

"Inside" refers to a physical location that is somehow separated, physically or symbolically, from another physical location that is exterior to it. The locations of inside and outside generate different spatial experiences and, by association, suggest different mental orientations toward the world. And so we use the spatial and experiential distinction between inside and out to help structure our understanding of the world and the actions that follow (Johnson 1987, pp30–7).

Which perspective do we adopt toward the enclosure architecture makes? If it has a roof and walls, do we imagine being within the sheltered *space*, or do we imagine being on the exterior, contemplating the *form* the shelter makes? Inside we are surrounded; we occupy space which has depth and shadow. Outside we are confronted by solidity and its surface. Inside we can smell, *feel*, hear as well as see the space for in-habitation, outside we can see the exterior surface of its shell and perhaps we can *see* into it. Inside we are occupants; outside we are spectators. Inside our movements are restrained by the limits of the space, we are subject to the forces within the space. Outside we are not subject to those forces, our movements are not constrained by those limits. Inside is more hidden, more private, to be discovered; outside is exposed, public, what is shown.

And which perspective do we adopt toward life and experience? For the most part, being outside and so maintaining "objectivity" is the preferred perspective in the West. Starting with René Descartes three centuries ago, that model of understanding is based on an attempt to detach human consciousness from what is considered the brute materiality of bodies and matter. In order for knowledge to be objective, it is believed, we must somehow rise above embodied experience and daily life with its necessarily material and practical aspects.

In this drive for objectivity, or an appearance of it, personal experiences and feelings, dreams, fears, and desires are all considered suspect since they pertain exclusively to the subject and are not observable by everyone. "Objectified" knowledge as reported by those who have used recognized techniques to gather that knowledge, or appear to have done so, takes on more importance and may seem more believable than one's own experience. The world becomes something *out there*, external to oneself – visible, measurable, and reported by others, particularly others deemed to be expert. What is *in here*, interior to the self, is given most credence when it is described in ways that distance the insights from the individual who generated them. They are made to seem as if they come from out there, from some generalized source of knowledge.

Our Western society lives on the surface, caring only about appearances. The outside has become the public facade, what we show or what we can show, the impersonal. It is as if the more public we become, the more impersonal we have to be. Look at the uniforms

Marking an inside

Inside "here"

"House" (cast concrete, Rachel Whiteread)

we have to wear to be socially accepted; we are read for what we look like; it does not matter who we are. We learn at school how to conform. We go through years of unlearning our inner nature and spontaneity to behave as society expects us to behave. To wear a facade has become a form of respect for others but also a form of protection for ourselves. It is also possible that the outside has become so important because gradually, by concentrating on it, we have forgotten what the inside is and we do not remember the road toward it.

The artist Rachel Whiteread understands the significance of the inside, the space of human inhabitation, the space that is more felt than seen. To make its significance apparent to others, however, she transformed the interior of a London terrace house to an exterior – to be seen. Filling the entire house with concrete and removing its walls and roof, she transformed space to form, making an inside (an occupiable space) into an outside (a hard, visible surface). She discovered what was there, bringing it to our attention yet the way she did so made clear that the inside, the space felt but not seen, can be given significance only when it becomes an outside – the solid, the form, the visible object.

The inside, what is perhaps unseen but felt, the realm of embodied experience, of fears and dreams, is too "subjective" to be trusted or valued. The sensory mode that best serves the distancing that objectivity requires is vision: in order to see, one needs no direct physical contact with the circumstance to be known and thus one can be quite removed from it. The senses of hearing, touching, taste, and smell all require closer contact or actual engagement so they are denied importance.

"Objects" are visible, clear, and take no effort to discover. What is inside is not visible or possibly not yet visible; it requires discovering. All too often we remain on the outside, contemplating the building, life, experience, the body (even our own bodies), remaining remote and disengaged. Rachel Whiteread's house, by representing an inside as an outside, is a poetic provocation that actually invalidates the inside. For the imagination this "inside," now transformed into an outside, no longer has an inside and therefore no mystery. The essence of inside, a whisper rather than an assembly of explicit words, is violated when it becomes an outside statement.

Yes, Rachel Whiteread made the silent voice of the inside come through to the outside and yet she made it so solid, only to be looked at, to be experienced as a spectator, never as an occupant. The vulnerability of the white walls and their moldings still belongs to the inside. My instinct is to push the door panel as if the entire surface, rather than being solid, were a flexible membrane. I would push it further to remove it from the shadeless spotlights, to bring back that surface that was once inside to its twilight nature.

For some time now in architecture the outside perspective has taken precedence, giving far more importance to form, idea, and appearance than to ways of living, to occupants' needs, and embodied experience. The tradition of architecture as autonomous objects that is so clearly presented in books, magazines and many buildings today neglects one of the reasons for architecture to exist at all – the enclosing of human activity. Architects remain on the outside, creating the building as object, looking at it but not imagining its inhabitation. They become lonely spectators, projecting their ideas upon the world, rather than discovering what is already there or could emerge.

It is time to be inside, to become participants and not just spectators. Then we will no longer be outside looking *at* or above looking *down* but inside – inhabiting, feeling. This is the difference between claiming an exterior and dominating position, with seeing as the single sense, and occupying an interior, intimate space that cannot be known or understood with a single look.

Outside

Because architects are specialists in the designing of form and the manipulation of materials, because they represent their ideas in drawings and models, which are also physical objects meant to be seen but not occupied, and because they hold the values of appearance and aesthetics so dear, and rightly so, there seems to be a natural tendency to adopt the position of being outside – the position of maker and spectator – and not to assume the position of occupant. Architectural education tends to support this distance from the life that buildings necessarily sustain (or frustrate) by encouraging students to adopt an overriding concern with formal issues, to use professional language, and to present abstract drawings and models, often with no indication of how the spaces are intended to be used.

At the first studio review I ever attended in architecture school, I was a bit unsure what to say about the vacation house a student had designed. So I asked him, "Would you like to live there?" The student looked very surprised and replied, "I never thought about that."

Similarly, the visual presentation of architecture in magazines, monographs, and books depicts few people and few, if any, indications of real, ongoing life. The plans may show the functions of different spaces because the magazine editors or the books' authors, rather than the architects themselves, chose to indicate the functions by number with an adjacent key or by implication, through particular furniture. Numbers, a key, furniture in the drawings, people in the photographs may, indeed, distract from the aesthetic appearance of the architecture. Their absence nonetheless reveals and reinforces a distance from everyday life. What typical contemporary drawings and photographs depict so well is space as a concept, not space as inhabited.

> Within the spatial practice of modern society, the architect ensconces himself in his own space. He has a *representation of this space*, one which is bound to graphic elements – to sheets of paper, plans, elevations, sections, perspective views of facades, modules and so on. The conceived space is thought by those who make use of it to be true, despite the fact that it is geometrical; because it is a medium for objects, an object itself and a locus of the objectification of plans (Lefevbre 1991, p361).

> The user's space is *lived* – not represented (or conceived). When compared with the abstract space of the experts (architects, urbanists, planners), the space of the everyday activities of users is a concrete one, which is to say, subjective (ibid., p362).

Architecture serves both to support and to symbolize patterns of living. Yet that service to something that is not itself architecture is often lost in the drive to create beautiful and memorable form. Too often form and use become oppositional and the purpose of a building, to meet both general and particular needs of occupants, is sacrificed to a concern for appearance or novelty. This assumed opposition between architecture and living, form and use, is clearly apparent in the Modern Movement which split architecture into two camps: architecture as art and architecture only as Functionalism. "On the one hand, 'building could be seen to have nothing to do with art at all' in the famous definition of Hannes Meyer. . . On the other hand to the high priests of aesthetics, the concepts of purpose, use and *telos* were denigrated as a 'mere' utility and architecture was to be viewed as 'autonomous' – answerable only to its own set of rules" (Wilson 1995, p45).

In these cases it's as if the architect has taken a position completely outside life and its many practical requirements, even viewing them with disdain. For Peter Eisenman, ideas about "living" are equivalent to "mindless convenience" and so he trivializes life.

Exterior architecture seems to have interested avant-garde architects at the expense of the interior. As though a house ought to be conceived more for the pleasure of the eyes than for the comfort of its inhabitants. . .
(Eileen Gray in Adam 1987, p233)

"Architectural Outlook" (Collage, Nils-Ole Lund)

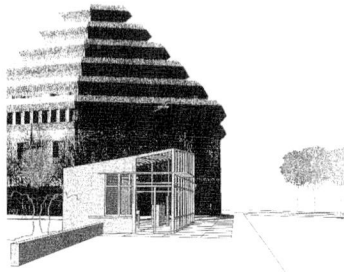

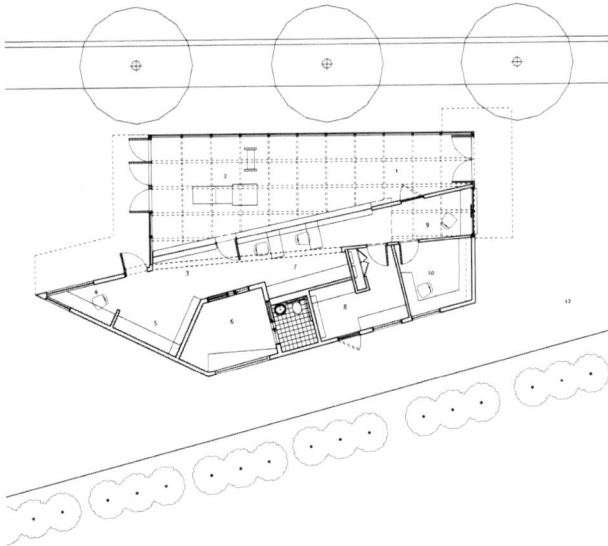

Visitors Center, Museum of Jewish
Heritage, New York (Claire Weisz
Architect + Mark Yoes)
a. Center and Museum
b. Plan of Center

I do not know what my houses mean for living . . . I'm not dealing with mindless convenience: Is the dishwasher next to the sink; is the bathroom next to the bedroom: My work is not about convenience – it is about art. I am not suggesting that people should necessarily live in art – I don't live in art – and I'm not suggesting that people ought to live in my architecture . . . I could do my work without purpose – my best work is without purpose. I invent purpose afterward. . . Who cares about the function? That is the reduction of architecture to mindless convenience. I build to transcend function (in Ellis and Cuff 1989, pp66–7).

When use is denigrated, activities key to a particular building type may be ignored and spaces and equipment for them omitted. When the Museum of Jewish Heritage, designed by Kevin Roche John Dinkeloo Associates in Lower Manhattan, was completed, it contained no space for ticketing, providing information, or conducting security checks, all activities that are part of visiting a museum. Before the imposing, 20,000 square foot, hexagonal museum, expected to attract some half a million visitors annually, could open in September 1997, a separate entrance pavilion had to be designed and built – within six weeks. The resultant free-standing pavilion by Claire Weisz and Mark Yoes houses the necessary support services plus a staff lunchroom, staff restroom, office space, storage, and telephones, all contained within 1,300 square feet. Significantly, designing very quickly for the everyday necessities of museums did not result in a prosaic or mundane building. Not at all. The Visitors' Center, composed of two trapezoidal boxes, one of aluminum and glass (the visitors' space) and one of lead-coated copper (the staff and security spaces), offers light and views to its occupants and, with its different facades and changing roof lines, makes an elegant contribution to the landscape of Battery Park City. Certainly function was no burden on design here.

More commonly, when attention is paid to the body's functional needs, it is a universal body, of standardized measurements and movements, expected to perform tasks in the most efficient and orderly manner possible, with few feelings, with little pleasure from sensation, rather like a machine. As Sherri Scribner has described, this body is clearly depicted in *Architectural Graphic Standards,* in male and female versions in frozen poses, to be accommodated as static, inanimate objects might be, always viewed from the outside (Scribner 1997).

The body so conceived is also portrayed in architectural texts as a motionless, male figure, viewed frontally, arms and legs outstretched, neither very young nor very old, strong and healthy but nonetheless imprisoned within a square and a circle. Originally drawn by Leonardo, the "Vitruvian man", is alone, robbed of life, clothing, objects, surroundings, and relationships. (Which does beg the question of whether this body needs architecture at all.) How well this image reflects the body that is often assumed in design: it too is singular, healthy, and static, perpetually independent of objects, surroundings, and people, apparently with little need for such things.

"Icon #1" (gouache and colored pencil on paper, Nancy Wolf)

There is no doubt that the "body" is curious and slippery. It is conceived of in many different ways, often being called: natural, material, lived, legible, social, medical, architectural, virtual, absent, or obsolete. These are not descriptions of *what* the body is; it is too many different things for that. These are descriptions of *how* the body is, how it is experienced, conceived or used. They are as much descriptions and conceptions as the Vitruvian man. One conception, illustrated by that figure, portrays the body as a physical object, closed and complete in itself, independent of other objects, possibly an inert container for a self that gives it life and directs its movements. This body locks the self away from other selves and from the world, separating the self even from its own body.

As an   object,
the body is unified and closed, complete in itself and ending at the skin, separate from its surroundings and from other objects. It is no more and no less than its materiality. It is solid.

As an   object,
the body is viewed from the outside. When we are or act as if we are outside, the sense we employ is vision since hearing, smelling, touching, all would require that we be inside. The emphasis on exteriority and vision distances us from bodily sensations and needs, and it may give us a sense of power, even an undue sense of power.

The body is at once the most solid, the most elusive, illusory, concrete, metaphorical, ever present and ever distant thing – a site, an instrument, an environment, a singularity and a multiplicity.
(Bryan Turner 1966, p43)

As an   object,
the body is often robbed of life, becoming an impassive and inert "thing," without will or intention. This body is at the heart of Cartesian thinking and, so, of modern architecture, modern medicine, and modern culture in the West generally.

Bodies are both objects and subjects: we point to them and we also point *with* them. The weakness in Cartesian thinking is to give all importance to the body as object. In medicine, this has led to a nearly exclusive emphasis on the physiology, biology, and chemistry of the body, neglecting culture, lifestyle, personality, and habits of diet and exercise (Leder 1998). In architecture the body may be seen only as a source of metaphor or measurement or only as some*thing* to be accommodated, whose needs and experiences as a living, acting person with particular desires may seem to be a burden on design.

Worse yet is when bodies are considered only as consumers, becoming the pretext for endlessly produced goods that represent a designer style or simply the drive towards compulsory production and consumption in fashion and in furniture. Seldom is an attempt made to go further, to think or rethink the object with people's comfort in mind. Seldom are forms and materials chosen to make the object more suitable to the body's comfort; more often the body must adapt to rigid shapes made for the convenience of the producing machine.

Indeed, it is surprising how little industry invests in items that benefit the body

"Lost City" (pencil on paper, Nancy Wolf)

*As buildings lose their plasticity and their connection
with the language and wisdom of the body, they become
isolated in the cool and distant realm of vision. With the
loss of tactility and measures and details crafted for
the human body – and particularly for the hand –
architectural structures become repulsively flat,
sharp-edged, immaterial and unreal.*
(Juhani Pallasmaa 1996, p20)

and how much it invests in objects created for the sake
of design only as appearance, which often signifies social
status. Clients have their favorite categories of product,
from the cheapest to the most expensive and so often,
as a consequence, architects choose among these same
categories as well, choosing on the basis of style and
cost alone. No matter what the cost or the style and
image, we lack products designed from the body. And
so, as occupants, we remain outside, unwelcomed by
the furniture, the building, or its surroundings.

*Large panes of smoky glass reflect the clouds in the
sky and the buildings opposite and the people on the side-
walk. There are no visible openings in the perfectly
smooth walls, no windows, no doorways: all is a hard
silvery surface, reflecting all but revealing nothing. It's
nearly impossible to tell where or how to enter or whether
anyone is presently inside. The building invites neither
the eye nor the body to engage. Coldly, regally, it says
look but keep your distance, observe but do not participate.*

With buildings like this one, we have created environments in the very image of our relationship to
matter, to bodies and to experience: observe but do
not feel. This kind of building exemplifies what
Juhani Pallasmaa calls "architecture of the eye" which
intentionally creates a sensory and mental distance
between body and building, generating feelings of
isolation and detachment.

The material used, glass or another homogeneous and
unarticulated surface, and the lack of reference to the
scale of the human body or attention to details used
by the body, proclaim that materiality is unimportant;
that architecture, like the Cartesian model of knowledge,
is best when it attempts to transcend both bodies and
matter. The building itself, not only its representation
in drawings, tries to be as abstract as possible, free of
materiality as well as life. Nancy Wolf's drawing *Lost
City* contrasts this attitude in architecture with an earlier one that prized a strong sense of materiality, human
scale, and articulated openings. Then we could clearly see doors and windows; we could see inside, we
could easily enter.

Many of us, architects and inhabitants, have become
virtually anesthetized to our sensations. We are distanced
both from past experiences and from present sources
of sensation. Body, self and world are obscured in the
haze of an intermediate realm of logic and rationality.
And so we live largely in a world of objects, relying
heavily on a language of nouns, missing qualities. Look
around the room where you are reading and see all the

items there. Each and everyone has a name, fixing its identity and purpose and distinguishing it from other things with other names and other purposes. A noun is only one thing and not something else. If it is mind, it is not body. If it is matter, it is not psyche. Adjectives call forth qualities, drawing attention to human feelings and experiences. Adjectives suggest states of being and feeling, they bring the listener closer to the situation, even *into* it. We may think we live in a world of nouns, but we depend, for survival, on qualities of living, on being warm (or cool) enough, rested enough, fed enough, energetic enough.

In the drive for "objectivity" insights and information coming from within oneself and from one's own experience are devalued and we are taught either not to draw upon those sources or to act as if we have not. In so many endeavors the self is unavoidably a source and an influence but this is not well acknowledged, explored or mined for its possibilities, for the possibilities of using one's own experiences and predilections in a full and reflective, as well as a critical, way. This often happens in architectural education. Students quickly learn never to say "I like" as a rationale for a design choice. That is both too personal and not sufficiently detailed an explanation. Yet it could be the beginning of a fruitful exploration: Why does the student like the choice she has made? Where does the liking come from? What larger or related concerns and consequences can be uncovered?

In their architectural education students are encouraged to forsake the values of their own culture in order to adopt those of the transnational culture of architecture, which is largely Western with its allegiance to the objectified model of knowledge and principles of design that are expected to be universal in their application. This means a devaluing of their own experiences and those of the very people in their home communities whom they may later serve when they become practicing architects. In reviewing his own architectural education in India, Sanjoy Mazumdar reports that very little attention was paid to social or cultural issues either in the general curriculum or in the studio projects. Religion, customs, family structure, gender roles, and cultural relationships, all being significant issues in everyday life in India, were neglected. Middle-class, largely Western, lifestyles were assumed, such as a reliance on the automobile even though that is the least common means of transport in India. Sanjoy concludes that ". . . the values inculcated alienated graduates from their local cultures and local social and physical contexts" (Mazumdar 1993, p235). What they learned were professional values, which brought them closer to architects from other countries while paradoxically distancing them from potential clients in their own country.

Distancing oneself from one's own experiences creates a distance from the experiences and feelings of others as well. Then we all live "out there," in a world of objectified knowledge, on the outside of our own experiences, with little empathy for the experiences of others. Professionals, including architects, may lose touch with the consequences of their decisions for the lives of others. They learn and use a professional language that is both technical and neutral, or positive, that separates the phenomenon from its impact on people's lives. The terms "urban renewal" and "urban redevelopment" serve that purpose very well: they transform what may be the wholesale destruction of buildings and neighborhoods that have long been home to their residents, that are beloved by them, into something that sounds like a welcome improvement.

Inside

One of the reasons for architecture to exist at all is to house and organize human activities, to support and enhance daily life. The earliest shelter, the tent, the room, the building, the park, the city do this. It seems likely that activities and their spatial

. . . the life of things can be kept at a distance as long as the naming of them with nouns comes between us and their self-presentation. Noun language does defend us against the display of colors, edges, curves, surfaces, hardness, softness, gloom or brightness, fixity, texture, gravity, working in combination and discombination, piling on top and alongside each other making thing as image. (Robert Sardello 1985, p29)

"Piazza" (bronze, Giacometti)

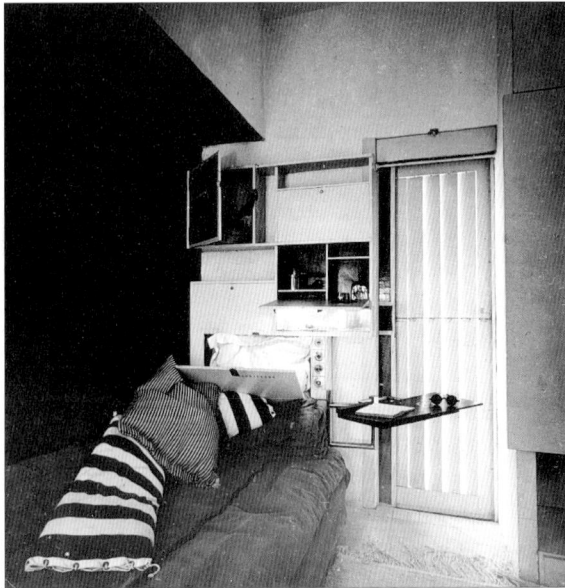

Alcove off living room, E.1027. (Eileen Gray) Maison en bord de mer, Roquebrune, France

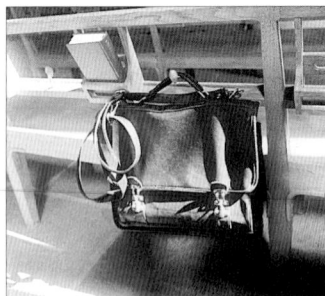

Chapel in crematorium, Stockholm (Gunnar Asplund)

patterns developed first, and that the physical manipulation of space to support and further facilitate the activities followed. "Schools began with a man under a tree, who did not know he was a teacher, discussing his realizations with a few, who did not know they were students. . . Spaces were erected and the first schools became" (Kahn in Lobell 1979, p47).

First there is a human activity, then the need for a kind of place that can support that activity. It is likely that acting in the world preceded building and the pattern of those actions already began to organize space before any structure was built. One example of such a spatial pattern is gathering around a hearth:

> The first sign of human settlement and rest after the hunt, the battle, and wandering in the desert is today, as when the first men lost paradise, the setting up of the fireplace and the lighting of the reviving, warming, and food-preparing flame. Around the hearth the first groups assembled; around it the first alliances formed; around it the first rude religious concepts were put into the customs of a cult. Throughout all phases of society the hearth formed that sacred focus around which the whole took order and shape (Semper 1989, p102).

Human activities need not be a burden as the pejorative use of the word "function" suggests. Instead, they can be inspiring, as they were to Alvar Aalto, Hugo Häring, Hans Scharoun, Gunnar Asplund, Eileen Gray, and Louis Kahn. None of these architects gave use more importance than form, or program more importance than aesthetics; none was a "functionalist" in the sense of compiling numerical spatial requirements to drive the generation of form. Instead, patterns of human actions and experience helped to inspire the creation of form and space. Each of these architects recognized and celebrated the connectedness between everyday life and physical surroundings, and not only designed for that connectedness but drew inspiration and pleasure from it. We recognize their legacy in the work of the contemporary architects described in this book.

In this tradition, the body is treated as subject, not only as object. It is recognized as the necessary and animate *condition* for human life, as giving us access to the world. Through the body we are. We come to this earth with a body that we leave to the earth when we depart. Our souls wear bodies; they can not make themselves manifest without them.

As subjects, our bodies are permeable, fluid, and open to objects, people, surroundings; without them our bodies are incomplete. Our bodies extend beyond the boundaries of our skin, into the world, incorporating what is different from us, depending upon what is different from us.

As subjects, we sense the world in all its richness: we touch, smell, hear and taste it.

As subjects, our bodies are alive, moving, changing, acting with intention and initiative.

Conceiving of the body as subject helps us realize that we build for bodies. A church, a prison, a cup, even a straight boundary wall are all built for bodies (and by bodies). Matter has to be used to supplement, to support, and to protect their matter. Shelters came from the need to protect the body; the door came from the need to let only somebody come through. Clothes, wagons, beds, pencils are designed and produced for the body's use; even mental or spiritual activities involve tools and settings to support the body's comfort as they pursue them. Desks and tables hold the book we are reading or the computer we are writing with; the prie-dieu allows us to kneel in prayer; the mat, the pillow and a specially designed stool aid our meditation. Eileen Gray's alcove includes a pivoting table that swings out over the bed and can be raised for reading or lowered for eating and writing. Storage is provided for the pillows to convert the bed to a couch. In the chapel at Gunnar Asplund's crematorium in Stockholm a small knob on the bench offers a place to hang your bag. Thus design responds to the body's positions, gestures, and belongings and, in doing so, welcomes its presence. And the body, in turn, enjoys engaging with its surroundings – touching them, hearing them, moving parts of them.

Kings never touch doors.

They're not familiar with this happiness: to push, gently or roughly before you one of these great, friendly panels, to turn towards it to put it back in place – to hold a door in your arms.

The happiness of seizing one of these tall barriers to a room by the porcelain knob of its bell; this quick hand-to-hand, during which your progress slows for a moment, your eye opens up and your whole body adapts to its new apartment.

With a friendly hand you hold on a bit longer, before firmly pushing it back and shutting yourself in – of which you are agreeably assured by the click of the powerful, well-oiled latch.

(Francis Ponge, "The Pleasures of the Door")

Conceiving of the body as subject gives credence to our own bodily sensations, helping us to design "from the body outward" as described by Galen Cranz. In her course on the proximate environment at the University of California at Berkeley she reports that students find this approach empowering because "it provides an authentic criterion to evaluate what is good and what is bad. It's authentic because it is grounded in their experience and does not reduce the body to a machine. The concept of the self being an integrated psycho-physical entity honors both the mind and the body (Cranz 1998, p216).

In her design studios at the University of Florida in Gainesville Kim Tanzer assigns full-scale projects – drawing projects and building projects – to help students make connections between their bodies and architecture and between inhabitants' bodies and architecture. After the students have made full-scale drawings with which they paper the floors and walls of the school or build full-scale enclosures, they and their critics can no longer take in the project merely by looking in one direction with their bodies immobile. They must move and look first in one direction and then in another, up and down.

The projects stimulated a high level of emotional response in the school, which Tanzer speculates was generated by the size of the drawings. "By their sheer size, the projects demanded a response, and a bodily response" (Tanzer 1992, p321). She and

*Full scale studio project
(Professor Kim Tanzer,
University of Florida,
Gainesville)*

*Door handle, Rautatalo Office
Building, Helsinki (Alvar Aalto)*

the students became very personally involved and vulnerable. Visiting critics in the built project "floated around the space, found it difficult to focus comments, to act professorial. They tried to find a place to lean, a view from which to see the project, the students. Finally they settled in" (ibid.). Tanzer concludes that full-scale projects remove the usual opportunity that work in miniature provides to dominate the world through vision. They also seem to reduce the usual objectivity, abstract language, and distance of the teacher and the visiting critics. They can no longer remain outside the architectural object, as spectators; they are now inside it, as participants.

The alternative Pallasmaa poses to architecture of the eye is one that stimulates all the senses, including the basic orienting system of the body. "A building is encountered; it is approached, confronted, related to one's body, moved through, utilized as a condition for other things. A building is not an end in itself; it frames, articulates, gives significance, relates, separates and unites, facilitates and prohibits. Consequently, basic architectural experiences have a verb form rather than being nouns" (1996, pp 44–5). With this approach to design, embodiment and materiality are embraced and movement, activities, and sensations become sources of design ideas. Then matter, all kinds of matter and its manipulation, becomes a rich resource for creating *qualities*. While architects most certainly design form and space, they also, necessarily, design form and space with qualities that affect the senses of touching, hearing, smelling as well as seeing.

It's hot and humid. The light is harsh and bright on the kind of summer afternoon one fears that the sun may never set. I enter the cool, dim foyer of the silent villa and walk toward the marble stairs but pause before I reach them. I lean on to the freshly plastered wall. Standing up, I lie against the wall, pressing one hot, wet cheek and then the other and then my forehead against its cool velvet surface, the color of fresh creamy milk. I run my hands along it. It is deeper than velvet and far cooler, not completely flat but slightly molded so that I feel its shape, its flesh. Its softness invites my embrace.

Some qualities may be described by nouns like the types of material used – concrete, bronze, wood, steel, and glass. But these may have been modified in order to create particular sensations: the concrete polished and the bronze tarnished, the glass etched or bent and the plaster shaped and smoothed. To design certain qualities requires careful observation of the site – how the sun will enter the building on winter mornings and early afternoons, where one might view the sun rise or the sun set, where one might hear the sea or avoid the sound of trains.

Architecture is given life and spirit by all the qualities that touch the human senses and the human soul: by light and color, sound and texture, by expansion and compression of space, by view and prospect. These might be considered literal qualities created by the manipulation of materials and space, but they can go beyond the literal to touch our souls. Architecture outside makes vision the primary, even the only sense and a distant observer the primary condition. Architecture inside whispers of intimacy, of one's closeness to the enclosure it always makes.

To grasp this, we may need to rediscover our own embodiment and our own bodily sensations by moving to another level of experience – to one of qualities and not only of things. We can touch surfaces, or imagine what they would feel like if we could touch them – the roughness of brick, the smoothness of marble, the grain of wood, the curve of the door handle. We can take off our shoes and feel the floor and the stairs and the grass under our feet. We can watch the light and shadow play in the room as a cloud passes across the sun and feel the coolness that comes with dusk after a hot day. We can sense the rhythm of our movements as we walk down the stairs. We can see colors without calling out their names. We can smell the asphalt after it has rained or the dust during construction or the sea air. We can feel the parts of our bodies that meet the chair. We can listen carefully and, after the fire engine's siren dies down, we may hear the cooing of two mourning doves.

In her course on stairs at the University of Pennsylvania Nadia Alhasani has students walk up and down different kinds of stairs barefoot, paying attention to the sensations in their feet and their whole body (Alhasani 1996). Galen Cranz conducts a series of experiential exercises to increase sensory awareness in her course at Berkeley on the proximate environment. In her seminar at the New Jersey Institute of Technology, "Bodies and Matter: The Erotics of Architecture", Karen begins each class with a deep breathing meditation followed by a short discussion of what the students experienced. The course also includes critiques of buildings from an experiential, embodied, perspective and silent walks through campus during different kinds of weather when students attend to sounds, smells, and other visceral sensations. Another possibility is what Murray Schafer calls a "soundwalk" to explore the soundscape of a given area with a map that draws the listener's attention to particular sounds and ambiances; it may also include eartraining exercises: the pitches of different cash registers or different door bells could be compared (Schafer 1977, p213).

In experiencing the world more fully and more sensuously, we experience its animism. Animism is the acknowledgement and experience of a world alive, a world with interiority, a world with anima. Animism offers an alternative to objectification and distance in two ways: it gives significance to our bodily sensations and so to the world around us and it gives an interior life back to objects and surroundings (and to ourselves). It restores the insides to the outsides.

> I think seeing architecture as animate is the key to connecting the dualities of life: self/other, inside/outside, mind/body. Seeing something as animate does not have to imply imbuing it with a religious spirit. It is a way to awaken perception, to see relationships and associations more clearly. It provides a way to interact with the environment and to realize the physicality, the matter, of the place. When we walked around the campus and noticed how things felt around us, we were seeing life as animate, with actions, feelings. . . the hard ground, the soft mud, the singing birds, the strong wind (Roxanne Tsirigotis, New Jersey Institute of Technology, Spring 1997).

When we move through space with a twist and turn of the head, mysteries gradually unfolding, fields of overlapping perspectives are charged with a range of light – from the steep shadows of bright sun to the translucence of dusk. A range of smell, sound, and material – from hard stone and steel to the free billowing of silk – returns us to primordial experiences framing and penetrating our everyday lives.

(Steven Holl 1996, p11)

Inside the world

The human mind is not some otherworldly essence that comes to house itself inside our physiology. Rather, it is instilled and provoked by the sensorial field itself, induced by the tensions and participations between the human body and the animate earth. . . By acknowledging such links between the inner, psychological world and the perceptual terrain that surrounds us, we begin to turn inside-out, loosening the psyche from its confinement within a strictly human sphere, freeing sentience to return to the sensible world that contains us. (David Abram 1996, p262)

Archetypal psychologists James Hillman and Robert Sardello recommend recognizing that the world, and not just ourselves, has subjectivity and that the soul of the world and the soul of the individual are inseparable. We can respond to the world not just with our minds, but also with our hearts, turning them toward, and even *into,* the world. And so we can become sensitive to "the displayed intelligibility of things, their sound, smell, shape, speaking to and through our heart's reactions, responding to the looks and language, tones and gesture of the things we move among" (Hillman 1982, p84).

In her landscape architecture course at the State University of New York in Buffalo Lynda Schneekloth adopts the idea of *soul work* from Hillman and Sardello. Lynda says, "The soul work is highly theoretical but it's tied to the world. . . I think this approach allows us to bring the worlds of ideas and the worlds of places and real things together in a way that we can establish a relationship." She asks students to visit, observe, reflect upon and then represent ordinary places in the vernacular landscape, particularly those that are usually ignored and "distressed," like the space under an elevated highway (Schneekloth 1998).

In her course syllabus Schneekloth writes, "Our work will be to listen to these landscapes and understand them – their origin, their reproduction, their condition and their possibilities. You are asked to enter into a conversation with these landscapes to understand what they say to us about their being, their imagination." In Lynda's class students take the side of the world; they try to sense the feelings of the place they are observing and possibly intervening in. They are consciously pursuing acts of perception that are participatory, that allow the place itself to "speak."

Listening transforms the relationship between designer and place, between designer and client. Listening doesn't mean a literal interpretation of the place's or the client's spoken messages nor a response to their explicit wants but rather the ability to understand, as Louis Kahn would say, what they aspire to. In these terms design, rather than being the projection of individual egos, is the process through which places become what they aim to be, for the people who are going to inhabit them. Designers thus become facilitators as well as directors of an orchestra; knowing the nuances of each instrument, they can lead the musicians towards the best expression of each piece.

Inside Out

"The more obvious process of living is a giving forth rather than a taking in. Living is ceaseless expression; ceaseless substitution, the putting of one thing into many forms both of action and of thought. . ." (Stokes 1978, p162).

Not only is the experience of being inside primary, so is the process of bringing forth what lies within. What is speaking but the outward expression of a thought or a feeling from within? The same is true of composing a song, of creating a dance, a drawing, or a building. Indeed, the process of making manifest what we imagine or what we desire is continuous, occurring all the time, as we speak, as we decide what meal to prepare and do so, as we choose to have a cup of tea or to go for a walk, as we write this book. These are quite obvious expressions of particular intentions. Inside out at an individual level is also the manifestation of psychological states: what one does or how one arranges one's surroundings or where one chooses to live may reflect emotional circumstances (Howard 1993). This is true on a collective level as well: our cities and towns embody the values and intentions common to our time and culture.

While individual designers and architects may share those values and intentions or work with clients who hold them, they also necessarily draw upon their own personal experiences, usually stored in the form of mental images, in making design decisions. These images may come from childhood, from places one has visited, and from architecture one admires. In her research Frances Downing has found that the images architects draw upon carry emotive, experiential, and objective information. Images with a strong emotive aspect refer to places where the designer has experienced intense feelings such as being comforted by the place, being grounded by it or feeling elevated in some spiritual way. Images that are experiential have strong sensual content, of light, of texture, of color, of scale. Objective information refers to more formal design features and physical properties (Downing, forthcoming). While the particular content and the specific place vary, certain kinds of places are frequently described: the secret place, the ancestral place, places of comfort, places of activity, places of desire.

Since architects do, necessarily and usefully, draw upon personal experiences and images in designing, it makes sense to make the use of such images more explicit in architectural education. In the design studios she teaches at Texas A&M University Downing often chooses a thematic memory appropriate for the project at hand and asks students to draw a sketch of a place where that kind of experience occurred. For a project on housing for non-traditional households, the thematic memory she chose was "contact and retreat." After remembering and drawing a place where they had experienced contact and retreat, students completed a series of drawing and analytic exercises, generating material and then a diagram for developing the project.

One of Frances's own memories of contact and retreat is sitting under the table in her grandmother's kitchen while others were talking or cooking around her. In this image she finds the contrasts of small/large, under/over, dark/light, separate/together. The image suggests spaces where you can be near but not directly part of an activity, where your presence is screened but not hidden, where you can control your participation without being remote. Frances finds that in her own design work, she frequently creates spaces with these features – alcoves, window seats – places where people can experience what she experienced under the table.

In a seminar called "Architecture for Utopia" at the New Jersey Institute of Technology, Karen also asks students to draw upon their own subjectivity in an explicit manner: to "dream an impossible or a possible alternative to circumstances that currently exist" and to present that dream in a story with images (Franck 1998). By omitting any specific requirement for what the stories should cover and by using free writing techniques that require continuous, non-stop writing with no erasing and no crossing out, students are encouraged to delve into their own experiences, their own wishes and fears.

The stories students write express and stimulate strong emotions; they touch parts of our minds that more rational and directed forms of knowing do not. Mariano Alemany wrote in the prologue to his story: "I fear that which claims to be true, rational, and absolute for it is also devoid of feeling" (ibid., p126). The stories are indeed imagined but they nonetheless convey withering critiques of current circumstances, much as science fiction does. While the project draws upon personal experiences and feelings, it is not a means of exalting one's own subjectivity. The themes and conditions the stories depict are fully appreciated by others and resonate with their own experiences, as demonstrated by the sadness and humor expressed by students when the stories are read aloud.

Some students portrayed the architect/planner as a solitary, isolated figure, who seems totally removed from daily life with little understanding of people or their needs. In Chris Menchin's "Memoirs of an Aging Xyster," a visionary finds the last untouched piece of land on earth and there he constructs a city, but fearful of the time when people will actually come and inhabit it, he withdraws into a small cubicle in the ground. In other stories buildings become sentient and autonomous of human action or inter-

The mental image is a self-portrait of secret wishes and desires, as well as ground for common cultural (and, claim some, species-wide) values and assumptions. . . The mental image presents a personal biography as well as a vehicle for the designer to manipulate future projects.
(Frances Downing 1992, p313)

"Grandmother's Kitchen" (Frances Downing and Tom Hubka)

. . . the movement goes
from the narrower
embrace of my empirical
human world and its
personal concerns
towards archetypal events
that put my empirical
personal world in a more
significant frame.
(James Hillman 1973,
p112)

vention. In Matthew Evans's "No One Asked the Building" a building transforms itself immediately after construction is complete, becoming far more beautiful than what the architect had designed. As the greedy developers seek to take full credit for this event and to exploit it, they begin to hear a deafening noise from the building that nobody else can hear. Lloyd Stephenson, who lives in Newark, imagined a community where the homes and public space are fully integrated so that families no longer live in isolation in a hostile environment but in close relationship to each other.

Exploring one's own subjectivity can be a path to understanding the experiences of others. Frances Downing points out that in working with clients architects discuss and share their mental images with the client and the client may do the same with the architect (Downing 1994, p237). Moving from the personal to the collective is central to "placemaking," a collaborative process outlined by Lynda Schneekloth and Robert Shibley (1995). All participants – professionals and inhabitants – draw upon their own individual experiences and knowledge and, through extended dialogue, generate plans for change that are derived from an understanding of people-in-that-place. The plans for change come in large part from the personal and also the shared knowledge of the place-dwellers themselves, rather than from the "expert" or "objective" knowledge of professionals.

What emerges from collaborations between architects and clients may well be a place that neither of them envisioned originally. Such was the case with the Jagonari building in East London. Once a group of Asian women had recognized the need for educational resources in their neighborhood, they approached Matrix Architects. Working with the architects in a participatory manner, the client group brought in images of buildings they preferred, went on site visits and made a special tour of buildings made of pink brick to choose the brick they wanted. Scale models with movable pieces allowed the group to compare alternative arrangements of spaces.

After initial consultations with Matrix, the Jagonari group chose a more substantial building with more of its own identity than the unassuming, single-story, prefabricated one they had originally envisaged. The decision to have a more significant presence on the street came from the group's participation in the design process: ". . . their confidence grew; they felt more comfortable taking space in the world and they moved towards a more emphatic statement" (Grote 1992, p164).

Jagonari is a four-story building with a distinctive street facade, an interior courtyard and a two-story day care building in the back. The grilles on the external elevation were designed to protect the windows and doors while adding to and acknowledging the Asian identity of the building. Connections are made to both European and Asian cultures with two kinds of lavatories and, in the kitchen, with a high-level western sink and a shallow, floor-level eastern sink. The solid front, the grille-covered windows and the protected courtyard give women a feeling of security while the colorful facade still marks their presence.

What architects design is not so much form or space as it is *experience*, or rather a variety of experiences that will vary according to the time of day, the season, the activities and events occurring and the characteristics, roles and positions of the inhabitants. To envision the desired experiences in advance, architects draw upon information from their own lives, from clients who are commissioning the work, future occupants, published sources, and visits to buildings of the same type. Many architects do considerable research before and during the design process to gain insight into the very particular needs of the people who will be using the spaces. To understand the needs of birthing mothers who are not constrained by the space, furniture and routines of hospitals, Bianca interviewed women who had given birth at home.

a

b

Jagonari, London (Matrix Architects)
a. Street front
b. Courtyard

With the information she gathered, she was able to design a space and furniture that could answer those needs and yet be located within a hospital setting.

For the Paimio Tuberculosis Sanatorium in Finland Alvar Aalto took careful account of the horizontal position of the patient, lying in bed, drawing upon his own experience of being a patient and on experiments he conducted. Radiators were arranged to give heat mainly to the foot of the bed, so the patient's head did not receive direct rays. The location of the windows allowed the patient, when prone, to see out. To avoid noise, one wall was sound absorbing and wash basins were designed so that the stream of water from the faucet hit the porcelain at a small angle and so caused little noise (Aalto in Schildt 1998, p103). Opportunities for patients to enjoy a view out the window from their beds are now incorporated into other health facilities, as in the Vidar Clinic in Sweden designed by Erik Asmussen.

In working with nurses and doctors on the design of the Lambeth Community Health Centre, London, Cullinan Architects learned that day patients at similar facilities often feel very anxious at the end of the day that the drivers of the vans who take them home will leave them behind. To prevent these feelings from developing, the architects designed the day room so that patients would have a direct view of the building's entrance. As it turned out, drivers frequently come into the day room and join the day patients for a cup of tea before taking them home. Perhaps it is the clear connection from entrance to day room, as well as the general warmth of the building and its occupants, that created this new pattern.

In visiting buildings of the same type as the one being designed, time and attention are needed to notice desirable or undesirable conditions and circumstances. Taking on the roles of future occupants, empathically or literally, allows one to experience the building from their perspective. In preparing to design Woodlands, a nursing home in London, Sunand Prasad worked two shifts in an existing nursing home and experienced, for those extended periods, the pungent smell of urine and the harsh sounds of walkers on linoleum floors or other hard surfaces. For Woodlands Prasad selected carpeting that is not heavily absorbent, that is easy to clean and that muffles the sound of walkers and of equipment. He also designed four different gardens, each closely connected to patients' rooms to ensure that the scent of flowers and plants, which varies over the course of the day and evening and seasonally, and the sounds of birds are part of the experience of patients, staff, and visitors.

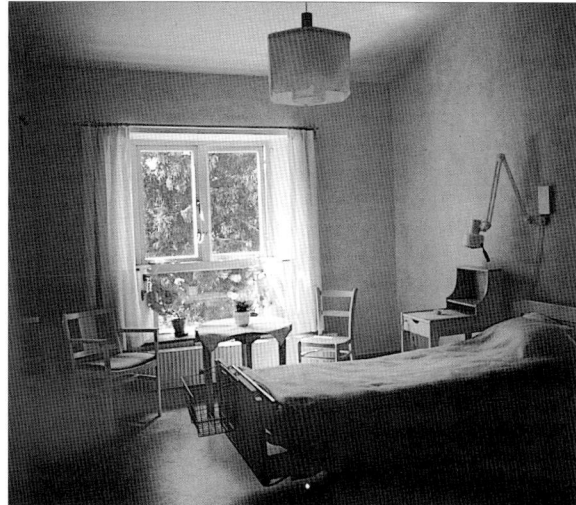

Patient's room, Vidar Clinic, Jana, Sweden (Erik Asmussen)

Garage/greenhouse, Orient, Long Island (A/B Studio)

The process of designing from inside out facilitates the emergence of what is hidden or obscured. For this to happen architects and designers need to listen, to uncover, and to let things happen: ". . . we want to examine things and allow them to discover their own forms. It goes against the grain with us to bestow a form from the outside, to determine them from without, to force upon them a way of any kind, to dictate to them" (Häring in Wilson 1995, p18). What is hidden may lie within the experiences and aspirations of the clients, the users and the architect and their collaboration; it may be within the pattern of activities to be supported by the design; or it may be within the site. It was from a rediscovery of what was already there in the social and built fabric of the community of Manteo, North Carolina, that Randy Hester (1993) was able to help preserve the key qualities of the town. Faced with the need for economic revitalization and redevelopment, residents were keen to maintain some of the original character of their community. Rather than determining which were the best-looking or the most historic buildings and spaces, Hester helped the townspeople discover those places that were important to their daily lives and to the social fabric of the community.

Among the places townspeople ranked most important were: a local drugstore and soda fountain frequented by teenagers and elderly citizens; the Duchess Restaurant where residents go for morning coffee and political discussions; and a gravel parking lot near the waterfront which people visit everyday to check out the tide and the daily catch and where community festivals are held. Although hardly noticeable to a professional architect, a developer or a visiting tourist, these everyday places were central to the residents' idea and use of their town and so they were kept and, after redevelopment, added charm and color to the town. However, because they were so ordinary and because they were so much taken for granted by the townspeople themselves, the importance of these everyday but "sacred" places was obscured; it took effort and work to uncover their significance.

Very often municipal officials and developers who choose a site for redevelopment may have little idea what is already there – possibly small but thriving businesses and committed residents. Penelope Coombes and her company, The People for Places and Spaces, in Sydney, Australia, take on the task of discovering the hidden identity and potential of a community that can then be built upon and promoted in future development. When there is conflict among the parties involved, Penny and her staff explore what is beneath the public positions, finding that there are solutions that will address each party's concerns once these concerns are uncovered.

What is already there in a neighborhood may be quite obvious – a building, a park, a streetscape – but neglected, its potential unrealized, its aspirations unfulfilled. In Cincinnati, Ohio, Maureen Wood recognized the possibilities inherent in buildings in her community. With the establishment of the Women's Research and Development Center, she has been able to transform the abandoned but very much loved Garfield School into housing with a community center and a future day care center and has embarked on a similar transformation of another empty school. Of course, redevelopment occurs all the time, in almost all cities. What is particular to the process of inside out is creating from the potential of the site and the needs of local residents.

And if the site is empty? There is hidden potential then as well. What if it is wooded, immediately adjacent to a railway line and station, yet the location for a new church? Many of the competition entries for the Myyrmäki church and parish center in Vantaa, Finland, placed the church as far as possible from the railway, thus using up the wooded land. In contrast, Juha Leiviskä boldly placed the church as close to the railway as he could, leaving as much wooded space as possible on the other side. Tall, solid walls protect the church from the noise of the railway, less than 15 meters from the altar; the walls on the other side are more open – to light and trees and grass. What had seemed a liability of the site was transformed into its asset.

Drawing only from personal experience or precedents published in magazines and books, or redeveloping only with a concern for profit, without discovering the needs and desires of people and site leads to built solutions that are merely products. Impersonal, inert objects, they speak only of individual experience, created by projecting subjects. The process of creating from inside out, however, speaks of individual and collective experience because the process itself is the subject, because it includes people as well as time and space and place. This process also includes tensions and struggle; behind those clean sheets of paper with their neatly drawn ink lines there is a complex story with its frustrations and its compromises. Creating from the inside out encompasses all the emotions of relating, including joy, something architecture is about as well.

Remember the boy at the end of A. Tarkowsy's movie *Andrei Rubliev*? The czar sends his men to the country looking for someone who can build a bell for the city's church. In the desolation of the war-torn land, one young boy stands up, saying that he will. Once he is taken to the city, a feverish process starts: metal objects are brought to him to be cast; people are hired to work under his guidance. Andrei Rubliev, the icon-painter monk who has kept a vow of silence for many years, follows the process from far away. The casting completed, the bell appears in all its shining splendor, but will it ring? People and authorities share this moment of suspense. Lifted up to the tower, the bell tolls and the joyful sound resonates throughout the town. As the citizens, overwhelmed by excitement, celebrate, the boy bursts into tears. Rubliev approaches him and, breaking his vow of silence, whispers, "You have made an entire city happy and yet you cry!" "I never built a bell before," the boy replies.

The process of creating from inside out is tension because it is an exploration of the unknown. Each project asks for a reinterpretation of existing parameters, for a reinvention of the means to perform existing roles. It is tension because it is a search for balance among resources, needs and purposes, because it is more than a participatory event: it is the struggle of new forms becoming manifest.

To the Greeks techne *meant neither art nor handicraft but, rather, to make something appear, within what is present, as this or that, in this way or that way. The Greeks conceive of* techne, *producing, in terms of letting appear.* (Martin Heidegger 1977, p335)

References

Abram, David. *The Spell of the Sensuous: Perception and Language in a More than Human World*. New York: Pantheon, 1996.

Adam, Peter. *Eileen Gray: Architect/Designer*. New York: Abrams, 1987.

Alhasani, Nadia. Defying dreams and gravitation: On the making of stairs. In *Triangulating the Bodies of Architecture: Proceedings of the 1996 ACSA Northeast Regional Meeting*. Buffalo, New York: State University of New York at Buffalo, 1996.

Arnheim, Rudolph. *The Split and the Structure*. Berkeley: University of California Press, 1996.

Cranz, Galen. *The Chair: Rethinking Body, Culture and Design*. New York: Norton, 1998.

Cuff, Dana. Through the looking glass: Seven New York architects and their people. In Russell Ellis and Dana Cuff (eds) *Architects' People*. New York: Oxford University Press, 1989.

Downing, Frances. Conversations in imagery. *Design Studies* (13)3: 291–319, 1992.

Downing, Frances. Memory and the making of places. In Karen A. Franck and Lynda

H. Schneekloth (eds) *Ordering Space: Types in Architecture and Design*. New York: Van Nostrand Rheinhold, 1994.

Downing, Frances. *Remembrance and the Making of Places*. College Station, Tex.: Texas A&M University Press: forthcoming.

Franck, Karen A. Imagining as a way of knowing: Some reasons for teaching 'Architecture for Utopia.' *Utopian Studies* 9 (1): 120–41, 1998.

Grote, Jamie. Matrix: A radical approach to architecture. *Journal of Architecture and Planning Research* (9) 2, 1992.

Hall, Edward. *The Hidden Dimension*. Garden City, New York: Doubleday, 1966.

Heidegger, Martin. Building, dwelling, thinking. In *Basic Writings*. New York: Harper & Row, 1977.

Hester, Randolph T. Sacred structures and everyday life: A return to Manteo, North Carolina. In David Seamon (ed) *Dwelling, Seeing, and Designing: Toward a Phenomenological Ecology*. Albany, New York: State University of New York Press, 1993.

Hillman, James. Anima. *Spring: An Annual of Archetypal Psychology and Jungian Thought*, 113–147, 1973.

Hillman, James. Anima. *Spring: An Annual of Archetypal Psychology and Jungian Thought*: 97–133, 1974.

Hillman, James. Anima mundi: The return of the soul to the world. *Spring: An Annual of Archetypal Psychology and Jungian Thought*, 71–93, 1982.

Holl, Steven. *Intertwining*. New York: Princeton Architectural Press, 1996.

Howard, Teresa. Inside out or outside in? The boundary between the emotional and physical environment. Paper presented to Group-Analytic Symposium, Heidelberg, Germany, September 1993.

Johnson, Mark. *The Body in the Mind: The Bodily Basis of Meaning, Imagination, and Reason*. Chicago: University of Chicago Press, 1987.

Leder, Drew. A tale of two bodies. In Donn Welton (ed) *Body and Flesh: A Philosophical Reader*. Malden, Massachusetts: Basil Blackwell, 1998.

Lefevbre, Henri. *The Production of Space*, trans Donald Nicholson-Smith. Oxford: Basil Blackwell, 1991.

Lingwood, James (ed) *House: Rachel Whiteread*. London: Phaidon, 1995.

Mazumdar, Sanjoy. Cultural values in architectural education: An example from India. *Journal of Architectural Education*, 46(4): 230–9, 1993.

Pallasmaa, Juhani. *The Eyes of the Skin: Architecture and the Senses*. London: Academy Editions, 1996.

Ponge, Francis. *Francis Ponge: Selected Poems*, trans C.K. Williams, John Montague and Margaret Guiton. Winston-Salem, N.C.: Wake Forest University Press, 1994.

Sardello, Robert J. Saving the things or how to avoid the bomb. *Spring: An Annual of Archetypal Psychology and Jungian Thought*: 28–41, 1985.

Schafer, R. Murray. *The Tuning of the World*. New York: Alfred A. Knopf, 1977.

Schildt, Goran (ed). *Alvar Aalto, In His Own Words*. New York: Rizzoli, 1998.

Schneekloth, Lynda H. Unredeemably utopian: Architecture and making/unmaking the world. *Utopian Studies* 9(1): 1–25, 1998.

Schneekloth, Lynda H. and Robert G. Shibley. *Placemaking: The Art and Practice of Building Communities*. New York: John Wiley, 1995.

Scribner, Sherri. *Lived Body Architecture: An Argument for Lived Bodies in Architecture and an Exploration of Women's Lived Bodies in Society*. Masters Thesis in Architecture. Newark, N.J.: New Jersey Institute of Technology, 1997.

Semper, Gottfried. *The Four Elements of Architecture and Other Writings*, trans Harry Francis Mallgrave and Wolfgang Herrmann. Cambridge: Cambridge University Press, 1989.

Stokes, Adrian. *The Critical Writings of Adrian Stokes*, vol. 2. London: Thames & Hudson, 1978.

Tanzer, Kim. Scale problems. In William Porter, Michael Dennis and Steven Grabow (eds) *Architectural Education: Where We Are*. Washington D.C.: Association of Collegiate Schools of Architecture, 1992.

Turner, Bryan S. *The Body and Society: Explorations in Social Theory*, 2nd edn. London: Sage, 1996.

Wilson, Colin St. John. *The Other Tradition of Modern Architecture: The Uncompleted Project*. London: Academy Editions, 1995.

*Vietnam Veterans' Memorial,
Washington D.C. (Maya Ying Lin)*

Chapter 2

From the Body

We walk down the path, descending along the shiny black granite wall. At the beginning the wall is very low; as we move further along, deeper into this shallow bowl, the wall becomes taller and the bowl deeper as the number of names increases over the course of the war. As the wall increases in height so it towers above us, we feel smaller, overshadowed by it. Its polished surface reflects us back: our bodies are layered over the engraved names of those missing and those who died.

Perhaps we search for a name we know and trace the letters with our fingers. The wall feels cool and damp after the recent rain. Next to us a woman reaches up, stretching her arms above her head and makes a rubbing of the name she has found. Beyond her a family crouches down, posing in front of the name they have found as a young man takes their picture. Some leave mementoes in the earth at the foot of the wall – flowers, notes, medals, articles of clothing, photographs. We proceed up the path and the wall gradually decreases in height as the number of names decreases. The architecture moved us as we moved with it, touching it, touched by it.

Maya Ying Lin must have designed the Vietnam Veterans Memorial in Washington D.C. envisioning the body as subject, while others envisioned it as object, adding to her memorial a statue of three GIs peering out from the trees. Perhaps Maya Lin recognized how much we live from our bodies: *from* because human perception and action extend outward from the materiality of flesh and organ and bone to items and sources of sensation that exist outside the boundaries of the skin. *From* because the body is the center of human experience with relationships born, maintained and changed to other entities. Our relationship to all else is structured from the position, location and attributes of our bodies.

It is from the body that we orient ourselves in the world. "Here" is where our bodies are located in space and "there" is some distance from them. The distance between the two is often described as the length of time it would take our bodies to get there, moving by foot or transport. Left and right, up and down, front and back, large and small, above and below are all defined in relation to our bodies. Many measurements used in architecture were originally derived from measurements of parts of the body – a foot, a yard of three feet or the size of a brick as what the hand could hold. Many abstract structures for thinking and understanding also originate in bodily experiences of perception, movement, and interaction with physical objects. These structures or "image schemata" include verticality, containment, balance, blockage, attraction, cycles and center–periphery (Johnson 1987). We experience these structures in our encounters with the environment and then we project them on to other situations, as metaphors, to organize shared understanding and knowledge. So, for example, we understand that an increase in quantity is oriented upwards. Our ways of inhabiting the world, physically as well as psychologically and intellectually, extend from our bodies outward.

What can we learn about bodies and their relationships to architecture if we think

The body, indeed, is where it all begins: as soon as one wonders what, where, or who one is, one looks to the body for the answers. (Ernst van Alphe 1993, p114)

and design from the body? We may recognize that as subjects our bodies are porous and permeable, taking in sensations, matter, and information as well as producing them. We may begin to realize that our bodies are so very open to objects, people, and surroundings, that they extend beyond the boundaries of our skin, into the world, incorporating into them what is different from us. We may notice that bodies are always moving (even ever so slightly), changing, and acting with intention and initiative (even when lying in bed and refusing to get up). And we may rediscover how much architecture, at many different scales, can support and enhance the activities and experiences of daily life.

Bodies: Open, Inclusive

Because the body is bounded by its skin and given solidity by bones, muscle, and organs, it is easy to think of it as solid, closed, and complete in itself, independent of its surroundings. Indeed, the development of a sense of self and a self-image depends upon the existence of distinct boundaries clearly demarcating self from other (Gallagher and Cole 1998). The development of modern science, technology and medicine required a conception of the human body as an independent entity; that conception is now commonplace. It takes effort to notice that bodies are also porous and permeable, deeply connected with their surroundings and with others and, by themselves, incomplete.

We can see this clearly at an organic level of survival. We breathe in oxygen from the world and exhale carbon dioxide; we eat food and drink water from the world and eliminate waste into it. The exchange between inner and outer is continuous. And to reproduce, at least in the traditional manner, semen must come from the male body, enter into the female body, fertilize an egg which develops into a fetus in the womb and the process culminates in the birth of an infant from the female body. And it is from the mother's breasts that the child receives milk.

We learn what our bodies are able to do only through interacting with objects and other bodies. We learn basic manual and bodily skills and more advanced ones through the repeated manipulation of objects. Think of shaking a rattle, feeding oneself, picking a flower and later learning to throw and catch a ball, to paint or to play an instrument. To learn new skills we pay careful attention to the gestures and motions required and to the manipulation of objects.

We learn that we are bodies at all and what kinds of bodies we are from external sources of information

The human body is radically open to its surroundings and can be composed and decomposed by other bodies. Its openness is a condition of both its life . . . and its death. . .
(Moira Gatens 1996, p110)

We continually project the body into the world in order that its image might return to us: onto the other, the mirror, the animal and the machine, and onto the artistic image. (Susan Stewart 1993, p125)

since we can never see our own bodies as complete entities; we can only see them in parts. So the feeling of unity, that we are whole and integrated, comes from a three-dimensional body image. To develop that image, we require information from the world – from mirrors, from viewing other bodies, from interacting with others (Schilder 1950).

On an everyday basis we depend upon our surroundings to know where we are and where to go. To live and to thrive we take *in* information through all our senses: often our bodies are so open to sights, sounds, smells, and feelings from the environment that they feel almost transparent. We become so intent on the view of the sunset, on the music playing, on the person sitting opposite that we are unaware of our own bodies. For all intents and purposes, our bodies vanish from our awareness as we attend to the world. At other times we become so deeply involved in an activity, in reading, in designing, that we forget our bodies and our surroundings. But neither sensory experiences nor activities have to be this intense for our bodies to be "absent" (Leder 1990). Over the course of a normal day we are so busy with the routines and objects of daily life that our conscious experience of embodiment recedes into the background then as well.

Our bodies are also open to their social and cultural surroundings. Before birth, our parents anticipate what we shall be like, what we shall do and they are part of a culture which shapes those expectations. When we are born, we are immediately dressed and held and washed and fed in ways that are particular to that culture and that historic period and its material objects. And as we grow up, the culture continues to shape our bodies through food, medicine, medical care, physical activities, through clothes, furniture, and buildings as well as through systems of belief. Indeed, the body's needs, movements, and desires are as much cultural as natural, perhaps more so. Even referring to nature and culture as separate phenomena is problematic: the body is an interaction of the biological and the cultural, each twisting around the other, much like a double helix (Casey 1993, p220).

The culture is not only "out there;" it is in here, in our manner of moving and sitting, in our ways of eating and greeting each other. Do we use forks and knives or chopsticks? Do we shake hands or bow? How do we wash our clothes? In the river, leaving them to dry on the rocks? In a small canal, rubbing the clothes on stone platforms, as in Taxco, Mexico or in washing machines? Do we hang the clothes to dry, even in places where

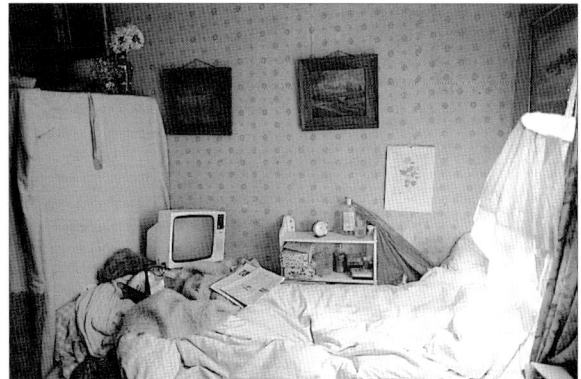

The absent body

Laundry, Taxco, Mexico

there is plenty of electricity or do we rely on machines to dry them? Each of these customs requires different positions and movements as well as different surroundings and objects. The mosque provides water and seats for washing the feet before worship; the Catholic church provides holy water for dipping one's fingers and crossing oneself. Rugs on the mosque floor make it softer for the movements of kneeling and touching one's forehead to the floor during prayer; the prie-dieu offers a place to kneel and a place to rest one's elbows as the hands are clasped.

We learn ways of inhabiting space in infancy and childhood and we may continue those ways regardless of the design of our surroundings. Among Bedouin families who have built their own concrete houses in Israel, the couches, chairs, and tables that furnish the houses are not used by family members; they rely instead on the traditional mattresses and pillows for sleeping and sitting. The shades on windows are often kept closed throughout the day; nothing is hung on the walls and residents never lean against them, still treating the house like the traditional tent (Sebba 1991).

Culture is in our very flesh, bones, and muscles. Just as diet shapes our health, life-long bodily patterns of moving and staying still shape our muscles and skeleton. In the cultures of Japan and China where women eat a diet low in fat, high in fiber and soy, there is a lower incidence of breast cancer than in Western cultures with their high fat and low fiber and soy diet. In Africa and India where people regularly squat as a manner of sitting, people's posture differs from that of people in the West who sit continuously for long periods of time in chairs. Squatting stretches the spine so people who squat experience less compression of the spine, which is therefore more likely to be erect with the head balanced and little strain placed in the neck muscles (Cranz 1998, p96).

While we are shaped by the cultures we live in, we also shape them through the invention and modification of customs, institutions, and artifacts. Many of those artifacts are extensions and enhancements of our own bodily capacities (Scarry 1985). The written, printed, and now the recorded word, libraries, photography, Xeroxing and the computer all extend and expand human memory and communication. The wheel and then carts, carriages, automobiles, trains, airplanes, and space craft have increased the speed and reach of human movement. Eyeglasses, microscopes, and telescopes increase the power of vision. Using these inventions modifies our way of engaging with the world and with others.

As we use them, many of these objects become extensions of the body; with them our bodies expand beyond the limits of our skin, beyond the limits of our reach. Because the preconscious system of motor capacities that facilitate movement and posture, which is called the body schema, is open and flexible, it can integrate the body with the environment and with these objects (Gallagher and Cole 1998). The body schema allows us to orient ourselves in the world. It is a set of directions and demarcations, organizing the ever-changing I–world relationship (Strauss 1966, p155). Unlike the body image, which has relatively clear and fixed boundaries, the body schema extends outward, incorporating objects into it so it may include the flute one is playing or the computer one is using or the cell phone one is holding.

With the body image, and with our anticipation of future movement and our memory of past movement, bodily experience extends beyond the skin. "When I go toward the door of the lecture hall, I am already there, and I could not go to it at all if I were such that I am not there. I am never here only, as this encapsulated body; rather, I am there, that is I already pervade the space of the room and only thus can I go through it" (Heidegger 1977, p335).

Through our patterns of inhabitation, space becomes a kind of possession. Each

Bodily existence floods over into things, appropriates them, infuses them with the breath of life, draws them into the sphere of daily projects and concerns. (Bernd Jager 1985, p219)

of us is centered in an invisible but nonetheless significant "personal space" or three-dimensional bubble that ensures that a certain distance will usually be maintained between our body and those of others. In determining how much space is required for a room, it is vital not only to know the number of people who will occupy it but the kinds of activity they will engage in and, accordingly, what spatial relationships they will maintain with each other in that culture – intimate, social, or public (Hall 1966).

Through our daily pattern of activities and routines, we acquire the space we are using; we lay claim to it by our actions. Sometimes this acquisition is actual and the space we occupy becomes visibly "ours;" other times it is only experiential. For instance, in the public realm of buses or theaters, the places we occupy are recognized as "ours" as long as we are there and we may mark these territories with bags or coats if we leave them for a short period. Spaces we occupy for longer periods, such as workspaces and certainly dwellings, we often personalize with mementoes, decorations, and many other belongings. The places where we live become the most intimate and most visible extensions of our bodies (Scarry 1985) and of ourselves (Cooper Marcus 1995).

Although many of the spaces we occupy on a daily basis do not belong to us, our inhabitation of them, often on a regular basis, makes them familiar, sometimes sufficiently so that we traverse them almost unconsciously, no longer aware of their features. In some sense we incorporate these places and spaces into ourselves. "Inhabiting is an act of incorporation; it is a situation of active, essential acquisition. Incorporation is the initiative of the active body, embracing and assimilating a certain sphere of foreign reality to its own body" (Lang 1985, p202). As the body seems to spill over into the tools and other objects it uses, so too it spills over into the spaces it occupies.

The degree of reciprocity between body and space varies. The body is receptive to the cues the environment presents, sensing how open a space is to intimate inhabitation and engagement. Designed space encourages certain ways of occupying it and certain attitudes and may forcefully discourage others. Oscar Newman (1980) has demonstrated one example of this in residential settings: spaces outside individual dwellings that are physically or symbolically designated as private and that are visible from the dwelling's interior encourage residents to have feelings of responsibility so that they personalize, maintain and use the space intensively and in doing so develop relationships with their neighbors. In contrast, residential spaces that are anonymous, apparently belonging to no one, encourage no feelings of responsibility, generate no patterns of intensive use and feel alien to residents.

Like tools, architecture compensates for human frailties and extends and enhances human capacities. As shelter it has long been able to keep rain, wind, sun, heat, dust, and cold out or to retain heat and coolness. With more recent technological inventions for heating, cooling, and ventilating, buildings can moderate and fine tune the climatic conditions in each room. And so built environments of all kinds help keep the body alive, healthy and comfortable. More recently, buildings may provoke illness caused by the toxic fumes emitted by some materials in rugs and furniture or by the inadequate circulation of fresh air. This indicates not only how open the body is to its surroundings but also how vulnerable.

Because of this basic vulnerability of the body, sheltering allows the myriad activities of daily life to take place; in many climates preparing food, eating, sleeping, conversing with others, and staying healthy would all be extremely difficult in the absence of shelter. This is well demonstrated by the problems that occur when shelter is destroyed through war, hurricanes or earthquakes. There are other pursuits – ones involving long periods of concentration, the use of delicate materials, furniture or equipment or special

As I go through the day, my extended body ebbs and flows, now absorbing things, now casting them back onto shore. . . I live in bodies beyond bodies, clothes, furniture, room, house, city, recapitulating in ever expanding circles aspects of my corporeality.
(Drew Leder 1990, p35)

conditions – that could not take place at all in many regions without shelter. In these ways, architecture serves as protection, an outer garment, shielding human embodiment and human activities from external conditions and creating more favorable internal ones. Thus we can be and do what we could not be or do otherwise.

Architecture goes further in responding to the human body: it extends and enhances human capacities. From the tower we are able to see, and be seen, over long distances and to send messages over those distances by voice or other means. Think of the muezzin calling people to prayer from the minaret or Paul Revere at the start of the American Revolution lighting the lantern on the steeple of the Old North Church in Boston to warn of the British arrival, "one if by land, two if by sea." With the amphitheater and then the theater, the concert hall and stadium, architecture allows a large number of people to see and hear a performance, all at one time. With the school, the university and the library, large numbers of people have access to formal knowledge. With the museum, many more people can enjoy works of art or other treasures once accessible only to a privileged few. With the use of steel structures and elevators architecture allows a great many people to live, or work, on a small piece of land and so to make intensive use of resources and amenities in that location.

With the fortress, castle, and casbah, architecture provided security from hostile groups and a means of defense against them. With the caravanserai, the inn, the hotel and the motel architecture has long offered places for travelers to stay. For centuries the soup kitchen, hospital, orphanage, homes for the poor or the elderly have extended care and support to those in need, in quite definite bodily need. By virtue of their purpose, their management, and their design, these types of places adopt very different attitudes towards the bodies of their occupants and the physical environment. At best hospitals, schools, and special needs housing give support and care; the prison and asylum remove people from the larger population and control their actions; places of leisure such as parks, restaurants or theaters offer a retreat and escape from daily routine and commitments (Franck 1994). Other building types – libraries, universities, some state and national capitols — accommodate practices that enable and empower.

Bodies: Moving, Making Space

The living body moves. Some movements are easily observable like shaking hands, waving good-bye, standing up or walking; climbing stairs. Others are smaller, subtler – smiling, changing one's gaze, tapping a finger, breathing. Others are not observable to the human eye at all and occur internally: digesting, the heart beating, blood moving through the body. Even thinking is movement; experiments show that thoughts trigger neurons in the brain's motor cortex connecting directly to muscles which then exhibit tension (Hanna 1979, p145). In addition to these internal processes the body's muscles are always at work, even to maintain its posture, even when sitting or standing still.

And the body is continuously changing as cells die and are replaced, as bones lengthen in the growing body, as stature decreases in the aging body, as hair or skin changes color, as lines appear, as we gain or loose strength, as we become ill or regain our health. From day to day, hour to hour we may feel differently, sometimes from changes brought on by internal conditions such as what we've eaten or drunk, and from external ones – hearing a sad song, seeing a loved one after a long absence. The significance of movement and change to human embodiment makes it clear that the body is a process. Indeed, the word "body" is misleading since it implies stability and solidity whereas a "soma is neither static nor solid; it is changeable and supple and is constantly adapting to its environment" (ibid., p5).

Designed for movement, the body thrives on it. Confined to bed, unable to move on their own, invalids must be moved by others or their skin will fester. Without moving for long periods of time, muscles wither and movement becomes difficult. Continuous and vigorous movement, once part of everyday life, must now be consciously undertaken as "exercise" in our sedentary modern world. Over and over again studies indicate that even moderate amounts of exercise help prevent illness, relieve depression and stress and extend people's lives.

The importance of movement for good health is not only a matter of strenuous exercise. In her book, *The Chair: Rethinking Body, Culture and Design*, Galen Cranz describes how frequent changes of position are needed to keep our spinal disks healthy and how the contemporary epidemic of back problems results not only from our way of sitting but simply from how *much* we sit without frequent changes of position – to reclining, perching, standing, or lying down.

It is through movement that we perceive and understand the world. Not only do we make bodily movements to see and touch and smell what is around us, we also understand surroundings and objects in the sense of how we might use or interact with them. The processes of knowing and understanding are not representations of what is "out there;" nor are they projections of what is "in here." They are instead ongoing linkages between inner and outer which involve, most importantly, acting in and upon the world or imagining such action (Varela et al. 1991). We understand the world through our actions and potential actions.

Nowhere is this clearer than in architecture. We understand its forms and its features via the kinds of movement they afford or imply. A doorway is understood as an opening for the human body to pass through. If the door is ornamented in some way or prominently located, we understand that it is the "front" door or formal entry. A much larger opening, a gateway, is understood as accommodating bodies riding on horses, in carriages or cars. The window suggests looking into or out of. The window in the door encourages looking before opening. The tower suggests that the body will move up or down. The most basic types in architecture are precisely those whose formal features imply basic kinds of human movement (Franck 1994).

It is through bodily movement, posture and activity that we engage with the world. We are not so much in space as of space. Our primary relationship is not facing space and objects as independent observers, pondering what lies before us. From the very first we actively and continuously engage with the world for survival and for enjoyment (Turner 1996). We enact space through a vast repertoire of movements and gestures from reaching, grasping, and nursing at the mother's breast to planting and harvesting and cooking to drawing and building to myriad more. As we act, both we and the space are transformed. "I am not in space and time, nor do I conceive space and time; I belong to them, my body combines with them and includes them" (Merleau-Ponty 1962, p102).

On stairs and ledges all over the city and the campus young people on skateboards have left traces of dark wax to speed up their travel. At night on the college campus, the skateboarders fly freely over their favorite spots. Sometimes they find the security guards joyriding, doing tricks in their small carts, each taking joy in movement.

With the positions and movements of our bodies we *arrange* space. A person walking in a straight line is making a path. Two people facing each other in conversation make the space around and between them intimate, wherever they are. A group of people sitting together facing each other is making a circle. People standing one behind the other, waiting, are making a line. A group of people facing a single person is making an audience.

Organized gestures . . . are not simply performed in "physical" space, in the space of bodies. Bodies themselves generate spaces, which are produced by and for their gestures. (Henri Lefevbre 1991, p216)

Skateboarding,
Nashville, Tennessee

Rollerpark, Greenport, Long Island

These are perhaps primal arrangements, once marked in the landscape by pathways or a circle of stones, later sculpted into forms we now call streets, highways, and hallways, living rooms and meeting rooms. Bodily orientation and patterns of movement in relation to the world and to others became the basis for built forms; the patterns continue in these and other forms. Sitting on the hillside looking down at a spectacle below became the stone seats and stage of an amphitheater, a coliseum and later an enclosed theater and, later still, a football stadium.

The young people skateboarding all over town pose problems for pedestrians and drivers and cause damage to steps and curbs and benches so a special playground for skateboarding and rollerblading is built with ramps and curved walls.

Architecture does not simply suggest movement; it frequently choreographs it, encouraging us to move in particular ways, adopting particular positions, sometimes quite insistently. How clear it is with stairways.

Short steps,
with no landings,
tell your body
to move straight
up, no pausing,
no turning.

Steps winding up a tower that flare out to meet the outer walls of the tower, becoming narrower as they approach the center tell you to place your foot on the outside of the tread, where it is wide. Your body moves round and round, spiraling upwards.

Grand stairways with narrow risers
and spacious landings invite slow
and gracious movement. We pause at the
landings, gazing out into the distance.

Through a very carefully synchronized series of movements of arms and legs, torso, feet and hands we ascend or descend the stair. "The enclosing balustrades (or walls) of the flight control the stair user's movement through the space, and the dimensions of the risers and treads strictly govern the cadence of gait" (Templer 1992b, p23).

The narrow stair
to the attic is
like a filled-in
ladder. There is
no space for
two people to go
up together. Each must
go up alone. There
is no place to
pause.

a

On the grand stair of
the library or the opera house,
many go up and down at the same time,
at different speeds, some together, some alone.
On the landings there is space and time to pause,
to talk, to look, and to embrace.

Stairs, like ourselves, are vertical bodies. Rooted to
the ground, they lift our bodies up or bring them down.
By taking us to different heights, they affect us emotionally. Indeed, they are very powerful artifacts for our
imagination as well.

b

c

*How different it is to go up than to go down. The body
is heavier; gravity must be overcome while climbing up;
gravity pulls us down when we return. Down and up:
the model is still our body linking, in its vertical structure, sky and earth. It is the tension between sky and
earth that stairs reproduce by linking the ground with
the floors above. To design a stairway – to choose the
rhythm of the steps, the solidity or lightness of the structure, the pauses and the views – is to create a mood as
well as journey for the body to make. In the Maison de
Verre in Paris, Pierre Chareau showed how stairs
dematerialize as they come closer to the sky and how,
consequently, the body's movements must become
lighter and more careful.*

Stairs
a. Round and round,
Back Bay, Boston
b. Straight down,
Truro, Massachusetts
c. Up, steeply, Monte
Alban, Mexico

And the banister. Does your hand grasp it by encir-
cling it completely in a "power grip," by grasping it in
a "sideways pull," or by pinching it (Templer 1992a,
p124)? Is it a rounded wooden banister that fills up your
hand voluptuously or is it a narrow metal one, stingy
and cold to the touch? Perhaps it is one of Aalto's brass
banisters, bound in leather so it feels both hard and soft.
Does your hand slide down smoothly, the full run of
the stairs without interruption, or does it have to stop
at certain points?

There are also banisters that are walls whose solidity is overcome by a stream of water running along their
surface. In the Alhambra garden in Spain, for aesthetic

Garden at Alhambra,
Granada, Spain

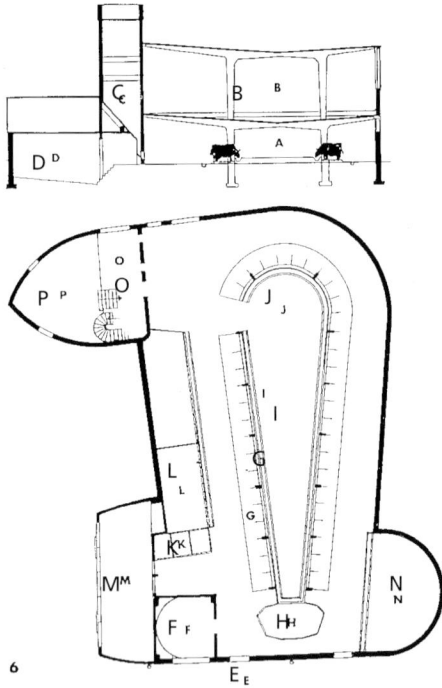

Cowshed at Gut Garkau farm, Germany (Hugo
Häring, redrawn by Peter Blundell Jones)
A Cowshed B Hayloft C Silo D Rootcellar
E Cow's entrance F Dairy G Spaces for 42 cows
H Bull I Feed trough J Trapdoor from hayloft over
K Baby calves I Heifers M Young bulls N Calves
O Silo over P Rootcellar

Reading area, Exeter Academy Library, Exeter, New
Hampshire (Louis Kahn)

and environmental reasons, but also for the body's pleasure, the designer chose to run a stream of water along
the top of the wall next to the stairs for the hand to
touch and for the body to refresh itself with the sound
as well as the feeling of water.

*I will never forget the feeling of this stream. No need
to bend or to kneel to reach it; it was just there, at the
level of my hand, and it was flowing down the stairs with
me.*

Discovering Movement, Positions and Relationships

The key patterns of movement and the key relationships
of one occupant to another and to the objects at hand
can serve as inspirations for design. The modern architect and theorist, Hugo Häring, believed very strongly
that the spatial order of a building should be taken from
the order of activities that the building is to house, an
order that must be uncovered, not imposed. "Häring
believed that in every situation demanding a building
there was an inherent order to be discovered and fulfilled. He called for an open-ended planning process
in which the designer became a kind of midwife at the
building's birth, expressing not his or her own individuality, but the individuality of the task at hand"
(Blundell Jones 1997, p97).

Among the several farm buildings he designed at Gut
Garkau is a pear-shaped shed for 42 cows and one bull.
In conversations with the farmer Häring discovered that
the natural feeding pattern of cows is to stand in a circle around their food. A circular form for 42 cows would
have created too much unnecessary central space so an
oval shape was adopted. Wanting to create a significant
position for the bull led to the selection of a pear-shaped
oval; the narrower end of the pear gives the bull an
appropriately dominant position among the cows (ibid.).
The pattern of relationships of the cows to each other
and the bull became the spatial order of the barn.

Louis Kahn drew insight and inspiration from his
understanding of the activities and related movements
a building should support. For the library at Exeter
Academy in New Hampshire he envisioned the ritual
of reading in a library as taking a book from the dark
to the light (Lym 1980, p83). Another ritual would be
to pass by and catch sight of beautiful books laid open.
At the Exeter library Kahn designed for both of these
rituals: the private reading carrels are located on the
periphery of the building in the light; the book stacks
are in the inner part away from direct daylight; in the
center is a void, where the entrance is located and

around which Kahn planned display shelves for open books (ibid., p84).

Bodies differ in size and strength and capabilities, and positions assumed vary dramatically with the activities being pursued. These differences can be taken into consideration and accommodated in design when attention is paid to the particular bodies, activities, and positions to be housed, when design is pursued from the body, and from a particular body at that. In designing day care spaces, Boston architect Gail Sullivan is very attentive to the size and reach of children and to the activities they enjoy. In the conversion of a large basement cafeteria to a day care center in Peabody, Massachusetts, Sullivan created an interior "play street" with the classrooms lining it as houses might line a street. The double-hung domestic windows between the hall and the classroom, set at children's height, provide visual access to each classroom (as expected by day care providers). The Dutch doors to the classrooms allow the upper part to be opened so that teachers can talk with people in the hallway without the children being able to run out of the classroom. A play pavilion with an indoor sandbox is greatly enjoyed. At Lexington Play Care a children's sink for water play is equipped with foot controls to avoid passing germs between children.

Sometimes when designers have little experience with the specific tasks housed by a particular building type or when they assume that the occupants' culture is the same as their own, errors are made. In Israel the open floor plan of new housing poses problems for Orthodox Jewish families: the kitchen is open to the living room but women, who are the main users of the kitchen, are not supposed to see their husbands while the men use the living room for religious study (Ginsberg 1991). So they must put up curtains or otherwise modify the visual connection between living room and kitchen.

Bianca, yesterday when I went for a walk in the late afternoon I saw a lot of people at the end of your street. Curious, I approached the small piazza where groups of men and women were gathered around the fountain, talking animatedly in Italian and some in Russian. Perched on the chain that blocks cars from entering the piazza were more people talking. Since the winter air was cold, people were wearing winter coats and scarves. What were they doing? It was Sunday. I looked around for an event that had just ended (church?) or that would soon start (a wedding?), but there was no indication of such an event. People's positions, the groupings and the cigarettes reminded me of a cocktail party

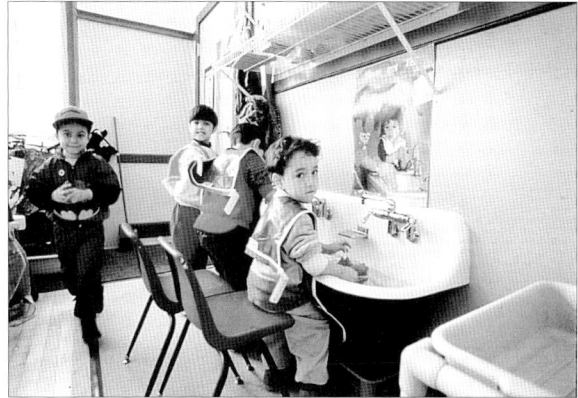

Lexington Play Care, Lexington, Massachusetts (Gail Sullivan Associates)

Typical class room entry, NSCAP Head Start, Peabody, Massachusetts (Gail Sullivan Associates)

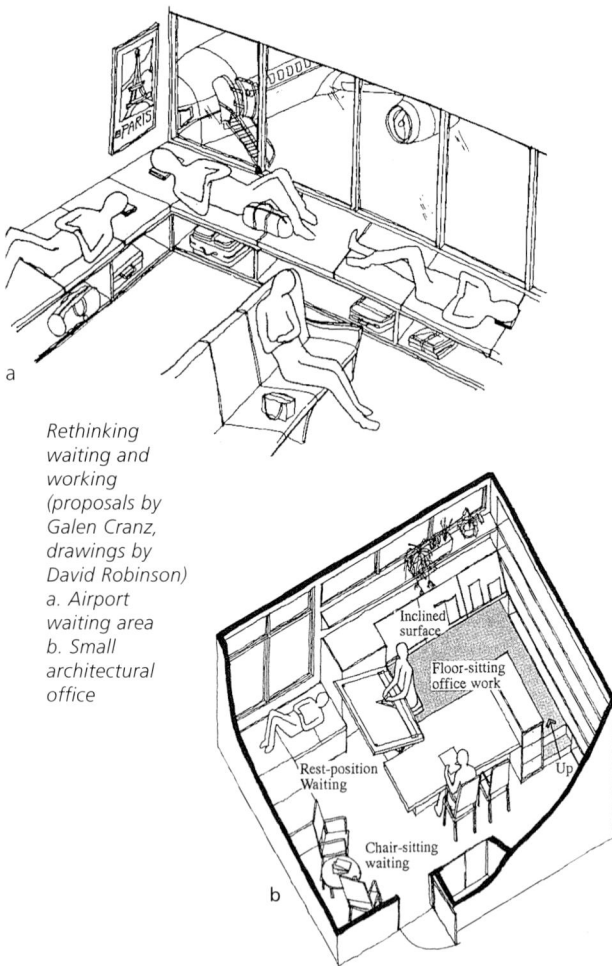

Rethinking waiting and working (proposals by Galen Cranz, drawings by David Robinson) a. Airport waiting area b. Small architectural office

without the drinks. It was simply the regular time and place for gathering and talking. And it was the right time, Sunday afternoon, and the right place, in the neighborhood, intimate, quiet.

How actions are carried out – who is present, how they relate to each other, the location and the props used – are all shaped by culture and history. The gathering of friends and acquaintances may take place in a piazza on Sunday afternoons, at cocktail or other parties by invitation, or in cafes where only men gather. Traditional ways of gathering may change over time, sometimes through a planned intervention. In Copenhagen, when the architect and planner Jan Gehl first proposed to close some downtown streets to traffic and to encourage the installation of cafes, critics of the plan predicted it would never work, claiming that Danes are not Italians, that they would not gather in cafes and plazas. Thirty years later, Copenhagen has closed most of its downtown streets to traffic; the cafes are so numerous and well used that planners have recommended that the city limit any licensing of additional cafes. Some provide blankets to customers to extend outdoor cafe-sitting into the cool days of October.

It is not only the manner in which activities are carried out that varies across cultures and through history; the bodily postures assumed may also vary. While the basic physiological repertoire of movements and gestures available to the human body remains the same, how we draw upon this repertoire, our postures and actions, their duration and repetition are also culturally and historically shaped. Today many people throughout the world sit on chairs but sitting on chairs has not always been so common and in many parts of the world squatting is still preferred. In the Middle East, India and Africa squatting is traditional and habitual.

The Western reliance on chairs and practice of remaining in them for long periods of time without assuming a variety of other positions, including squatting, very likely contributes to the severity of back problems (Cranz 1998). To alter this situation, Cranz recommends a change in the design of homes, schools, workplaces, and public spaces so that they offer opportunities to assume various postures, including lying down in, for instance, waiting areas in airports. She envisions an ideal office environment where interior design and furniture allow a wide choice of postures while working – reclining in a lounge chair, perching on a high stool, stretching out on a carpeted platform or sitting on its edge, standing and working at a chest-high surface or reading at a slanted surface, taking a break to drape oneself over a large inflated ball to promote flexibility of the spine.

This variety of positions, particularly in public or in places of work, is counter to current cultural patterns of sitting in chairs, patterns that are deeply embedded. The change would not just be in design but in culture to make these postures acceptable. "Can we really change the practice of sitting in chairs? It is embedded so deeply in our culture that it seems natural, meaning virtually biological, and therefore not susceptible to change. . . This is in fact unconscious knowledge, which is harder to change than either the rational technical knowledge we learn in schools or the informal knowledge that people tell us in the process of living. The difficulty of changing an unconscious practice like chair sitting includes resistance to the subject by dismissing it as absurd or trivial" (ibid., p209). Bringing the topic forward for discussion and for acknowledgement of the possible consequences is the first step.

The postures assumed during childbirth have also been culturally and socially ordered. Even though the most physiologically sensible position is squatting and squatting is a commonly assumed position in many cultures, modern Western medicine has encouraged a prone position on a hospitable bed, which is prominently situated in the delivery room, with the medical staff of doctor and nurses playing the more active role and the birthing mother the more passive one, recipient of the actions and decisions of others. The positioning of the birthing mother on a bed, in the center of a room, easily visible from the door puts the mother on stage, giving her little privacy and no sense of control (Lepori 1992).

In her research on the physiology of birth and the kinds of position and movement reported by women who had given birth at home, Bianca uncovered the advantages of moving between a variety of different positions during labor, each easily assumed and changed as the mother chooses. The supine position imposed by most obstetricians obstructs and complicates delivery rather than facilitating it. It produces the lowest contraction efficiency, increases maternal discomfort and reduces the amount of blood reaching the placenta, thus increasing breathing difficulties for the baby. In addition, the necessary internal rotation of the baby within the pelvic canal becomes more difficult and more painful for the woman when she is kept in a fixed position on the delivery bed.

In contrast, Bianca's research shows that when a woman is free to move around the delivery room to find the positions that are most comfortable to her during labor

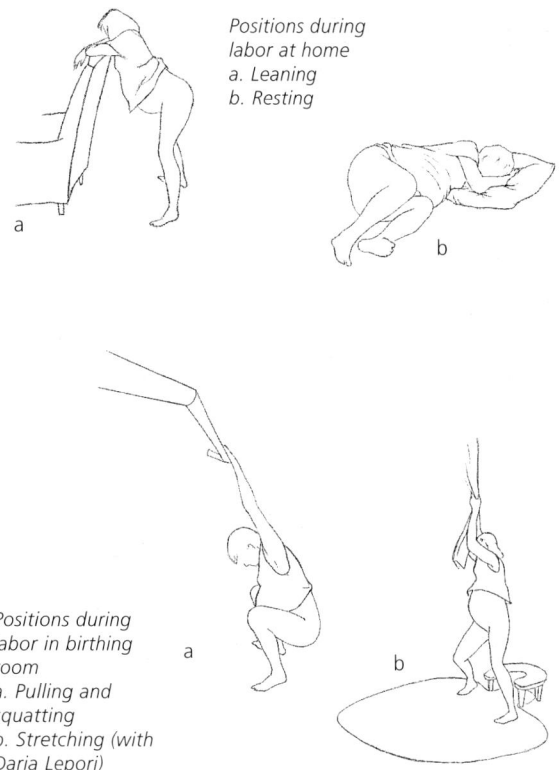

Positions during labor at home
a. Leaning
b. Resting

Positions during labor in birthing room
a. Pulling and squatting
b. Stretching (with Daria Lepori)

Rocking dance of labor

*Forced stillness of labor
and delivery*

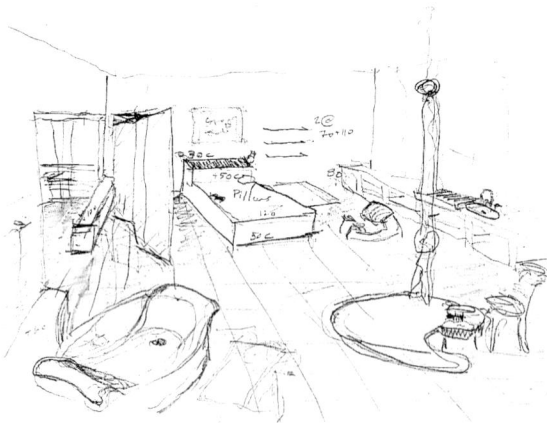

*Sketch of birthing room, Fermo Hospital, Fermo, Italy
(R. Bianca Lepori)*

and delivery, she experiences less anxiety and less pain, more efficient contractions, shorter labor, and better cardio-pulmonary functioning during delivery. Interviews with women who have given birth at home show that they never expose themselves at the center of the scene, such as the prominently placed delivery bed implies. Instead, women who are free to follow their natural urges during childbirth tend to choose an empty, protected area, such as a sitting room, not a bedroom. There they kneel, crouch and adopt other postures that relax the pelvic floor and allow gravity to help the birth take place.

The findings indicate that in design, the central focus of a delivery space should be eliminated. Imitating a cozy home environment is not a significant change when women are still forced into rigid practices that benefit the medical staff rather than mother and baby. Women don't really need particular colors or a homey atmosphere as much as a space in which they can move around and change positions whenever they wish. The backup support of the contemporary medical world is needed but in more flexible, women-centered spaces.

Bianca's prototype design of the space and furniture for a birthing room sustains the woman's freedom of movement and her power to choose different positions and different actions during labor and delivery. Instead of a bed placed in a dominant position either in the middle of the room or in the center of a wall, the center of the room is left open and a platform is placed to one side. On it a woman can sit, kneel, lie down, rest; since it is low, she can easily stand again or kneel on the floor with her elbows resting on the platform. Rungs mounted on the wall, a low wall, movable birthing stools, and towels hanging from the ceiling offer opportunities for stretching, hanging, leaning, squatting, and pressing. Most women need to hold on to something during contractions. Since water can relieve pain and accelerate dilation, a specially designed bath allows for floating, reclining and giving birth in water as well.

The choice of positions and movements and the very encouragement of activity puts the mother, physically and emotionally, in control and places the staff, both symbolically and actually, in a supportive role. The body, more than ever, is considered in its wholeness: this includes the woman's emotions, her strength and her vulnerability, her need to be secluded and in control. The design is not intended to replace existing spaces and practices for giving birth but to add another option. This option is to be placed within a hospital setting so that all of the medical technology that is presently available could be used if necessary.

The process of designing the birthing pool lasted for several years. I started the design when women were giving birth in very uncomfortable baths. I saw their heads falling uncomfortably to one side or their bellies sticking out of the water. I also saw that the sides of the pool, when they were high enough to contain more water than traditional baths, were tall and rather unsafe. Women had to climb in and out of them, often without any support. There was also the need for practitioners to be able to approach the woman; their needs had to be considered as well as the mother's.

The woman has to be able to float and so one side of the bath had to be almost 2 meters long. In order to float and also spread her arms, the pool couldn't be too narrow but it couldn't be too large either because that would make it difficult for practitioners standing outside the pool to be of help. Some women felt the need to push against the tub walls; some wanted to sit down; others wanted to stand or squat. The shape that evolved is meant to meet all these needs as well as to welcome the woman in a soft embrace. Midwives tell me that it is a uterus. This is enough to reassure me.

The pool is equipped with a door to facilitate entrance and exit and we have added an underwater light not so much for medical control as to offer the possibility of turning other lights off with only the underwater light remaining on. This increases the uterus effect of the pool and also acts upon the endorphins. The protocol for water birth included a sieve to remove organic matter, so we explored the possibility of including a vacuum system that could simplify removal and that is now part of the kit as well.

This is what we offer but the Italian market is mostly oriented toward simpler and therefore cheaper versions of water birth baths that are not designed for the woman's pregnant body but simply respond to the fashion of the moment. The same could be said for the birthing room layout. The need for movement has been taken very literally by factories that are now pursuing the business of verticality at any cost and send their distributors to me to show me products I could use in my conversions. It is rather moving to listen to their speeches on verticality. But I have to interrupt them to explain the importance of the horizontal position, the resting one, which is necessary though unprofitable since it requires only a simple platform rather than the complex multi-layered bed, the bed that ends up located in the middle of the "new room for active birth," for the woman to be on stage once again.

The research and design approaches taken by Galen

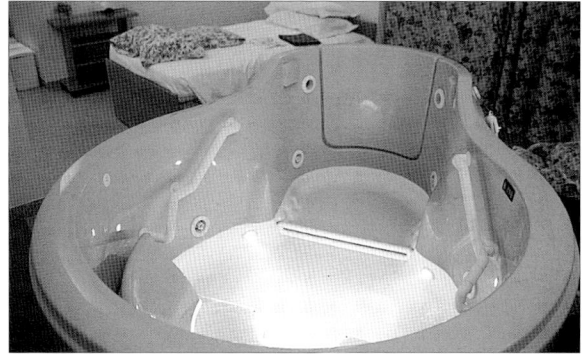

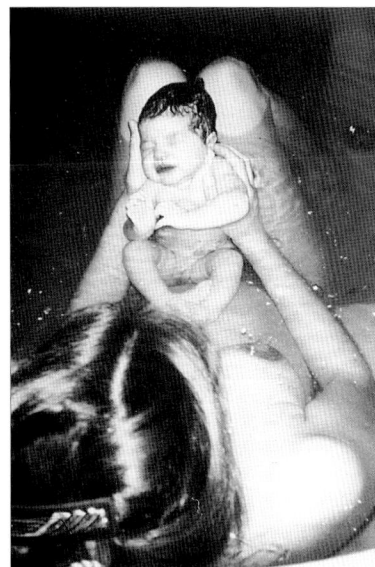

FROM ABOVE:
Birthing pool, Lugo di Romagna, Ravenna, Italy (R. Bianca Lepori)

. . . space is not only the
space of "no," it is also the
space of the body, and
hence the space of "yes,"
of the affirmation of life. . .
(Henri Lefevbre 1991,
p201)

and Bianca start with the body and analyze its physiology and its needs in thorough detail. They have been able to distinguish current cultural expectations about appropriate bodily positions from what makes sense physiologically and each recommends changes in those expectations and in the design of space, furniture, and equipment. When these changes are adopted, the room and its furnishings open up to the body, inviting its inhabitation, giving it comfort and pleasure – creating the space of "yes."

"Once we have left the *waters* of the womb, we have to construct a space for ourselves in the *air* for the rest of our time on earth – air in which we can breathe and sing freely, in which we can perform and move at will. Once we were fishes. It seems that we are destined to become birds. None of this is possible unless the air opens up freely to our movements" (Irigaray 1993, p66).

Space of Yes

Architecture designed from the body supports the pursuit of myriad activities by people of different sizes and needs and desires. It is the kitchen sink with its own built-in step that the child can pull out to reach the faucet to turn on the water. It is the light, movable chairs in a park that allow people to follow the sun on a spring day and to find shade at the height of summer, that give people the chance to be alone, in a pair, or in a group. It is the ledge, window sill, or wall wide enough to sit on, the rail or counter or wall the right height and material for leaning. It is the small bench built into the wall next to the apartment door where you put packages as you open the door. It is the shower heads at a stadium that are high enough to accommodate the very tallest basket ball player. It is an architecture that attends to small and large movements, that supports variety and choice, that recognizes that life is movement and rest of individual, fleshed bodies. It is Galen's ideal workplace and it is Bianca's birthing room.

Activities are performances, requiring preparation, enactment; they depend upon props and supports, lighting and furnishings, enclosure and exposure, storage, entrance, and exit. These sequences, the props and qualities needed, the coming together of how many, the separation and solitude of how many require *discovery* and then the choreographing of the movement of bodies and objects. This means that before and during design, the activities that are to take place, and the furniture, equipment, and spatial arrangements they require must be considered. A furniture plan for the types, number of pieces, and possible arrangements is crucial to understanding and supporting the future use of a space.

The committee meeting is not going well. Everyone is sitting on chairs or a low couch around an even lower coffee table. Because there is no conference table, there is no place to put papers at an easily accessible height and there is no place to write. The committee members try to take notes on pads balanced on their knees. Sometimes the papers slide off and fall to the floor. There is a tentativeness to the conversation; the candidate being interviewed feels unsure of herself and becomes defensive. The next time the committee meets in a conference room, around a table. The candidate places her own papers and books on the table and speaks firmly and with conviction. Committee members place their papers and notes on the table as well, glancing at previous notes and making additional ones. The meeting goes well.

In their admiration of architecture as object and their treatment of the body as object, each viewed only from without or above, too many architects treat activity as secondary to appearance, an unavoidable but burdensome necessity. Activity and its requirements, however, need not be reduced to "function" or denigrated as "mere use." It can be the wellspring of design. The result can be places and furnishings that respond with understanding and support to the needs of occupants and that are a pleasure to see and feel – the space of "yes."

When the body is recognized as radically open to its surroundings, we can begin to see how it is continually unfinished, always a potentiality (Shilling 1993; Turner 1996). We can also begin to see how surroundings and objects respond to the body's needs and so partly complete and extend it. How well do they respond to the body? What are the particular needs to be met in a new design or a renovation? What is the particular potential or potentials we wish to realize with the design of a space and its furnishings? How will the architecture of that place meet, support, and extend the open body?

Perhaps more so than any other modern architect Eileen Gray designed space and furniture with an understanding of the open body and the power of architecture to complete it at a very intimate scale, attending with great care and detail to the movements and gestures that are part of the tasks of daily life. The house she designed for the engineer Jean Badovici on the Côte d'Azur, called E.1027, accommodates with great sensitivity both the larger movements of entering, eating, sleeping, relaxing, sunbathing as well as the many smaller gestures of shaving, reaching for a piece of cake, putting a cup down on a table, or reading a clock in the dark. In designing the entrance Gray studied all possible movements of the act of entering, considering the sequence of actions from putting down an umbrella to hanging up coats and hats (Adam 1987). The house contains two bedrooms, a servant's room, utility rooms, and one large central room (21 x 46 ft) which provided a living area, a dining area with a built-in bar, and a guest alcove, defined by screens and built-in furniture.

The use of terraces was also thoughtfully considered, even to the provision of a sandtrap for sunbathing. The terraces became additional "rooms" of the house and some furniture was designed for use both indoors and out. The amount of sunlight allowed to enter the house could be finely adjusted with a variety of shutters; one type was invented and patented by Gray and Badovici. Gray even determined how to achieve the best views during overcast weather.

Inside the house many items of furniture could be easily moved or adjusted to serve different functions; others contain details that addressed multiple needs. Tables could be pushed together when more surface was needed, table legs lengthened or shortened to create a coffee table or a table for writing. A cantilevered bedside table could pivot to serve as a reading stand or lowered to eat or write in bed. In the main bedroom reading in bed is accommodated with a white light inserted into the headboard which also has a blue nightlight, an alarm clock that can be read in the dark and outlets for an electric kettle and a footwarmer. In the living area a large divan could also be converted into a bed. A narrow table for tea, which can be increased in length, is covered with cork to avoid the noise of dishes, cups, or cutlery. Circular trays to hold cake can be rotated to be easily reached.

Gray also designed the conversion of Jean Badovici's apartment on the rue de Chateaubriand in Paris which was only 430 square feet. As her plan shows, the apartment is designed around activities and the spatial and furniture requirements to support them. She located the entrance, bath, and kitchenette and bar in the smallest possible space; this allowed for a spacious living and working area. A curved metalic curtain screened the bathroom and a dropped ceiling over the service area allowed for an ingenious circular storage space in the ceiling, reached by a retractable ladder.

For furniture and room dividers in the house and the apartment Gray used a wide range of materials: steel, chrome, leather, canvas, cork, zinc, glass, wood, and aluminum. In the house she made screens from the sheets of metal used in flour mills

One must build for man, so that he may rediscover in the architectural construction the joy of feeling himself, as in a whole that extends him and completes him. (Eileen Gray in Adam 1987, p236)

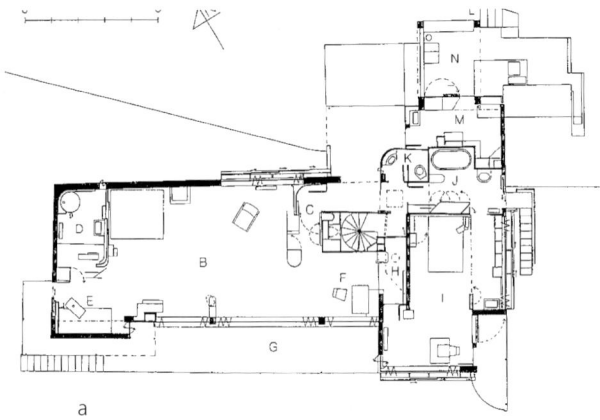

a

E. 1027, Maison en bord de mer, Roquebrune, France (Eileen Gray, plans redrawn by Stefan Hecker and Christian F. Müller)
a. Plan of upper floor
A Main entrance B living room C wardrobe D shower E alcove
F dining area G Terrace H Bar I Bedroom J Bathroom K Toilet
L Service entrance
M Winter kitchen N Summer kitchen

b. Plan of lower floor
A Guest room B Servant's room C Heating D Toilet E Workshop
F Terrace under the house
G Shed

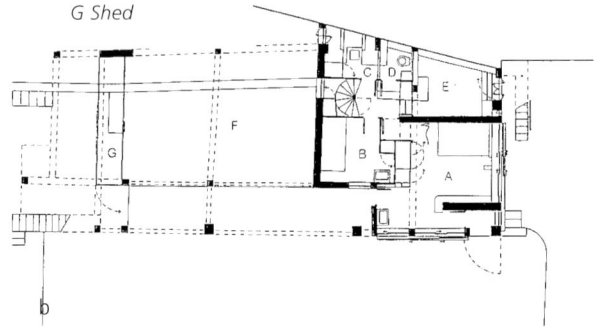

b

a

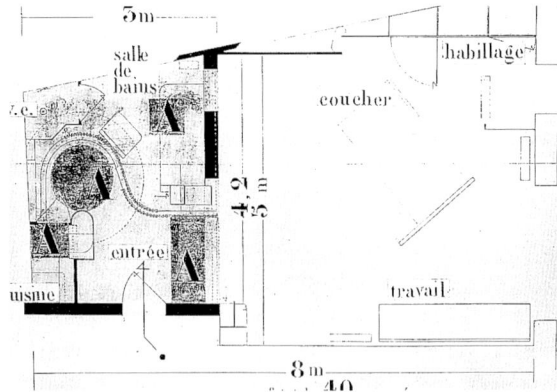

b

Apartment, rue de Chateaubriand, Paris
(Eileen Gray)
a. Metalic curtain concealing service area
b. Plan
c. High storage cupboard

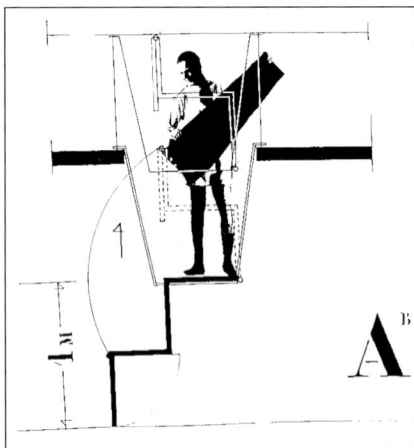

c

to sift flour (ibid., p206). She covered the outside of the bathtub with a coat of aluminum and the interior of the wardrobe with celluloid. On the floor of the bathroom were mats of perforated felt and on beds she often placed blankets of fur. From her very fine work in making lacquer furniture, screens, and wall panels and in designing rugs Gray brought great sensitivity to the sensuous qualities of materials as well as to the body's movements and gestures.

For the design of the Shiranui Psychiatric Hospital and Stress Care Center in Omuta City, Japan, Itsuko Hasegawa gave careful thought to how the natural environment of the building might improve patients' well being and aid their recovery and, accordingly, what the best site for the building would be. Based on existing research, visits to other hospitals, meetings with patients and staff, and her own experience, she proposed a beach location. "This would provide the natural rhythm of tides, the soothing open space of the sea, the motion of the waves and the reflection of light – all of which contribute to make one feel a part of nature" (Hasegawa 1993, p7).

Hasegawa believes that nature itself is a great healer. Afraid that suicidal patients would be attracted to the water, a fence had been planned to separate it from the building but Hasegawa successfully persuaded the director to omit the fence, suggesting that experiencing the change in tides and the reflection of the moon on the water, without the interference of a barrier, would be beneficial. "To provide a view of the ever-changing sea, all the patients' rooms are placed along the water's edge in a segmented linear pattern to approximate amorphous gentle curvature. The building is surrounded by reflected light from the water, creating a relaxed and warm atmosphere" (ibid., p7). Oversized windows in patients' rooms bring in light and breezes from the sea; the corrugated metal roof brings in the sound of rain. The walls of the balconies, made of polycarbonate, give a feeling of transparency, and bring in more light, reflected at different angles by the angles of the walls.

Meeting over a period of three years, Hasegawa and the hospital's director, Yuichiro Tokunaga, were able to develop a joint vision and Hasegawa was able to translate her insights about patients' needs and the changes they undergo into the interior design as well. The director is very pleased with the building, finding that less medication is prescribed and people recover more quickly than in the previous building.

The six nurses' stations are centrally placed but angled so that while nurses have a clear view from them, as

Tea table, E. 1027, Maison en bord de mer, Roquebrune, France (Eileen Gray)

A house is not a machine to live in. It is the shell of man, his extension, his release, his spiritual emanation.
(Eileen Gray in Adam 1987, p309)

a

b

Shiranui Psychiatric Hospital and Stress Care Center, Omuta, Japan (Itsuko Hasegawa)
a. View from waterfront
b. Patient's room

Shiranui Psychiatric Hospital and Stress Care Center, Omuta, Japan (Itsuko Hasegawa)
a. Balconies facing water
b. Lower floor

a   b

Plans: roof, upper level and ground level, Shiranui Psychiatric Hospital and Stress Care Center, Omuta, Japan (Itsuko Hasegawa)

1 Bathroom 2 Psychological remedy rooms
3 Library 4 Terrace 5 Body sonic room
6 Nurses' station 7 Ward
8 Examination room 9 Day room
10 Staff room 11 Meeting room 12 Shop
13 Cafe 14 Entrance 15 Locker room
16 Machine room
17 Working remedy room 18 Tatami room
19 Dining room
20 Living room 21 Workshop

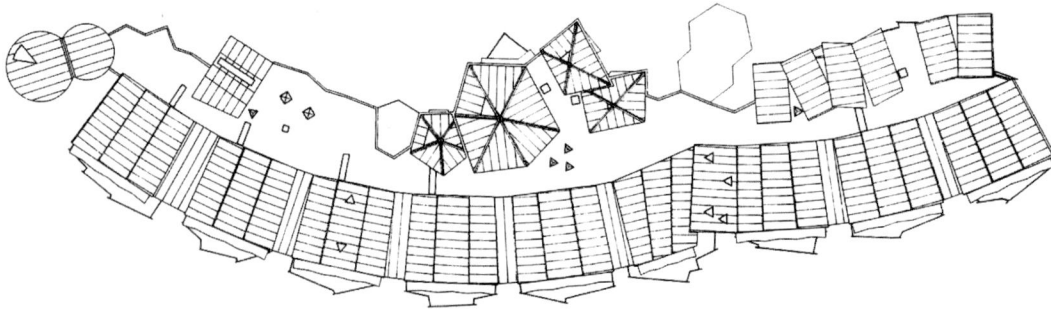

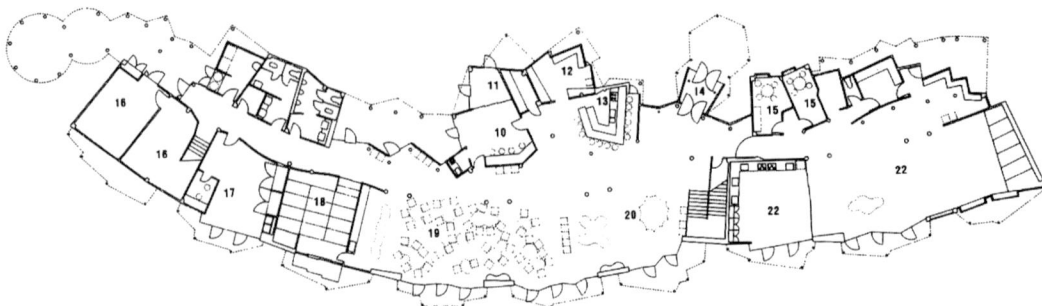

one approaches a station, its presence is not obvious.[1] When patients who have suffered nervous breakdowns first enter the hospital, they are placed in private rooms close to a nurses' station to be under observation. As patients get better, they are moved further away; thus they see the progress they have made. The rooms furthest from the nurses' station house four patients; each room has three doors so patients can enter and exit without crossing another patient's space. Movable bookcases allow each patient to make his/her own space as enclosed or as open as they choose depending on their desire for contact or retreat. This ability to choose, and a small window or a grill over each bed for ventilation, give patients some control over their environment. The rooms for suicidal patients have tiny bathrooms, each with a window right opposite the toilet so that the patient feels connected to the outside world.

On the ground floor are larger meeting rooms and the dining space. The walkway along side of a public room, distinguished by a change in floor surface, a lower ceiling and a few columns, allows people to be in the room without feeling they are invading an ongoing activity or that they have made a commitment to stay. The 19 tables for dining are all different shapes and sizes. Picking a tiny table, with room for only one or two people, sends the message that you wish to be alone while sitting at a larger table suggests you may be approached. If the dining room is not yet full, these clues provide important but subtle information to those who come later.

There is a variety of spaces for patients to go; little spaces for congregating in small groups or places to be alone. Each is different, providing a rich choice of alternatives. A variety of surfaces adds to the choice and richness. Materials on the interior reflect the light differently; glass marbles in the floor and in the ceiling add more detail and color and a feeling of playfulness. When it rains, one can still be outside protected by translucent canopies. For the approach and entrance to the building and to common spaces inside, Hasegawa has created a series of gentle layers, allowing one to make small, gradual decisions. The broken facade created by the balconies and the canopied spaces in the front of the building creates soft boundaries between indoors and outdoors.

The path people mark in the ground by repeatedly taking the same route is called a desire line. When architecture is designed from the body, from its needs, desires, and aspirations, when it completes and extends the body in the best ways possible, it creates a series of "paths" for the body to follow easily and comfortably that enhance our experience of daily routines, and that may bring about change in our lives. So often what these desire lines might be is obscured by layers of cultural expectations that prescribe other paths or by architectural priorities that place value on other issues. Fortunately Eileen Gray, Alvar Aalto, Itsuko Hasegawa and other contemporary architects have uncovered these desire lines and made them into architecture.

Note
1 We are grateful to New York architect Glynis Berry for this information and these comments about the Shiranui Hospital, which she toured with the director in 1992.

References

Adam, Peter. *Eileen Gray: Architect/Designer*. New York: Harry N. Abrams, 1987.

Blundell Jones, Peter. *Hans Scharoun*. London: Phaidon Press, 1997.

Casey, Edward S. *Getting Back into Place: Toward a Renewed Understanding of the Place-World*. Bloomington & Indianapolis, Indiana: Indiana University Press, 1993.

Cooper Marcus, Clare. *House as A Mirror of Self*. Berkeley, Calif.: Conari Press, 1995.

Cranz, Galen. *The Chair: Rethinking Body, Culture, and Design*. New York: W.W. Norton, 1998.

Franck, Karen. Types are us. In Karen A. Franck and Lynda Schneekloth (eds) *Ordering Space: Types in Architecture and Design*. New York: Van Nostrand Reinhold, 1994.

Gallager, Shaun and Jonathan Cole. Body image and body schema. In Donn Welton (ed) *Body and Flesh: a Philosophical Reader*. Oxford, England: Basil Blackwell Publishers, 1998.

Gatens, Moira. *Imaginary Bodies: Ethics, Power and Corporeality*. London: Routledge, 1996.

Ginsberg, Yona. The use and meaning of "home" among religious families in Israel. *Center for Environmental Design Research Working Paper Series* (26). Berkeley: University of California, 1991.

Grosz, Elizabeth. *Volatile Bodies: Toward a Corporeal Feminism*. Bloomington: Indiana University Press, 1994.

Hall, Edward. *The Hidden Dimension*. New York: Doubleday, 1966.

Hanna, Thomas. *The Body of Life*. New York: Knopf, 1979.

Hasegawa Architects. *Itsuko Hasegawa*. (Architectural Monographs No. 31) London: Academy Editions, 1993.

Hecker, Stefan and Christian F. Müller. *Eileen Gray*. Barcelona: Editorial Gustavo Gili, 1996.

Heidegger, Martin. Building, dwelling, thinking. In *Basic Writings*. New York: Harper & Row, 1977.

Irigaray, Luce. *Sexes and Geneologies*, trans. by Gillian C. Gill. New York: Columbia University Press, 1993.

Jager, Bernd. Body, house and city: The intertwinings of embodiment, inhabitation and civilization. In David Seamon and Robert Mugerauer (eds). *Dwelling, Place and Environment: Towards a Phenomenology of Person and World*. Dordrecht, Netherlands: Martinus Nijhoff, 1985.

Johnson, Mark. *The Body in the Mind: The Bodily Basis of Meaning, Imagination and Reason*. Chicago: University of Chicago Press, 1987.

Lang, Richard. The dwelling door: Towards a phenomenology of transition. In David Seamon and Robert Mugerauer (eds) *Dwelling, Place and Environment: Towards a Phenomenology of Person and World*. Dordrecht, Netherlands: Martinus Nijhoff, 1985.

Leder, Drew. *The Absent Body*. Chicago: University of Chicago Press, 1990.

Lefevbre, Henri. *The Production of Space*, trans. Donald Nicholson-Smith. Oxford: Basil Blackwell, 1991.

Lepori, Bianca. *La Nascita e i suou Luoghi*. Como: Red Studio Adazionale, 1992.

Lepori, Bianca. Freedom of movement in birth places. *Children's Environments*. 1994, 11(2).

Lym, Glenn Robert. *A Psychology of Building: How We Shape and Experience our Structured Spaces*. Englewood Cliffs, N.J.: Prentice-Hall, 1980.

Merleau-Ponty, Maurice. *Phenomenology of Perception*, trans. Colin Smith. London: Routledge & Kegan Paul, 1962.

Newman, Oscar. *Community of Interest*. New York: Doubleday, 1980.

Scarry, Elaine. *The Body in Pain: The Making and Unmaking of the World*. New York: Oxford University Press, 1985.

Schilder, Paul. *The Image and Appearance of the Human Body*. New York: International Universities Press, 1950.

Seamon, David and Robert Mugerauer (eds). *Dwelling, Place and Environment: Towards a Phenomenology of Person and World*. Dordrecht: Martinus Nijhoff, 1985.

Sebba, Rachel. The role of the home environment in cultural transmission. *Architecture & Comportment*. 7:3, 1991.

Stewart, Susan. *On Longing: Narratives of the Miniature, the Gigantic, the Souvenir, the Collection*. Durham, North Carolina: Duke University Press, 1993.

Strauss, Erwin W. *Phenomenological Psychology*, trans. in part by Erling Eng. New York: Basic Books, 1966.

Templer, John. *The Staircase: Studies of Hazards, Falls and Safer Design*. Cambridge, Mass.: MIT Press, 1992a.

Templer, John. *The Staircase: Histories and Theories*. Cambridge, Mass.: MIT Press, 1992b.

Turner, Bryan S. *The Body and Society: Explorations in Social Theory*. 2nd ed. London: Sage, 1996.

van Alphe, Ernst. *Francis Bacon and the Loss of Self*. Cambridge, Mass.: Harvard University Press, 1993.

Varela, Francisco J., Evan Thompson and Eleanor Rosch. *The Embodied Mind: Cognitive Science and Human Experience*. Cambridge, Mass.: MIT Press, 1991.

Shonandai Cultural Center, Fujisawa City, Japan (Itsuko Hasegawa)

Chapter 3

The Animism of Architecture

We build for the living even when we build for the dead. The interior of the container holding the dead body is dark and still with a plain, womb-like surface of velvet. The exterior surface of wood veneer and the coffin's surroundings in the chapel or the cemetery are for the living and represent the creative expression of living people. The coffin's exterior as well as the surroundings, being the container of the activities and emotions of living people, conform to various rules that are aesthetic and cultural as well as functionally and financially bound.

The living have created the coffin, the living will experience it; they will approach and act and react to it with emotion. Being primarily functional – for containing a still body, for storing it – the inside of a coffin can be compared to the inside of a cabinet or a drawer or to a shopping list whose literal and symbolic languages coincide. Due to its stillness and its inability to respond to environmental stimuli, the body doesn't need and wouldn't enjoy any structural variation in the container's shape; it wouldn't appreciate varying shades of color and texture or the play of light and shadow.

Our workplaces can be very functional: my table may have the right dimensions, my chair may be perfectly comfortable but what a difference it makes to have a ray of sunlight, a window with a nice view, a friendly tactile relationship with my desk and a spot of gorgeous color to look at every now and then. What a difference from having four blind walls and a blank view in front of me, unfriendly materials and dull colors.

Architecture is given life and spirit by all the qualities that touch the human senses and the human soul: by light and color, sound and texture, by expansion and compression of space. If the functional nourishes our physical needs, the poetic nourishes our soul. If the former relates to people and objects as machines, the latter relates to living human beings.

Since all things are alive and related and since we make and unmake with energy, the art of making and unmaking can not simply be a mechanical one just as the product can never be just an inanimate object or a logical-mathematical system. Both making and unmaking are creative expressions of living people that, once completed, facilitate living expressions.

In designing for the living, why not consider, along with the body that moves, the body that feels, and the body that dreams? Users as well as designers need to be aware of how these different bodies pertain to our nature and are therefore involved in the use as well as the design of architecture. The three bodies are always one; thus anything one of them may experience affects the others, anything one of them does affects the other two. This means that, even when involved in something very practical that seems to concern only the body that moves, the other two are involved in their own ways, absorbing and filtering sensations.

If the going up and down of stairs is for the body that moves, the material the steps are made of, the way they meet or do not meet our feet, are for the body that feels through its senses. The glittering quality, the opacity, and the smoothness of

Yeats's tower, Ireland

materials, as well as their shapes, are for the body that dreams, the one that draws upon images, and that, through specific experiences, reconnects to its nature and to the collective it belongs to.

> Below you the earth
> Above you the sky
> Within you the ladder.
> (Sandor Clores in Heathcote 1997, p15)

This body is an admirable instrument, of which I am sure that those who are alive and who all have it at their disposal do not make full use. They draw from it only pleasure, pain, and indispensable acts, such as living. Sometimes they become confused with; sometimes again they forget its existence. . . ; and, at one moment mere brutes, at another pure spirits, they know not what multitudinous bonds with all things they have in themselves, and of what a marvellous substance they are made. And yet it is through this substance that they participate in what they see and what they touch: they are stones, they are trees, they exchange contacts and breaths with the matter that englobes them. They touch, they are touched; they have weight and lift weights; they move and carry their virtues and vices about; and when they fall into a reverie or into indefinite sleep, they reproduce the nature of waters, they turn into sand and clouds (Valéry 1932, pp30–1).

Matter Matters

It is through our senses that we perceive the world; it is through them that our relationship with the world is made possible. The angel in Wim Wenders's film, *Wings of Desire*, from its disembodied position, recognizes how precious are the bodily senses which we take for granted. Missing a physical body and asking for the opportunity to have one, he confesses to his angel friend something that sounds like:

Stone wall, Malta

I want to know what it is like
to touch gently the nape of a neck
to feel the roughness and softness of the soles of feet
to feel the wetness of dew
the heat of a warm tea on a cold day
to touch her cheeks and sense the warmth
to come to know the ordinary things of life
those simple things that man
has come to forget.

Man . . . fabricates by abstraction, ignoring and forgetting a great part of the qual-
ities of what he uses, and concerning himself solely with clear and definite conditions,
which can most often be simultaneously satisfied, not by a single material, but by sev-
eral kinds. He drinks milk or wine or water or ale indifferently out of a gold, glass,
horn or onyx; and whether the vase be wide or slender, or shaped like a leaf or a flower,
or with a quaintly twisted foot, the drinker considers the drinking alone. Even he who
made that cup was unable to do more than harmonize very roughly its substance, its
form and its function (Valéry 1932, p65).

How does it feel to touch a stone wall, or a marble column, a sponge, a jean jacket
or a silk shirt? What does a steel bridge suggest? What a concrete or a wooden one?
What is the message of a glazed wall, a brick, a granite, or an aluminum-veneered one?

Although the use of materials refers to history, to the evolution of tools and technology, their language goes beyond specific periods of time. The qualities they embody
relate to a collective way of feeling, perceiving, and responding. Through their nature
they send out messages that affect the environment and our experience of it. Materials,
rather than just being functional to the creation of goods, buildings, and environments,
act upon the quality of our perceptions and experiences each with its own particular character and voice.

I certainly wasn't more than seven or eight when I started to feel attracted by Matter, or more
precisely by something "shining" in the heart of Matter. . . I used to withdraw in the con-
templation, the possession and the savoured existence of my god of Iron. Iron, yes, I said
Iron. . . And now still I see, with particular accuracy, the series of my 'idols.' In the country
a plough's bolt that I was carefully hiding in a corner of the courtyard. In town the hexagonal dress of a little reinforcing metal column that was coming out of the nursery floor which
I got hold of. . . Why iron then? And more particularly, why that piece of iron (it had to be
as thick and massive as possible) if not because in my experience as a child nothing was
harder, heavier, tougher, more enduring than this marvellous substance grasped in a form
that was full at its maximum? Consistency: that undoubtedly has been for me the fundamental
quality of being.(Teilhard de Chardin, from "Comment se pose aujourd'hui la question du
transformism" in Vigorelli 1963, pp49–50).

Although industry is changing the traditional use of materials by producing plas-
tics that have the transparency of glass, glass walls that have the strength and resistance of brick and stone ones, laminates that look like metal, metals that may look
like fabrics, each of them carries its original character so intimately related to our own.

This powerful ability to transform, adapt, and interchange materials and play with
them, which has evolved from the world of craft into the one of engineering and technology, does not prevent materials from being true to themselves. On the contrary,
they seem to stretch their original attitudes, sometimes with irony, other times with
submission or with courage, as in Calatrava's silver threads holding massive polished
stones, or with delight, as in the "garage" designed by Hideaki Arizumi and Glynis

Garage/greenhouse, Orient, Long Island
(Studio A/B)

Traditional roof, Japan

House extension, London (Teresa Howard)

Berry of Studio A/B. Back-to-back panels of policarbonate transform the building from a simple garage into a garage/greenhouse.

The use of materials seems to follow its own evolution. With time, materials gain new applications, are made into new shapes, expressing aspirations nobody could have dreamed of before. In this evolving world of matter and form, where form allows matter better to express itself and matter allows form better to express itself, some materials are a leitmotiv, a recurrent presence. These are the ones that relate us more to the earth, to tradition, to metaphor and practical solidity, to an organic rather than a mechanical universe.

Among these materials timber and stone change with the level of technology used in their production, which nonetheless preserves the qualities they naturally possess. They are and they suggest the raw materials that people have found in nature since the beginning of time. As a building material, timber goes back, with rock, to the origin of dwelling. Originally the tree itself was used with little modification: tree trunks and branches as posts, beams and rafters. Now it is sliced into beams and planks, still showing its veins and keeping alive the warm memory of its origin.

Without entering into either the excesses of the Hungarian architect Imre Makovecz, who sees trees as creatures with a close relationship to people due to their vertical orientation, pointing both towards the sky and deep into the earth, and still uses dead trees as structural elements, or into the skillful geometry of the ancient Japanese art of joinery, we can appreciate the strength, versatility, and flexibility of wood. We can see how it contributes to the creation of warm, welcoming buildings of different shapes, functions, and sizes.

For the extension to her brick house in London, Teresa Howard chose pine for most of the framing and Douglas fir for the large beam and main column, since it grows more slowly and so has a finer grain and greater strength. It also has a soft brown-orange color that seems to emphasize its strength as well as its lightness. Unlike ancient barns or buildings whose dark timber supported a solid overloaded roof, contemporary timber-framed buildings can be very light, particularly if they have a glazed roof or skylights. Then their insides become outsides, as if the roof were a pergola training a plant whose leaves have not yet sprouted.

Strong as well as relatively light, easily cut into pieces of differing length and width, wood can be easily transported and handled while also conveying a feeling of cleanliness. It doesn't seem to keep the memory of the machines that have cut it nor of the dust it has produced during the process. For this reason, as well as by virtue of its texture and its irregular natural patterns, it is reassuring and calming. It speaks of perfection and naturalness, of the stages of life it has undergone as a tree, showing signs of aging and wear once it has been cut and used.

Because of all its qualities, timber is matter *par excellence*. ". . . in Greece the word *hyle* that has the same meaning as primordial matter, stands for timber" (Chevalier and Gherbrant 1986, p65). Its soft yet solid consistency makes it a material with "plastic" attitudes: it surrenders to carving and to the shapes that want to be carved into it. Very flexible, when laminated, wood can be bent into curves of different shapes, as Alvar Aalto did and generally Scandinavian designers do so well in their furniture.

Walking down the stairs tonight what a feeling: the velvet, skin-like Victorian mahogany handrail – reassuring, elegant, softly cut – accompanied my hand, absorbing and sharing my temperature.

Far harder to cut than wood, but more easily broken if they fall, marble and granite are also very much alive. The silent harmony of their patterns preserves the memory of the slow or abrupt changes that the earth has undergone. They speak of solidity as well as change; this might be the reason why they are used so often for sarcophagi, statues, monuments, and memorials as well as for public buildings of government, education, culture, and commerce. Made of crystals they also speak of preciousness and eternity.

Sandstone is a softer material that also preserves the memory of both the slow and the abrupt changes the earth has undergone. More modest than marble and granite, it does not show off its crystals, but only opaque grains. It is less smooth, thus less caressable; being more porous, its surfaces absorb light rather than reflect it. It is warmer though, calmer and more reassuring than granite or marble. Depending on the metals it is composed of, it can be incredibly colorful, more joyful than the elegantly tinted marble and granite. Sandstone is more for everyday life although used in monumental buildings: in a sacred building of Saqqara it is used as if it were a wooden lintel and ceiling beams.

Made of crystals like marble and granite, onyx is more subdued, but also more precious than sandstone.

It continues changing, it emits odours, it warps, cracks and changes with the house and with the dwellers: it ages and matures, like wine. (Imre Makovecz in Heathcote 1997, p19)

St. Matthews Episcopal Church, Pacific Palisades, California (Moore, Ruble, Yudell)

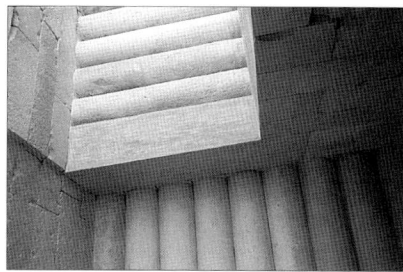

Sandstone interior from 3000 BC, Saqqara, Egypt

Onyx, Verona bank (Carlo Scarpa)

Of a sculpture of granite cubes counterbalanced with silver threads on sharp pointed cones and spindles, Calatrava says: "You feel the pain the steel points inflict on the granite and the potential injury to its polished surface." (Peter Buchanan 1987, p53)

*Window in stone wall,
Portugal*

Kew Gardens, London

*Kasai Rinkai Koen,
Tokyo (Yoshio
Taniguchi)*

Permeable to light, its nature has the quality of transforming light into a variety of patterns offered by the nuances light assumes by passing through it. It is seldom used as a building material, although it replaces glass very well when light but not sight is required.

Elastic and transparent, glass seems not to belong to the world of matter. Between the visible and the invisible, a fragile vehicle for sight, glass was originally a material for small-sized elements such as windows. Generally inserted in the necessary voids in the thickness of a wall, and so, when standing for what is not there, it often needed bars and shutters to create the barrier it could not be. It allows for seeing out and seeing in, for light to enter.

Stone, marble, brick, and concrete create solidity and mass, darkness and enclosure within; glazed openings bring in light and view, visual access to the outdoors and, to a large extent, the feeling of openness. When the structure is light, as it was first constructed at the end of the nineteenth-century with cast iron, the eye experienced no limits between inside and outside. Cast iron structures holding a great many panes of glass, sometimes with barrel roofs also of glass, created spacious, light-filled conservatories, train stations, and the remarkable Crystal Palace in London or the Kew Gardens conservatories of the Victorian period. Today steel structures are used to create similar kinds of public spaces with much larger panes of glass.

A glass pane doesn't invite touch because its transparency is deformed by finger tips. It is sensitive, though, to the knocking of hands and vibrates back, with a subdued sound, an echoing sensation. While it creates a connection for the eyes, it also separates what, through the eyes, it unifies.

A new kind of glass, tempered and multi-layered, offers the qualities of glass while adding rigidity as well as safety. Thus glass can be extended from the size of one window pane to an entire wall, the "curtain wall." It then becomes a barrier, thus less elastic and heavier. Its immateriality is lost and, rather than just letting light pass through it also reflects it, thus contributing to an illusory approach to the building and its surroundings. "The reflection of light or of reality certainly doesn't change their nature; however it implies a certain amount of illusion, of lying. . . Mirrors give

an upside down image of reality" (Jean Chevalier and
Alain Gherbrant 1986, p415).

Let us not forget that mirrors also welcome us if we
are determined enough to look at them, and ourselves,
as Antoine Predock invites us to do in the facade of
the Mandell Weiss Forum in San Diego.

Brick suggests absorption rather than reflection.
Particularly when the bricks are hand-made, their irregular sizes and the humanity of their imperfections speak
of life as stones and timber do. With their rather rough
texture bricks are very "material" and modulate walls
and facades with great dignity, never with an ostentatious
look. Like timber they can create carved surfaces articulated by moldings of different depths.

Brick may be one of the most traditional materials
since it has kept its dimensions, more or less, over time
and cultures. It is always used for what it is, the smallest
prefabricated element of the building industry, the one
that requires hands to hold each piece one by one and
place them layer upon layer, bonded by cement. Being
made of earth, brick relates to the ground and, more
than other material, blends with it.

Brick is not for contrast with the environment: discrete
even when in daring forms, it brings the earth towards
the sky. This metaphor is very well embodied by Ralph
Erskine's Ark, in London, its solidity bound to the ground
from which it seems to have been born. The rooting
of the glazed building is powerfully and delicately
expressed by the waving effect of the brick texture that
is reminiscent of water, whereas the brick pillars remind
us of the scaffolding necessary to hold the ark in place.

Contrary to brick's general application, Erskine's brick
is used plastically, not statically. The round shape breaks
with the tradition of brick, but even more breaks with
the tradition of a building becoming narrower as it grows
out of the ground. Although the traditional law of statics
teaches that walls have to narrow rather than widen,
the power of the architect here was in transforming and
adapting matter to an idea rather than making ideas
adapt to it. People's creativity and ingenuity transform,
giving new forms to materials by emphasizing their
archetypal qualities.

Simple, of the color of the earth of which it is made,
adobe carries the essential qualities of brick; it is a
building module, a rational form of a loaf of ground
that with time fades away, again into the ground. The
dwellers of New Gourna in Egypt knew this and so,
when they wanted to return to the old Gourna they
flooded the new settlement that Hassan Fathy had
designed and built in adobe.

The Ark, London (Ralph Erskine)

Adobe bricks drying, Egypt

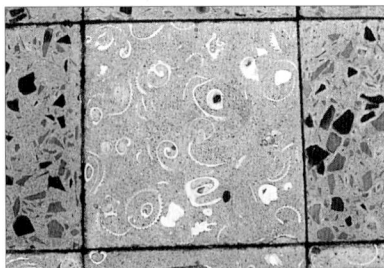

Shells in concrete floor, Shonandai Cultural Center (Itsuko Hasegawa)

Traditionally, in most countries, building materials for those who are settled and have financial resources have been strong and heavy in order to give a sense of solidity and safety, in order to last, to be a valid investment. No matter how precious, they have to cohere in order to create a solid mass in which functions are stabilized. To this purpose both brick and concrete, as manufactured materials, respond very well.

Since the Romans, concrete has made possible extremely large and daring constructions of great strength and durability. Today, together with steel, it is the material of pillars for bridges, thick walls for atomic power stations, and foundations and walls for buildings worldwide. Many of these uses hide the concrete, together with the steel buried within it, under ground or behind false ceilings or between partitions.

More than other materials concrete has contrasting qualities, with a distinctive shadow side that relates to its use as a material for the hidden part of the building, where it is rough and mechanical. Its light side comes through when architects explore its primary plastic qualities which transform it from a heavy material into a very light, malleable, friendly, yet strong one.

Made from light, loose elements that are easily transported, concrete solidifies once it sets, becoming powerful and heavy, adapting totally to the purposes it has to meet. Unlike wood and stone, that need to be carved, concrete is molded and thus its shapes and texture are determined by the mold into which a blend of the cementing material, water, sand, and gravel, is poured. By changing the proportions and the consistency of the elements of which it is composed, by adding colored pigments, glass, stones or shells to the mixture, its gloomy grey color and its aggressiveness are replaced by delicate, light surfaces, rich in nuance.

Concrete is the most plastic of the traditional building materials. With it, space can become organically and dynamically sculpted, thus breaking with the concepts of the rigidity and weight of building matter, as does Steven Holl with his shaping of ramp and stairs in the Kiasma Museum, Helsinki.

Concrete can be treated with care and revealed to the eye, its feeling of roughness can stimulate our imagination, as in buildings designed by Louis Kahn who often combined it with wood, which seems to balance concrete very well. In his British Center for Art at Yale University, one can see the light-colored oak of the wall panels contrasting with the thin concrete columns and floors. At the Museum of Anthropology at the University of British Columbia Arthur Erickson shows the solidity

a

b

c

Flexibility of Concrete
a. University of British
Columbia Anthropology
Museum, Vancouver
(Arthur Erickson)
b. Kiasma Museum of
Contemporary Art,
Helsinki (Steven Holl)
c. Kresge Auditorium,
Massachusetts Institute
of Technology,
Cambridge (Eero
Saarinen)
d. Yale Center for British
Art and Studies, New
Haven, Connecticut
(Louis Kahn)

d

Entrance to the Louvre, Paris (I.M. Pei)

and potential massiveness of concrete against the lightness and transparency of glass.

Like concrete, steel allows the construction of feats of engineering – extremely tall buildings and very long bridges. So often it is hidden, becoming rough and rusty, sharp. When freed from the constraints of concrete, steel regains its nobility and becomes genuinely agile. It holds up buildings on its own. On its own it is more daring and more direct than when buried in concrete. Then, we can read the tensions it holds between connecting joints. Buildings with an entirely exposed steel structure are a sort of x-ray of themselves.

When combined with glass, steel structures become particularly essential: no flesh, but only bones. It is as if steel had suddenly made a choice to become itself, freeing itself from its hidden dedication. By coming to light, like concrete, its form changes, as does its color; it becomes more precious, it acquires new life, makes buildings more agile. Produced in straight bars it is seldom used as a plastic material, rather it contributes to the shaping of buildings that are polygonal, that look very much like gigantic toys. With glass, rather than with concrete, steel is the high-tech emblem of the close of the twentieth-century.

Steel has helped to separate load-bearing structures from the outer skin, reducing the facade to a thin membrane. Even when non-structural, steel is a determined material that, either in sheets or in bars, rigidly holds a shape whether in cars, airplanes, or handrails. Its shining quality speaks of the hardness of its nature, almost as glass does.

Other metals are softer, therefore non-structural; they are used to dress up the structure or to create objects and furniture. They may shine also, modulating and reflecting light. While not as essential to construction as steel, metals are essential components of it. More malleable, they weather and relate to particular times or styles. Some of them are alloys, like bronze that was utilized before iron by blending together copper, silver or lead, or like aluminum, softer and lighter, used very frequently today for cladding and furniture. Whereas in the past metals were used for domestic tools and garments, today they are very much part of construction, bringing the moon's qualities to it. "The word metal is related by Rebe' Allean to the root *me* or *mes*, which is the most ancient name given to the moon" (Chevalier and Gherbrant 1986, p88).

Seeing Through

Almost like fabric, perforated metal and metal nets are used to create a separation between realms, adding privacy and mystery to the building which appears through it as a woman's face through a veil. Whereas fabric, except for tents, generally belongs to interiors, perforated metals are used mainly on the outside. Whereas fabric dresses up the inside of buildings and balances their rigidity, as Scarpa often did in exhibitions and museums, creating spaces of intimacy and bringing to the solidity of construction the quality of impermanence, perforated metals create mutable surfaces used on their own or against solid facades. When used as a screen against the outer skin of a building, perforated metal becomes a thin membrane that, like successive layers of clothing made of gauze and lace, decomposes, enriches, and gives depth to a facade.

When fabrics are used outside like tents, they can be stretched over steel frames to make very fluid forms, with materials that are nearly transparent like gauze or heavier and more protective like canvas. For the Asajigahara Rest Area at the Nara Silkroad Expo, Hasegawa was inspired by people who wrap themselves in cloth: "the Muslim kurta, the Iranian chador, and the Indian sari. The image I had in mind . . . was of a group of people in such a dress; but I also wanted to suggest nomadic tents 'pao' of different sizes and the mountain ranges along the Silk Road" (Hasegawa 1993, p57). Inside one can see reflections of trees and water on the tent.

Different degrees of seeing through can be obtained by different perforations, different colors, and by a combination of materials. For a canopy at the Shonandai Cultural Center, Itsuko Hasegawa alternated curved, denser sheets with a more flexible, open net that moves slightly in the wind, its blue and purple panels catching the light, animating the space, much as does the water below. More solid, because of its stability, its density, and its role as almost a second wall is the round screen Steven Holl designed for Makuhari Housing, creating a kind of film over the bright colors behind it.

It is again Hasegawa who, in curved screens of yellow and gray/green at the Shonandai Cultural Center, introduces the moon-like qualities so lacking in the construction field. As if she were building with textiles, the effect is flowing surfaces to be lived in. Almost as in fashion today, the feminine quality of transparency is introduced to add sensuality to the built form. At Cona Village, a low-cost housing development, screens of soft gray with muted patches of pinks and blues offer a soft barrier for the spaces behind and enliven the facade.

"The Fashion of Architecture" (collage, Nils-Ole Lund)

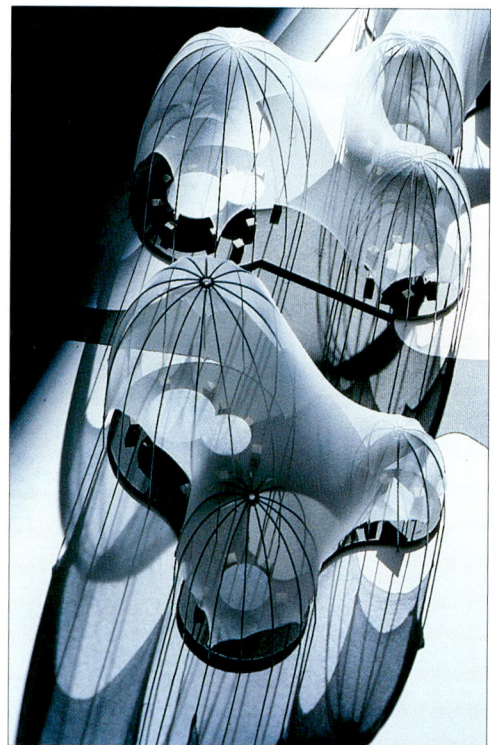

Asajigahara Rest Area, Nara Silkroad Expo, Nara City, Japan (Itsuko Hasegawa)

a

b

c

d

Seeing Through
a. Shonandai
Cultural Center,
Fujisawa City,
Japan (Itsuko
Hasegawa)
b. Makuhari
Housing, Chiba,
Japan (Steven
Holl Architects)
c. Shonandai
Cultural Center
d. Cona Village,
Amagasaki City,
Japan (Itsuko
Hasegawa)

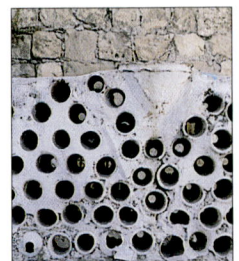

Vernacular seeing
through, Hebron, Israel

The effect of "seeing through," so popular in the countries where women live in spaces concealed from men, is also captured with brick structures, with wooden screens and shutters or even with concrete inlaid with bottles. A screen over a facade conveys a more subtle message – suggesting through concealing. The field created by transparency is a very delicate one. It eliminates the obvious while offering depth and evoking a sense of mystery.

New approaches to design such as the one of Günter Bëhnisch in Stuttgart decompose the facade "separating the individual functions of sun screening, spatial enclosure, escape balconies articulating facades three dimensionally into a series of plans (Bëhnisch 1998, p1142)." This creates texture, lightness, delicacy, despite the rigor of its dynamism; an intriguing trend that adds mystery and texture thanks to the variety of materials used as well as to the interplay of shadow and light. It also adds depth to the surfaces materials create, animating them so they literally vibrate.

Water and trees are very much part of architecture and its context for which they provide soft, vibrating, reflecting, moving, and singing volumes and surfaces. They also provide coolness, scents, relaxation, and relief, as in the water garden designed by landscape architect Dan Liley in Dallas next to the Allied Bank tower by I.M. Pei. "Instead of providing the standard hard surface plaza, Liley has used water and 200 bald cypresses. . . Instead of hard surfaces which reflect and absorb heat, only to emit it again, the water and trees provide a cool oasis. . . The hard surfaces are restricted to paths and places to sit and relax in. Visitors are surrounded by the sound of water splashing and hissing in fountains and waterfall, and, as time goes on, they will be shaded by a forest of trees growing out of the middle of water" (Prince 1988, p70).

The wall of falling water in Paley Park screens out the sounds of Manhattan traffic; it creates an oasis of cool air and tranquility. Running or standing, moving smoothly and silently or violently and with voice in fountains of spray, in waves or flat surfaces, water always speaks of movement and depth, of nature and of ourselves.

Matter as Field

As quantum physics reminds us, the entire universe, whether or not we perceive it, is pulsating; quantum physics also reminds us that matter creates energy fields whose pulsations are in constant exchange. The fields of materials are in constant exchange with each other

Water garden, Dallas (Dan Liley)

Paley Park, New York City (Zion & Breen)

Fountain at Centre Pompidou, Paris (Niki de Saint Phalle and Jean Tinguely)

"Rose & Boat" (monotype with hand color, Ellen Wiener)

and our own fields are in constant exchange with the fields we encounter. If this is the nature of physical reality and therefore the nature of the world we live in and the one we build, as Ellen Wiener's art suggests so well, then a true quantum approach to architecture grasps this dynamic quality of matter. Quantum leaps have to happen in each of us first, in the ways we experience as well as in the ways we design the material world.

How does the material feel? What does it suggest? Answers to these basic questions illustrate how materials, objects, buildings, and people create fields. It is as different to sit next to a person dressed in white than a person in red or black as it is to walk in a crowd of singing people compared to a crowd of shouting or praying people. Each color the person is wearing as well as the singing, the shouting, or the praying emits a different kind of energy that creates different fields. What kind of field does this particular place generate? How does it interact with my own field?

It is not so much a matter of the likes and dislikes of an "I": that is, the feeling subject over "felt" objects and people. It is instead the relationship between fields, without boundaries, that attract or do not attract each other. And if they do attract each other, they do not necessarily do so all the time. There is movement, change within fields, particularly within human fields.

The concept of field acknowledges the autonomous existence of the material world, of its qualities that are not the result of passive accidents, but of active, interrelating forces. The concept of field also helps individuals be less personal, less judgmental about something they seem to dislike. By considering preferences as dependent on the fields of people and the fields of matter, it may be easier to understand how the energy of certain forms and materials is appropriate to one person's field but not to another's.

Since we live in a world made of interrelating fields, there is no isolation, there is no way of doing something without interfering with something else. If not even the atom can be observed without its nature being modified, think how powerful are the modifications we make to and through materials when we use them for building and how significant are our insertions into environments.

Wood, brick, metal, concrete, glass, aluminum – each has its own archetypal qualities and distinctive character. Each has its own peculiar field that can change our experience of the same object as well as the quality of the experience we are involved in. To eat with a silver fork is not like eating with a stainless steel, plastic or wooden one. They weigh, sound, smell, and feel different; they

Willowbrook Green Apartments, Los Angeles (Ena Dubnoff)

Monochromatic field, Andalusia

Burano, Italy

interact differently with the taste of food. The field of a stainless steel fork is more impersonal than the one of a silver fork. Being stain-less, the steel one has a smooth, hard and impenetrable surface whereas the silver one is more porous, less cool to the touch and shows the marks and dents of use. The lightness and fragility of a plastic fork may make eating less substantial, some sort of necessary process, depriving the meal of its ritualistic nature. A wooden fork doesn't give much chance of concentrating on the food either. So weightless yet substantial that, when it touches your lips, it could be a sort of food in itself.

The fields materials generate are related to their dimensions as well as to the intensity of their color. How different the fields generated by a pot of grass, by a patch of grass and by a lush lawn. Even more different from a pasture. The field water generates in a cup is different from the fields created by water in a transparent vase, an aquarium, a bath, a pool, a pond, a river, the ocean. The smaller the field the more we are in control of it; the larger one may overwhelm us. From smaller to larger, a field transforms from object into subject. Whereas glass can give fragility to a small object, the fragility of glass, when used as the surface of a mirrored curtain wall, becomes impenetrable; its transparency is translated into a field of reflection and thus rejection, rather than a welcoming invitation to seeing through.

Shape as well as scale changes the field of materials, modifying their character. A curved iron bar is softer than a straight one, a wooden beam cut at a 90 degree angle seems harder than a trunk-like one. Plastic can look like metal or fabric depending on its shape. Depending on its shape, glass can be like water or solid crystal. Shapes have their own archetypal character that goes beyond the simple category of type. They speak their own symbolic language that mainly refers to the body that dreams and to the one that feels. Materials then become a quality of the shape and support shape better to express its intention.

Through the qualities of shapes and materials architecture speaks; but we also resonate with these qualities according to our individual field and to the collective code rooted in each of us. Thanks to this collective code we resonate differently with different shapes and materials, with their different character and symbolism. How do we want to affect people with our design? This can be rather worrying for someone who is making space and shapes; how to provide something that satisfies people and yet originates from only one individual or small group of them?

Window, Chapel of St. Ignatius, Seattle University, Seattle, Washington (Steven Holl Architects)

The four bonsai trees are fields that attract different people who are each fields of their own. I may perceive and experience space as if I were a pink or a brown or a green tree. From a pink, brown or green point of view I can perceive, but I can also design. As a tree of one or another shape I can design for trees of shapes that are different from mine. Furthermore people who are once attracted by one type of bonsai may be attracted by another one on a future occasion. People change; their polarity changes and therefore their taste changes together with their needs. As a pink bonsai how do I design for a green one? How for green, brown and pink bonsai together?

Combining Materials and Beyond

One might think that the more materials are combined, the more their field will visually vibrate, but this is not necessarily so. Think of a big bookcase. Think of its books arranged according to their height; think of them arranged by the material of their covers or by color. Think of books of two colors arranged randomly all over the bookcase. Think of the books of two colors distributed to make stripes: first a stripe of one shelf, then two shelves, then three and four until you have divided the bookshelf horizontally into two colors. Think of the stripes being vertical as well. Think of the books being all the same color.

Now, what about the bookcase? What is its color, its material? How does it frame the books? Does it match the two colors? What happens when all the books have the same color? What if the frame of the bookcase is of the same color too? And, what is that color? Furthermore, what is the color of the room? The same, similar, darker, lighter? What if the walls are decorated with patterns and the books are all different colors?

Matter speaks through color too. When Bianca chose turquoise-green copper for the roof of the extension to the building she was converting in Arezzo, she did so because she wanted it to stand out as a joyful statement

Bonsai trees, Brooklyn Botanic Garden

Kiasma, Museum of Contemporary Art,
Helsinki (Steven Holl Architects)

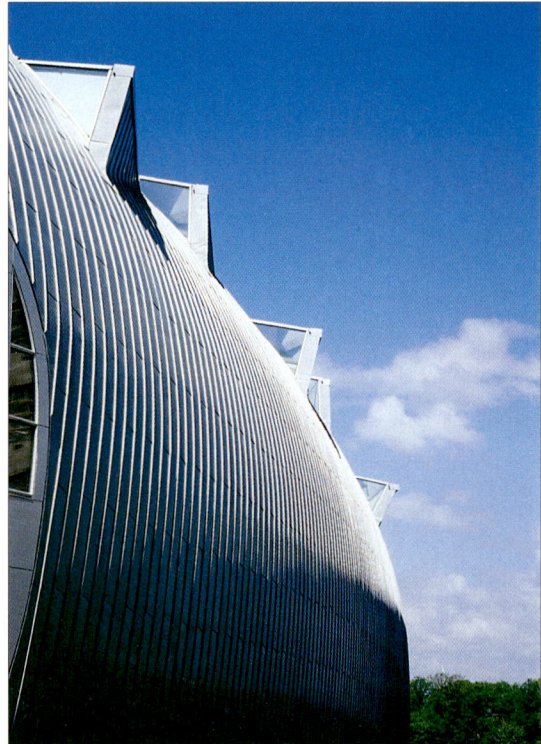

rather than to blend in with the pink terracotta and dark yellow context as traditional copper would have done. This kind of joy in contrast can also be seen in the canvas awnings on the facades of Willowbrook Green Apartments, Los Angeles, designed by Ena Dubnoff.

It is both the form and the combination of materials with their colors that give a building so much of its identity. The Kiasma Museum of Contemporary Art in Helsinki, designed by Steven Holl, is composed of a variety of contrasting materials whose qualities stimulate the senses of sight and touch. On the interior the walls are plaster, the sculptural stairs and ramp concrete, and the floors integral colored concrete. The exterior side walls are made from thick aluminum sheets that have been sanded, causing the aluminum to reflect the light in different ways. Not shiny, it may look almost white or very dark, depending on the position of the sun and the way the light hits it. The dramatically curved roof and wall are sheathed in zinc panels finished to a weathered patina that will continue to darken over time. The north and south elevations contain brass panels that also have been treated to have a copper-colored finish.

Lecture Hall, Institute of Technology, Otaniemi, Finland (Alvar Aalto)

exterior side walls are made from thick aluminum sheets that have been sanded, causing the aluminum to reflect the light in different ways. Not shiny, it may look almost white or very dark, depending on the position of the sun and the way the light hits it. The dramatically curved roof and wall are sheathed in zinc panels finished to a weathered patina that will continue to darken over time. The north and south elevations contain brass panels that also have been treated to have a copper-colored finish.

During Finland's dark season, the museum acts as a kind of lantern as light from its windows and skylights warms the city. Holl also designed many interior details including paper dispensers in the public lavatories, door fittings, and wash basins, all of aluminum cast in molds. The rear wall of the auditorium is covered with a dark blue velvet-like canvas, which also covers the seats.

The fields created by a building stimulate our senses while they also meet our needs for warmth and coolness, for light and shadow.

For the main lecture hall at the Institute of Technology at Otaniemi, Finland, Alvar Aalto chose deep-red brick, granite, copper, and glass. The main approach to the building, along the administration wing, reveals an amphitheater: the exterior wall of the lecture hall steps back creating benches of granite; above it are bands of skylights, topped by a copper roof.

I walked into the lecture hall just after the morning session of an international conference on mathematics, when the participants had all gone to lunch. The space between the rows of seats was wide enough that I could walk freely and easily without worrying about bumping my legs or tripping. Slim wooden desks could be pulled up and out from the backs of seats to provide writing surfaces. The air in the spacious hall felt cool and fresh and filled with soft, clear light. There was no whirring of air conditioners or fans on this warm summer day, no buzzing of light fixtures. The atmosphere was calm and peaceful.

The reinforced concrete structure of this fan-shaped hall is dramatically curved, composed of longitudinal structural ribs and deep lateral shells. The ventilation system is integrated into the spaces between the ribs and within the lateral sheets (Trencher 1994). The bands of glass that serve as skylights, so prominent on the exterior of the hall, are placed deep above the light baffles so they cannot be seen on the interior, creating a diffuse light. On sunny days they can be left open and on winter days the electric light from the hall illuminates the amphitheater on the building's exterior. Electric lights placed in coves at the back of the hall cast their light upwards against the curved baffles.

Of Light and Shadow

We see objects and buildings because of the light that touches them. One could say that for sight all objects are the result of the light that hits them to the extent that if there is no light, there is no object. Objects and buildings seem to take hold of light to make their appearance in the world. "Let there be light," the biblical version of the world's creation, refers to making visible, making understandable, to something that becomes manifest. The movement from darkness to light is birth and renewal: new born babies come to the light and everyday objects come to light again and again, with the dawning of each new day.

It is not so much the opposite qualities of day and night or the opposing fields of complete darkness and full sunlight that are of importance here as it is the qualities of shadow and light. Shadow is not the absence of light but the result of beams of light encountering an obstacle. It is the softer and cooler side of light, the one that

Community garden, New York City

a

b

Trellises
a. Indian Institute of
Management, Bangalore
(Balkrishna Doshi)
b. Alicante, Spain

between the trees, which conveys a feeling of coolness, transforming the experience of a site, designing new patterns not only on the ground and walls but also on objects and bodies as well. Through the interplay of shadow and light, architecture becomes literally animated and people and nature participate directly in this animism. Like trees, trellises, grilles, and openings in walls create similar, changing patterns of light and shadow outdoors, giving us protection from the sun and enlivening the space with pattern and movement.

Light and shadow play an interesting role in the interface between outdoors and indoors. The facade of a building is the frontier between the outside spaces where shadow modulates the natural light and the interior spaces where it is the natural light that modulates the shadow. On the outside, the stepping in of the window panes from the facade's surface, the cornices, shutters, and balconies all cast shadows that animate and give depth to the building's surface. In this regard it is interesting to notice how the smooth curtain wall, by preventing light from playing games with shade, remains superficial in its articulation. It maintains its two-dimensional quality of rigidity and impenetrability, despite the transparency of the material of which it is made.

Curtains, shutters, and shades contribute, in a permeable way, to the modulation of natural light indoors. They filter and break down sunlight. On a summer's day a few streams of light come through the shutters into a protected, cool room, which absorbs its vibrations. Planes of light cut through the shutter's openings, bringing messages from some other dimension, reminding us, inside, of the presence of the outside. Our eyes open, we can stand there in the veiled mystery of light, protected from its glare.

How pleasant and vitalizing is the light that streams down, unobstructed, from a skylight in the roof or through a clerestory in the upper part of a wall. How different this is from light coming through a window. Light from above lifts our minds and souls. While lifting our souls up, the light comes down, making a space in the shadow for reading or working, for being active and vital. When the openings are large compared to the size of the room, they minimize the enclosure, opening the space to the sky.

Except for places like the Pantheon where light streams through the oculus or ancient Roman houses with a *compluvium* (an opening in the roof for rain to enter and be collected in a rectangular basin), traditionally light coming directly from above has been artificial light that generically lights a space by taking away darkness as well as shadow. How different it is to have a meal around a table lit with candles than to have a dinner where people float in a room that is fully lit from the ceiling. How special to see the gestures of people coming out of the darkness rather than dispersing themselves in the anonymous atmosphere of homogeneous electrical glare! Faces are different, colors are deeper, words are softer.

Whereas natural light coming from the ceiling adds to a room's atmosphere, artificial light, if it floods the entire space in an equal manner, creates anonymity precisely because it creates no shadows. It is an obvious light, allowing no games of shadows, appropriate for some activities and tasks when everything in the space must be seen equally clearly and completely, when nothing in particular is to be emphasized or "highlighted." And so homogeneous lighting invites no feelings toward anything in particular and creates no seduction of objects, environment, or people.

The sources and kinds of light and the atmosphere they make help tell people how to behave, how loudly to speak, how gently to move, how much intimacy is invited. How quickly the conversations in restaurants soften when the lights are turned down

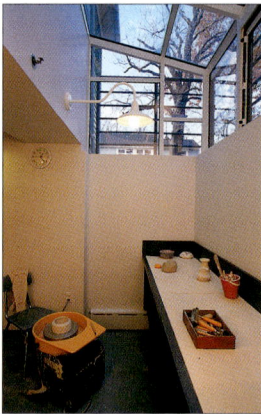

Beacon High School ceramics studio, Brookline, Massachusetts (Gail Sullivan Associates)

and the candles lit. How quickly students begin to move around in their seats when the lights are turned on after a slide lecture even as the lecturer continues speaking.

With light and shadow designers choose the mood to be stimulated. It is best if the kind and amount of light can be changed to suit the mood and to meet specific needs. Therefore it is important to provide a system that can vary natural and artificial light to match the rhythm of our days and to meet our changing needs and moods. Like eyelids of different consistency, texture, and patterns these systems will modulate our emotions as well as the light that stimulates those emotions.

The more public a space is, the less light can be modified to suit individual moods and requirements. Nevertheless, the choice of general lighting should satisfy as many people as possible, as well as being complemented, if possible, with focused lighting to support specific tasks. In the grand two-story space of the main post office in Manhattan, small brass lamps over the counters can be turned on by visitors as they write a letter or place a stamp on it. Within this public place, a private realm is created by the light, by the gesture of switching it on and the activities that follow.

In the Academic Bookstore in Helsinki, designed by Aalto, two large central skylights bring natural light into the middle of the store while electric lights within the ceiling give additional, general lighting. Then smaller, narrow fixtures discreetly illuminate the horizontal displays of books and hanging fixtures bringing light and intimacy to each table in the cafe. Similarly, in the library at the Institute of Technology in Otaniemi, deep skylights, with electric lights hanging within them, a clerestory, ceiling lights, and hanging lamps offer a variety of light sources that help define different spaces.

Academic Bookstore, Helsinki (Alvar Aalto)

Artificial light can also be used to illuminate particular objects, such as paintings and sculptures. It may be directed toward a ceiling, a counter, a molding, or a flight of steps: here light guides people through the act of moving through darkness, having them focus precisely on the steps on which they are going to place their feet. This lamp here, on my desk, low and bright, is creating a space of light almost as in a Caravaggio painting. The space of life in the rest of the room is unimportant, unnecessary while my attention is focused on this table holding papers as I concentrate on this book, on my present, on what I want to see now. Through emphasizing one area of activity, a stage is created for it. For this reason the appearance of light fixtures is less important than the kind of light they generate.

Living Through

As we have seen, the world of matter, of materials shaped and combined to make buildings, of light and shadow, air and water, is alive and enlivens us. It is not only the basis of our physical existence, it is also the source of emotions, dreams and aspirations, the basis of our psychic existence as well. What is built is not only of practical import but of psychological significance also. This is not yet widely acknowledged or understood either by architects or psychologists.

> One has the impression that men do not know exactly what they are doing. They build with stone and do not see that each of their gestures when laying the stone is accompanied by the shadow of that gesture, by the shadow of the stone and the shadow of the cement. And it is the building of shadow that matters (Giono 1935, p27).

To explore this connection between "stone" and "shadow," between matter and psyche does not mean that we should dematerialize the former but rather that we consider its relationship to people and their inner life. We can observe everyday how men and women reflect themselves in the gestures they make, in the clothes they wear, and in the homes they inhabit. We invest strong feelings and a sense of self-identity in the places where we live and in the ways we furnish and transform them.

There is a human tendency to spatialize ideas, emotions, and situations and so "spatial archetypes provide one of the most profound keys to understanding the psyche . . . And spatial archetypes are expressed most directly through architecture . . . when it is at its best, a mediator between the self and the cosmos" (Lobell 1983, p70). The dwelling, more than any other built form seems to be a mediator between self and cosmos, and also, within itself, a cosmos mirroring the self.

Teresa Howard, architect and psychotherapist, recognizes the significance of both the physical and the emotional contexts of people's lives as well as the links between them; in her dual professional roles she helps people restructure both contexts. In her work as an architect on London housing estates she found that a rehabilitated house was pointless unless residents could also make an emotional investment in the dwelling, transforming it from "house" to "home," an investment that can be facilitated when their voices are truly heard and responded to in the planning process.

"Being an architect for me wasn't what I subsequently learned it is for other people, a kind of sculpture or a kind of art. It was very much about providing, or discovering, the kinds of places people need for themselves, for their emotional selves to grow and develop and feel safe, for relationships to function effectively" (Teresa Howard).

To explore the link between house and self-identity, Clare Cooper Marcus has adopted Gestalt therapy techniques for her interviews. After asking people to draw their feelings about home in a picture and asking them to describe what they have drawn, she then asks them to speak to the drawing as if it were the house, starting with the words, "House, the way I feel about you is . . . " (Cooper Marcus 1995, p8). After some time, she asks them to change seats with the house, that is to move to the other chair, and to respond as if they were the house. Thus a conversation between person and house takes place, often becoming quite impassioned and generating deep insights.

From her research Clare has discovered how much we express aspects of our unconscious in our homes, much as we do in dreams, both in our choice of dwelling and particularly in the objects we place in them and the way we decorate them: " . . . we all, to some degree, display in the physical environment messages from the unconscious about who we are, who we were and who we might become. Unable to comprehend all that is encapsulated in the psyche, we need to place it 'out there' for us to contemplate, just as we need to view our physical body in a mirror" (ibid., p17).

References

Bëhnisch, Günter. Interview. *Detail*. October/November, 1998.

Buchanan, Peter. Structural adventurousness, expressive engineering – Calatrava. *Architectural Review*, September 1987.

Chevalier, Jean and Alain Gherbrant. *Dizionario dei Simboli*. Vol. 1. Milan: BUR Dizionario Rizzoli, 1986. (Passages translated by R. Bianca Lepori.)

Cooper Marcus, Clare. *House as A Mirror of Self*. Berkeley, Calif: Conari Press, 1995.

Giono, Jean. *Que ma joie demeure*. Paris: Bernard Grasset, 1935. (Passage translated by R. Bianca Lepori.)

Hasegawa, Architects. *Itsuko Hasegawa*. (Architectural Monographs, No. 31) London: Academy Editions, 1993.

Heathcote, Edwin. *Imre Makovecz: The Wings of the Soul*. (Architectural Monographs, No. 47) London: Academy Editions, 1997.

Heschong, Lisa. *Thermal Delight in Architecture*. Cambridge, Mass.: M.I.T. Press, 1979.

Lobell, Mimi. Spatial archetypes. *Revision*, 1983, 6:2.

Prince, Martin. Dallas oasis. *Architectural Review*, August 1988.

Tanizaki, Jun'ichiro. *In Praise of Shadows*, trans. Thomas J. Harper and Edward G. Seidensticker. New Haven, Connecticut: Leete's Island Books, 1997.

Trencher, Michael. *The Alvar Aalto Guide*. New York: Princeton Architectural Press, 1996.

Valéry, Paul. *Eupalinos or The Architect*, trans. William McCausland Steward. London: Oxford University Press, 1932.

Vigorelli, Giancarlo. *Il gesuita positivo: Vita e opere di P. Teilhard de Chardin*. Milano: Casa Editrice il Saggiatore, 1963. (Passage translated by R. Bianca Lepori.)

Chapter 4

Space Therapy

The Constructor . . . finds before him, as his chaos and as primitive matter, precisely the world-order which the Demiurge wrung from the disorder of the beginning. Nature is formed, and the elements are separated; but something enjoins him to consider this work as unfinished, and as requiring to be rehandled and set in motion again for the more especial satisfaction of man. He takes as the starting point of his act the very point where the god had left off. In the beginning, he says to himself, there was what is: the mountains and forests; the deposits and veins; red clay, yellow sand and the white stone which will give us lime. There were also the muscular arms of men, and the massive strength of buffaloes and oxen. But there were in addition the coffers and storerooms of intelligent tyrants and of citizens grown over-rich by trade. . .

Here I am, says the Constructor, I am the act. You are the matter, you are the force, you are the desire; but you are separate. An unknown industry has isolated and prepared you according to its means. The Demiurge was pursuing his own designs, which do not concern his creatures. . . But I came after him. I am he who conceives what you desire a trifle more exactly than you do yourselves. . . (Valéry 1932, pp94, 95).

The activity of the Constructor, which refers to the profession of the architect, man or woman, is a special one that contributes to the re-creation of physical word. The way one designs thus becomes one's own way of contributing to this re-creation while the marks left in the world, through design, tell us about who has made them. Seen from this perspective, design becomes a way of serving as well as providing a service, an activity that can be performed not only in different ways but also at different levels, from the more practical to the more poetic.

It may be helpful to refer to the research carried out by Lorenzo Ostuni, an Italian scholar of symbolism, on the four levels of service implicit in the ancient word *theraps* (servant) as it was used in the classical Greece of the fifth century BC. When, in this context, the chiefs of the clans chose the servants they wanted from among the foreigners taken prisoner, they were careful to select the ones they believed to be suitable. In order to be chosen, the servant had to seduce the master, to reach out towards him and somehow conquer his mind and his soul. Beside conquering the master through particular talents based on knowledge and skill, he had to study him, learn about his likes and dislikes, and approach him in a way that would please him. Seducing the master was the prisoner's way of choosing. Through seduction, the person seduced, in this case the master, entered into a vulnerable relationship of dependence, reversing the emotional balance between the two, making each dependent upon the other. Furthermore, when culminating in selection, seduction involved both parties, each one interested in winning over the other person as a whole being rather than simply as a servant or a master. This first meaning of *theraps*, as seduction, corresponds to the first level of *therapeia* as practice and art.

The second level of *therapeia* corresponds to the second phase when the chosen servant entered the clan and began performing a service. As well as establishing dependence, the first level, seduction, had created between the two parties a reciprocal dignity that seemed to be basic to the servant's tasks. By doing what the master wanted and also what was good for him, a servant was performing a service that was practical as well as intuitive.

Architecture is also a service involving practical and intuitive activities. Yet any production of architecture as service only, without the seductive input that transforms a practical exchange into a personal engagement, is purely functional and routine. The seductive input brings sensitivity, an ability to tune in with people and site to the design task.

Because, in the Greek clans, servants came with the skills and knowledge of their own cultures and therefore often they were some of the most cultured people in the clans, their service could include a further level, the one of education. In the clan of Alcibiades, for instance there were over 100 servants: Alcibiades himself was illiterate, but the most talented of his servants were the tutors as well as the doctor of his children. The third level of *therapeia* thus corresponds to the third meaning of the word *theraps*, the one concerned with education and cure.

This third stage may remind us of the responsibility architects and designers have to society, to education, and to the cure of symptoms of pathology within the environment. In order to "educate" and cure, designers and architects have to have sufficient knowledge and skill. They have to have an understanding of the situation; they have to recognize the nature of the design that is needed; they have to be acquainted with the topic and have experience of it. Furthermore, they have to embrace the situation with their cultural and technical expertise. It is best if their involvement includes the humanities, science, and art as well as practical skills. Since the task of designers and architects is to create the environments where people live, they have to know at least as much, if not more, than those to whom they are giving their services. For this reason in ancient Egypt the knowledge required of an architect extended to the secret knowledge; in order to be an architect one had to be an initiate.

Initiation leads into the fourth level of *therapeia*, the one that was practiced in the sacred sanctuaries and was concerned with healing rather than curing. Here the approach to health was not strictly physical, but was "spiritually oriented and took the concept of total man into consideration" (Tansley 1984, p68). The fourth meaning of *theraps* has to do with cult and refers to the level of *therapeia* practiced in those sanctuaries where the pilgrims, coming from different places, relied on a god for the future healing of their disease, where ". . . healing was intended to be the restoration of harmony to the complexity of the body of man" (ibid.).

Hence, the fourth meaning of *theraps*, more than the others, relates to the nature, of the individual designer or architect, to his or her spiritual sensitivity and brings into the profession of architecture a dimension of transcendence. Whatever they do, whatever they know, however they relate, designers and architects can become channels for what wants to be expressed. Like pilgrims of ancient times, as well as ancient healers, some of them may be invested with pure energy and light which translate into a building's qualities. By trusting their natural power of intuition, it is possible for some of them to make manifest through their buildings the harmonies with which people will resonate.

Tell me (since you are so sensible to the effects of architecture), have you not noticed, in walking about this city, that among the buildings with which it is peopled, certain are mute; *others* speak *and others, finally – and they are the most rare –* sing? *It is not their purpose, nor even their general features, that gives them such animation, or that reduce them to silence. These things depend upon the talent of their builder, or on the favour of the Muses* (Valéry 1932, pp22–3).

Let us leave the fourth level to the special cases in which the architect and the designer are truly poets who can experience, practice, and convey all four levels of the art of the *theraps* without even thinking of them or planning a strategy toward reaching a particular result. The purpose here is to concentrate instead on the first three levels, the ones that contribute to the creation of buildings that, far from being mute, speak at least correctly.

The word "therapy," borrowed from physiotherapy and psychoanalysis and as applied to architecture, reminds us of its twofold nature: the one manifested through its mechanics, the other manifested through its qualities. With the depth of the fourfold meaning that goes beyond the curing of symptoms, space therapy focuses on the one hand on towns, neighborhoods, and houses as bodies, each made of parts cohering to make up a pulsating organism, each telling its own story, singing its own song. On the other, it focuses on the emotional quality of those stories and those songs.

Space therapy provides a framework of analysis leading to a design that goes beyond the casualness of form, and that, at the same time, emphasizes its power. Based on the principle that built form is always the image of an intention, space therapy challenges architects, planners, and their clients to ask precise questions and to leave space open for the answers. It shows that answers come naturally once the proper questions have been asked, after the motivating intention has been honestly formulated. Space therapy invites designers to be humble, to empty themselves of their preconceptions and to be responsive, yet also to be accurate and precise regarding what they observe and what they facilitate.

An attitude of *theraps* in architecture is an opening up to the task and the situation at hand. It requires the application but not the imposition of skill; it promotes sympathetic exchanges as well as synergistic collaboration. It allows for creations that arise from the needs of particular people and circumstances rather than from preconceived or standardized principles. It means being in the present and listening to the needs of people and site. Through an exercise in humility consisting of recognizing what we do not know, a *theraps* attitude in design helps to uncover new perspectives and thus helps us expand personally as well as contributing to the expansion and transformation of the collective.

Thanks to the fourfold meaning of the word *theraps*, the aim of space therapy is to unify the practical aspects of architecture as service with the more existential ones that relate to people and their well being, perceptions and emotions and thus to the building of shadow. Since "the building of shadow" is at least as important as the building of stone, as Jean Giono reminded us in the previous chapter, the making of architecture has to take both of them into account. They both have to be thought of during design. This will give depth to architecture and bring it back to its original meaning, which is not simply building (*tecto*) but building with archetypes (*arche*).

The archetypes are the psychological centers from which comes that which is not yet said and yet not made. According to Jung, archetypes are buried deeply in the collective unconscious, they can not be known directly by the conscious mind. However they do shape various concepts and forms of human expression – art, architecture, music, literature, relationships, social structures, cosmologies, world views – and through these, the archetypes can become evident indirectly. (Mimi Lobell 1983, p69)

Paths, Roads: A Way to Convey

My client's house is on top of a hill. It was built in 1700 and there are no longer any roads leading to it. The hill is wild, full of bushes, vegetation and white rocky patches. We climbed up once to check the structural conditions of the house and again last week to take a few more measurements for the working drawings. Every time we go up, we take a different route. Sometimes we get lost; other times we find our way very quickly. Walking down the hill, one day, my client said, "Pensate a come deve essere stata importante l'invenzione delle strade" (Think how important the invention of roads must have been).

Now we can go up to the house on top of the hill any way we like since we have undifferentiated ground but the moment we build a road we fix a path; we establish a way of connecting, of approaching and living, a way of perceiving. We give a unique version of that environment as we give a unique version of a narrative depending on the way we want the events to flow.

Where and how would I build that road? From where would I like the speech to start, through which sentences and experiences do I want to lead its readers, in what sequence? Would I lay the road along the contours or just cut it through them, making it go up the hill as fast as possible? Would I take the time to walk the proposed route before deciding to have it built and would I choose the nicest spot for an opportunity to rest? Would I give space to natural beauty or just draw on the map what looks right? Would I choose the short cut that seems the most economical or would I try to find a way to be economical by responding to the suggestions of the site?

The potential road leading up to the house on the hill is a connector that suggests other connections that create space. A pathway between two rooms is a small road just as a street between two rows of buildings is a corridor. Roads, corridors, and pathways, by making the connections between spaces, are key elements because they decide how space will speak to us. Choosing a pathway is the first step towards the creation, and thus towards the exploration, of space. By choosing a pathway we choose the sequence, the distribution of spaces: we organize the layout of its speech, the sequence of the sentences of which it is made.

Paths in architecture create the layout, the sequence of spaces and events; they lay down the structure of the narrative by introducing a diagram of distribution, the skeleton of the building to be. This will be dressed up by the flesh – and bones – of the building, of the neighborhood, the town. With the layout, a structure is given to the sequence of experiences, to the relationships within the building and to the relationship between building and context. With paths, layouts are the simplest forms of representing the design, the first choice towards a synthetic or rhetorical expression, an explicit introverted or extroverted narrative, whose beginning is established by the entry point.

The entrance is the beginning of the narrative, established by the designer and experienced by the people who will use the space. They will be led, through the arrangement of partitions, or other kinds of barriers such as low walls, along a sequence of spaces of different size, proportion, orientation, color and texture, that become the sentences telling the story of a particular place. Depending upon their punctuation, thus on the degree of separation of its parts, a space can be made of separate, self-contained spaces or interconnected ones. Full stops, commas, colons, brackets, exclamation marks articulate and give color to space just as they do to speech.

Pathways as structures of the speech of architecture are the key elements of a rigorous reading as well as of a rigorous design. Pathways give order – or dis-order – to space whose distribution can not be accidental or arbitrary even in the most spontaneous settings. As in nature, where everything has its own order, where spontaneity, beauty, and even wilderness are based on a bio-logic-mathematical system, architecture needs an underlying pattern of organization.

This pattern of organization is equivalent to the choreography behind any dance, a choreography that is independent of the costumes, the colors, the people performing the dance because it generates different performances according to the kinds of costume, color and people performing it. It is the choreography, though, that holds the whole with its structuring strength.

Once the pathway is established, and thus two-dimensional or three-dimension-

Tree is leaf and leaf is tree.
House is city and city is house
A tree is a tree, but it is also a leaf
A leaf is a leaf, but is also a tiny tree
A city is not a city unless it is also a huge house, only if it is also a tiny city.
(Aldo van Eyck)

al structure is determined, more or less sophisticated elements/words can then be used to build up the three-dimensional story and give color to the events. By laying down the horizontal and vertical distribution of a space as well as by the choice of elements we may remain at the second level of "therapy," the one of serving a purpose, or we may enter the other ones, of educating, curing, and healing.

Having laid out a correct framework, and thus having established the relationship between the parts, materials, shapes, and colors become the specific words of our designed sentences. Their combinations can become simply discursive phrases or poetic images. The choice of materials, views, elements, and proportions, can transform an analytical layout into an imaginative adventure. The way stairs begin or end, their landings, the way the light comes in, the way handrails intersect, the way water flows, the way walls and ceilings connect make architecture and, furthermore, make buildings speak poetically, with nuance, or in plain, straightforward language.

New Pathways and Old

The project was small but extremely difficult. Seven doctors in a surgery, or joint practice, wanted new, larger accommodation without having to move from their location fronting Walworth Road in south London since their patients were so accustomed to coming there. The doctors had purchased a second building, fronting Manor Place, immediately to the rear of their existing surgery as well as the narrow "backlands" site (referring to the buildings and courts at the back of buildings fronting the street) which had been a stable yard.

In addition to the spatial constraints of this deep, narrow site there were also regulatory requirements: pedestrian access had to be maintained from Manor Place across the site to the backs of shops on Walworth Road. And of course the doctors and their staff had specific needs as well – for security and flexibility, for a staff and doctor entrance separate from the patients' entrance, and for reception, waiting areas, and consulting rooms that were closely related so doctors could come to the waiting areas to greet their patients. After two firms of architects had failed to find solutions to this site and programmatic challenge, clients met with the firm of Penoyre & Prasad who not only designed the conversion and new building with the participation of the doctors and staff but also gave invaluable help in raising funds to pay for the building. The final design

Walworth Road Surgery, London (Penoyre & Prasad)
a Axonometric
b Courtyard, entrance area, window to waiting room at left

a

b

Reception and waiting area on ground level

Section showing clerestory, curved roof and roof lights

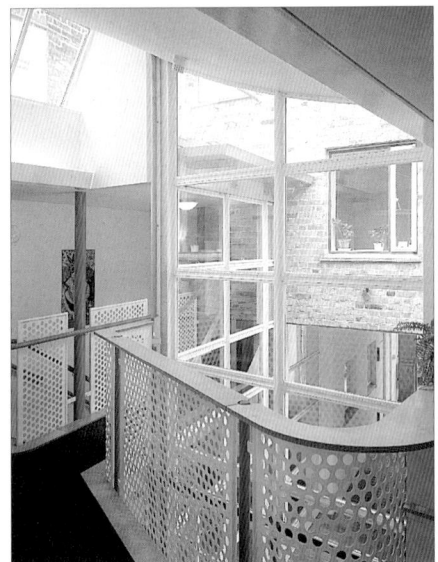

View towards street from upper waiting area

was achieved after several solutions were tried and met with precise criticisms from the clients.

"One of my friends says the best way to start a conversation with a couple you have not met before is to ask 'How did you two first meet?' Everybody loves to reminisce, and the process reveals what makes them tick. Perhaps it is because our architects approached us and our building like this that the Walworth project has been so fruitful" (Higgs 1992, p28).

Despite the project's many requirements and constraints, or perhaps inspired by them, Greg Penoyre and Sunand Prasad's final design met their clients' needs for a new and better building that is warm and welcoming as well as secure, that supports the multiple pathways the regulations and the brief required, and that has the added bonuses of a light and airy two-story reception area and a roof terrace.

The entrance is now from Manor Place. An existing archway there, with a gate, leads into a courtyard that provides the required public access to the site and also leads to the two-story, glass-fronted reception and waiting area of the new surgery. A stair behind the elegant, curved reception desk allows staff easy access to the second waiting area upstairs, which also benefits from the two-story glass wall at the entrance. Consulting rooms are located on the ground level and first floor, treatment rooms on the ground level, and staff facilities on the top level, with a roof terrace above.

Staff circulation extends from a discreet street entry on Manor Place up the front of the building to all floors, to the staff lounge and to the terrace. A stairway in the courtyard leads to the rear of the second level, as required by the fire regulations, and a bridge on that level links the new building to the former surgery on Walworth Road, which contains a clinic and multipurpose space and counselor's rooms. There are many pathways in this small and complex project, but each has its clear purpose, its intended users, and its own identity given by its location and its design.

The density and complexity of the spaces and spatial relationships within the new building and its relationship to the street, the courtyard and the existing building are in keeping with the context, with the quirky character of the small buildings and odd-shaped courts of the backlands. At the same time the generous use of glass at the entrance and the dramatic double curving tin roof feel modern and, even better, the interior feels light and open, even on a gray and rainy day.

Indeed, light has been carefully considered throughout. A low, corner window on to the courtyard brings

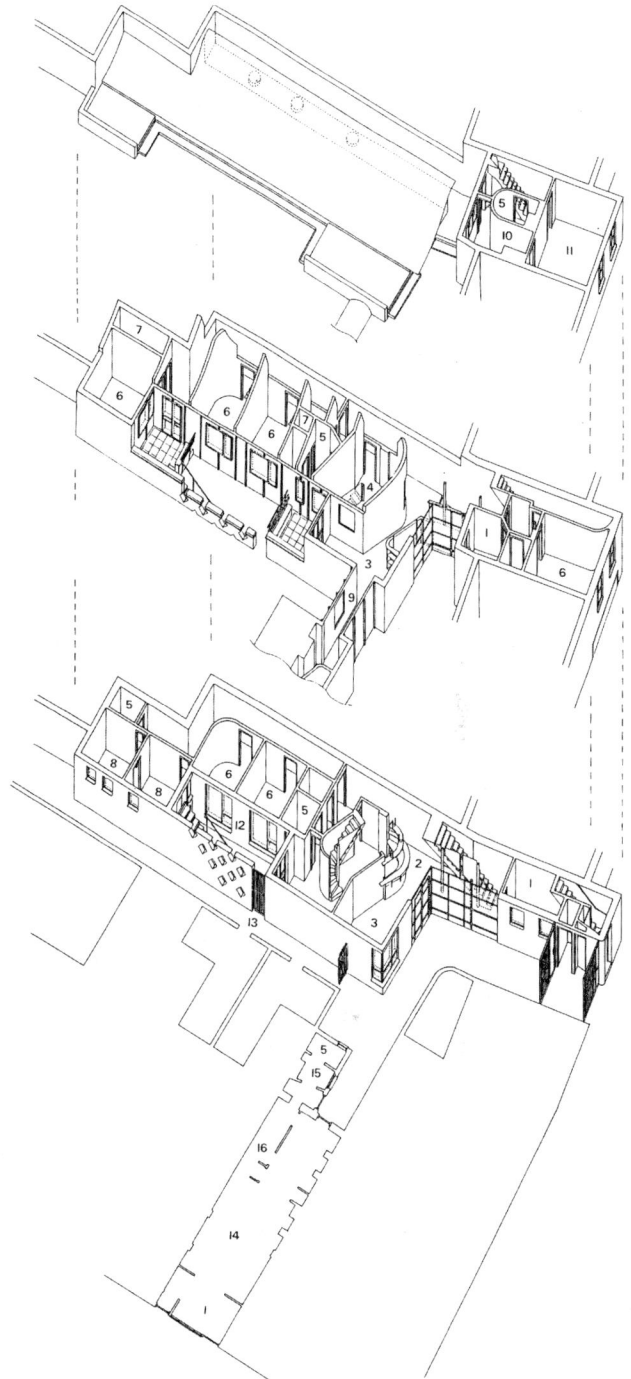

Isometric plans, Walworth Road Surgery, London (Penoyre & Prasad)

1 Interview room
2 Reception 3 Waiting area
4 Administration/office 5 WC
6 Consulting room 7 Store
8 Nurses/treatment 9 Bridge link to 206 Walworth Road
10 Kitchen 11 Staffroom
12 Courtyard
13 Public access
14 Multi-purpose/clinic space
15 Nappy changing 16 Stairs to staff and counselor's room

additional light into the ground-floor waiting area and adds another connection to the outdoors. The corridors on the next level have circular roof lights with a yellow surface, making for a warmer light from the sky. Even the lighting fixtures on the wall are yellow. Glass blocks inlaid in the corridor floor bring light to the ground floor; a clerestory brings in light from above and the curved ceiling makes consulting rooms on the second level appear more spacious (Hannay 1992, p31).

Literal and Poetic Narratives

Each expression is a symbol of the thought that it translates to the outside. In this sense, language itself is nothing but symbolism. (Mircea Eliade 1976, p189)

We use words differently according to what we want to say, the kind of message we want to convey. If the message is simple information, clarity is essential; the sequence of words and sentences has to follow a specific logic. If, more than information, what we want to convey is also a mood, an emotion, something that pertains to poetry and the world of art is also needed.

It is also true that architecture is based on articulation, signifying or not signifying as it may be. Like speech it carries its user through a sequence of spaces/sentences, each made up of different elements/words. Like speech, spaces and places can be stories created out of imagination, technical reports or instructions, slang descriptions, poems, or folk songs.

> Important: Lire ces instructions avant la mise en service de votre telephone portatif.
> Wichtig: Lesen Sie zunächst dieses Informationen durch, bevor Sie ihr Mobiletelefon einsetzen.
> Importante: Leggere queste istruzioni prima di utilizzare il vostro telefono cellulare.
> Onemli: Luften cep telefonunuzu kullanmadan once asagidaki bigileri okuyunuz.
> Belangrijk: lees deze informatie voordat u uw mobile phone in gebruik neemt.
>
> (Erickson, mobile phone instructions)

In contrast to the specificity of lists and instructions, contemporary space, like music and art, is based nevertheless on the undetermined. As Mircea Eliade says, since we refuse the world and the meaning of existence as known and accepted by our ancestors, we express this refusal by eliminating the ways of the past, by blowing up form and flattening volumes and by disarticulating languages. As Eliade suggests, this may be "a way of manifesting a nostalgia for another world, auroral, fresh, unedited" (Eliade 1976, p183).

> I am here   ,   and there is nothing to say   .
>
>   If among you are
> those who wish to get   somewhere   ,   let them leave at
> any moment   .   What we re-quire   is
> silence   ,   but what silence requires
>   is   that I go on talking   .
> Give any one thought
>   a push   :   it falls down easily
> ;   but the pusher   and the pushed   pro-duce that enter-
> tainment   called   a dis-cussion.
>
> (John Cage, "Lecture on Nothing")

Between the repetition of items in lists and instructions and "undetermined" sentences, both conveyed through words however different they may be, there is an entire realm of everyday talk as well as talk that reminds us of everyday life and emotions. They need organization, a framework that gives them freedom of expression. In architecture this is the structuring strength of paths that allow the imaginative strength of its elements/words to blossom.

> The children scattered. Jack went with them sparing a last bemused look over his shoulder at the wonderful parrot. (King 1985, p223)

These two sentences are like two very small and simple buildings or even just two rooms, one smaller or simpler than the other. They are quite clear and use words in a straightforward, visual, and colorful way.

To avoid exposure to the strong afternoon sun the living rooms must have a westerly aspect. (Yoshida 1963, p8)

Though an equally simple sentence, the last passage is less visual than the previous one. But talking about seeing it indicates how things should be rather than telling how things are or went. It conveys an atmosphere, and how to create it, whereas the previous passage tells about the mechanics of events.

The case offers two padded compartments that measure 11' x 13' x 2.5 each. The padded computer compartment features disk pockets, pen and business card holders and two straps to secure the computer. The other padded compartment comes with adjustable dividers to fit power-suppliers, A.C. adaptors, external disk drivers or keypads. (*Mobile Office*, May 1992)

As a kind of list, such a statement is a static sequence of separate words. It can be compared in architecture to plain functional situations, where every room is located in relation to its practical purpose, as it is meant to be in laboratories, offices, and prisons; it is distribution and organization that matter rather than this being a tool for creating experiences.

Daughter, dear daughter, I've done you no wrong,

I have married you to a great lord's son,

He'll make a lord for you to wait upon,

He's young but he's daily growing.

("The Trees They do Grow High", English ballad)

Songs use words to describe events, moods, sensations. Through their simple stories they stir emotions and create moods.

Mais moi je rêve. . . Je rêve à la douceur, multipliée indefiniment par elle-même, de ces rencontres, et de ces échanges de forme de vierges. Je rêve à ces contacts inexprimable qui se produisent dans l'âme, entre les temps, entre les blancheurs et les passes de ces membres en mesure, et les accents de cette sourde symphonie sur laquelle toutes choses semblent peintes et portées. . . Je respire, comme une odeur muscate et composée, ce mélange de filles charmeresses; et ma présence s'égare dans ce dédale de grâces, où chacune se perd avec une compagne, et se retrouve avec une autre. (Valéry 1945, p118)

In poetry the sequence of words (the path) loses its predominant position over the words. The choice and the sound of words create the language of poetry together with their sequence. Far from being a list of actions or items, the sequence is made up of images. There is no longer a sequence of words, but a blending of the structure and the images in which it is dressed.

Ignoro el número total de las cámaras; mi desventura y mi ansiedad las multiplicaron. El silencio era hostil y casi perfecto; otro rumor no había en esas profundas redes de piedra que un viento subterráneo, cuya causa no descubrí; sin ruido se perdían entre las grietas hilos de agua herrumbrada. Horriblemente me habitué a ese dudoso mundo; consideré increíble que pudiera existir otra cosa que sótanos provistos de nueve puertas y que sótanos largos que se bifurcan. (Borges 1985, p14)

As Mircea Eliade has written, "There must not be opposition between the use of words and the one of images: these two modes of expression might possibly be complementary to one another. In general the form of language is analytical, discursive, as the human mind of which it is the instrument and of which it follows and reproduces the path with as much accuracy as possible; on the contrary symbolism is essentially synthetic, and therefore, in a way, intuitive. This makes it more appro-

priate than language to serve the intuition beyond reason" (ibid., p121).

The word image is very popular today; like many others it carries only its most superficial meanings, referring so much to appearance that appearance replaces substance. According to the British archetypal psychologist Noel Cobb,

> Something becomes an image through an act of "taking in," breathing, becoming inspired by the world. This process . . . is the essence of aesthetic response – in the original Greek sense of *aitheis*, which at root is a gasp and "Ahh!" of wonder and recognition, a sniffing, a breathing in of the world. Without this taking in of the world, there is no awakening in the heart, no poetry, no making, no craft or crafting. Events remain events, soulless occurrences, they do not become experiences. Pictures remain two-dimensional happenings of form and composition, unless through the soul they become images (Cobb 1992, p18).

In order to grasp the concept of image as Cobb describes it, it may be useful to focus on works of art. Let us look at two statues. They are very similar but one of them reveals the body through its clothes while on the other the clothes simply hang. The way clothes are falling off the body of the first statue reveals the form of the body underneath. The body gives form to the clothes that become a sort of metaphor for what is underneath. A carved drape of a woman's dress is meant to express what is behind it as if we cannot speak of certain things directly, but only suggest them. What the second sculpture shows instead is a kind of carving that looks like a dress but there is rigidity and a stiffness, which says that the artist is concerned with how things look rather than with how things are. He is concerned with the appearance of the thing.

Let us look at the woman's breast on the second statue; it is in the right place and the clothes hang over it. The literalism of the statue consists in remaining somehow on the surface, dwelling on appearance only. By remaining on the surface this sculpture misses the essence of the thing itself. It looks like a woman and that is enough. In contrast, the first sculpture minimizes the difference between the inside and the outside by approaching the inside through the metaphor of its appearance. The sculpture expresses, through the dress, the form that is living beneath it. This is the reason why this sculpture is alive. It in-spires (literally "is breathing in," in contrast to ex-pires, "is breathing out"), therefore we "take it in." The other statue just looks like heavy and lifeless matter. As Cobb suggests, it remains an event,

a

Statues
a. The form revealed
b. The form carved

b

a soulless occurrence, never becoming an experience.

In architecture there are crude and more sophisticated forms of symbolism, the ones that belong to the surface appearance and the others that inspire and demand to be taken in. These forms of symbolism are the ones that make buildings speak, speak clearly, or sing.

Beyond the Literal

One proposal for the RIBA competition to design "A Single Family House" indicates what therapy could mean in design. It offers a service to client and site, honoring, respecting, and praising them both.

The building required is a one-family house to be built in Brockhall Village, Lancashire, on a site whose views the client wanted to emphasize. He was also very specific about his requirements for formal rooms, a kitchen, a children's wing and an office wing, the last two directly accessible from the outside as well as from inside the house. As explained by the designers, the design intention toward the building's posture, and thus toward the site, is to locate the house so it sits open, on the edge of the existing ridge, which is developed into a retaining wall for the garden.

The scheme, which was short-listed in the competition, tells its story through simple, decisive paths that stretch from the entrance in the two main directions of the formal rooms and the kitchen. From each of these a path extends further, on one side to the office, on the other to the children's wing. Both of these extensions are connected to the outdoors, thus on the one hand they develop the main story of the house, on the other they have their own stories to tell.

What could have remained merely a diagrammatic distribution or a linear organization of spaces becomes instead, in the development of this scheme, a combination of intersections of views in different directions and different outdoor experiences, which transform the linear path into a varied and surprising journey. This is due in particular to the courtyard adopted for the house. The paths of circulation as well as the various aspects of family life are held together by the "silent outdoor center, at the heart of the house."

The choice of the courtyard, functional to suit the needs of the family, becomes the poetic as well as literal answer to these needs; this outside room feeds the spaces around it with light, air, and vitality, becoming an extension of each of the internal spaces. "The three sides of the courtyard occupy the three major elements of the brief: the formal group, the kitchen group, and the children's wing. The fourth side of the courtyard is

Design for a Single Family House (RIBA competition entry by Frank Lyons, Anthony Aldrich, Alicja Andreasik, Dominic Morse and Michael Westley)
a. Plans and sketches
b. Roof plans and garden

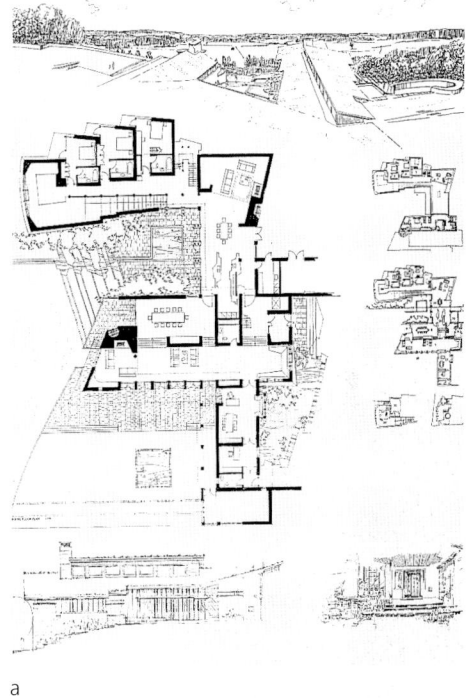

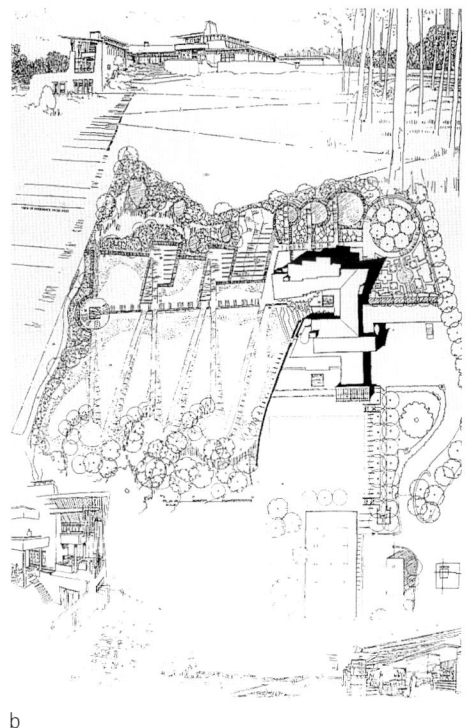

a

b

open to nature and to the views, thus binding the family positively into the landscape and nature. The openness of the courtyard also means that all the accommodation, even that in the deepest part of the plan, is able to benefit from the views that the site affords."

The rammed earth chosen for the walls, which have timber-framed windows, the earth and wood chosen for the roof, and the timber and stone chosen for the floors all add a special texture and flavor. The small, still pool that sits in the heart of the courtyard is a symbol of life and also of growth and the perpetuation of life thanks to the fountain bubble that generates, from the pool, a stream which runs through a series of irregular pools into the formal garden.

From the choice of the building's posture and the diagrammatic design up through the symbolic choice of forms the design evolved to propose a sensual combination of materials and detailing, those with the power of evoking images and a sympathetic response. The project suggests how a *theraps* attitude in design might approach the multilayered complexity of the practise of architecture by establishing first of all a rigorous choreography, a precise planning of steps, the exact geometry similar to the 90 degree corner that Matisse used to say was always behind each curve he drew.

Naming

According to the Italian poet Mario Luzi, the spoken language has lost its ability to *name* and is therefore no longer capable of having a true relationship with reality; it hides its muteness in an insane production of words used to say anything at all. This degeneration, says Luzi, can be avoided by returning to the origin, by re-establishing the original relationship between the phenomenon and the word, and by enabling the organization of reality into relationships that cease to be mysterious.

If materials, shapes and building elements have their own symbolism, their own meaning in relation to our perception, the true "naming" of their qualities may be a useful step toward a production of architecture that has something to say. What is the intention of the project and what is my intention toward the final result? What do I want people to feel, where do I want them to stop, what do I want them to look at? How would I like them to approach a surface, an entrance, a garden, a door? What will my choices mean to them?

Through naming, through this kind of reflection and analysis, one may discover that the choices may have led to a particular shape, material, element, or color that either contradicts the original design intention or shows that the intention is confused or overly concerned with carelessly producing for profit.

Naming may be useful for decoding the existing situation, for understanding why we react differently to various materials, places, and spaces. It can be an exercise in learning from our feelings and sensations, from our own responses. Naming is an invitation to re-learn qualities through the way we resonate with them as well as the way other cultures and other people do.

While discussing the conversion of a hospital ward, the person in charge of buying the furniture showed great concern about the choice of colors. The ones they had recently adopted were too strong she said, and people could hardly bear to look at them. She mentioned in particular an elderly lady who could not face a yellow cupboard located in front of her bed. Yellow has different meanings according to different schools of thought. For Jung it represented intuition and therefore the irrational, contrary to sensation, which for him was related to green. In the Indian tradition yellow is related to the third chakra, the stomach, the place of practical intelligence. This may explain why books on color suggest that yellow stimulates the intellect. Like green and red, yellow is a primary color, with high vibrations that may be too disturbing for somebody in pain or confined to a hospital bed.

Decoding that which exists may thus help us grasp the collective codes that bind it together, the ones that are rooted in each of us as well. Since the end of the nineteenth century psychoanalysis has been particularly relevant for the discovery of the communal patterns that bind our psychological behaviors. In so doing it has brought into the province of science what previously had been confined to mysticism and the occult schools of East and West. For these disciplines certain "signs" have deep meaning for the individual psyche and soul; they activate deep reactions or convey particular concepts. Circle, triangle, and square, for instance – each has its own symbolism, according to different traditions. Aside from what triangles represent for different religions, they depict a dynamic balance between three points. Furthermore, when laid horizontally they represent something different from when they are placed vertically, in which case the apex of the triangle indicates a synthesis of a vertical tension as well as a balance. The square traditionally represents the earth and thus a static balance. Circles suggest an undifferentiated continuum, the archetypal whole we come from and will go back to. Often geometries as well as numbers carry a symbolism that affects people far beyond the visual, as Vitruvius understood so well.

Largo Corelli: A Diagnosis

The 1996 competition for 100 Piazze in Rome included the redesign of Largo Corelli, a square in the *borgata* (suburb) of La Rustica, in the eastern area of the city. La Rustica, a typical example of post World War II speculative building, is surrounded by motorways, divided into two by the railway and further segmented by a road connecting the two exits of two motorways. Largo Corelli stands at the junction between the road that connects the motorways and three others.

The brief for the competition called for a "model design" that would create a reference point for the rehabilitation of the entire *borgata*, with identifiable routes to support a new urban design for the square and the area around it. Proposals were to focus on the rehabilitation of the area and were to emphasize the relationship between the church and other public and private services. Particular attention was to be given to the design of green areas to connect the square to the marketplace where a playground for children was also needed. Consideration was to be given, also, to the relationship between the square and the location of the ancient underground Roman aqueduct running nearby.

The brief anticipated a design that did not concern the rehabilitation of the square alone but that of the entire neighborhood. A more localized approach would not be enough to give the *borgata* new vitality, just as a surgical intervention to the heart would be insufficient to revitalize a patient whose body is badly lacerated with limbs missing.

At the heart of La Rustica, the square finds itself in a defective, fragmented, and disoriented organism: fragmented because of the railway and the roads that cut through it, disoriented since the natural boundaries do not coincide with the political ones. Within the natural boundaries of La Rustica exist three different districts and so the inhabitants do not recognize themselves as part of one unified entity.

Although a "square" is literally an open space surrounded by buildings, Largo Corelli presents itself more as a junction where five streets meet, a traffic roundabout. It is not a place of commercial or social activity: the presence of a church and the nearby marketplace makes Largo Corelli more of a parking place than a meeting place. What is missing within the heart of La Rustica is precisely the kind of beat its inhabitants cannot produce because there is no pleasure in going out for a walk or reaching the

View of Largo Corelli, La Rustica, Rome

school, the church or the market by foot. Indeed, it is nearly impossible to walk at all in La Rustica particularly because of the speed of the traffic on the road connecting the two exits from the motorway, loaded with lorries as well as cars, narrow, mostly without lighting or sidewalks. The inhabitants are forced to drive for their own safety.

In order to give La Rustica a chance to breathe normally, it seemed necessary to rebalance the suffocating elements, such as the traffic artery through its center, to redesign the street system and create possibilities for pedestrian circulation and pedestrian activities. The obvious proposal, before progressing with any design, was to revitalize the pathways, thus diverting the traffic flow by routing part of the traffic away from Largo Corelli through the creation of a "pacemaker" that would calibrate the arriving and departing flow and also rescue it from being a junction.

The redesign of the street system, which corresponds to the second level of therapy and responds to the first part of the brief, restores the integrity of the physical body of La Rustica and improves the quality of life of its inhabitants. This, however, does not necessarily heal its soul. Though part of Rome, La Rustica is a neighborhood that does not belong to the capital; it does not belong to the archetype of the Eternal City but only to the one of the suburbs, everywhere alike and thus without identity. To confront these aspects the third level of therapy needs to be entered.

The images that we can grasp today from La Rustica and from Largo Corelli in particular are not coordinated; nor are they based on particular hierarchies or views. They are anarchic in the worst sense of the word since they frustrate any kind of orientation. There are no elements that guide by analogy; there is no dialogue between elements. Each of them is involved in its own monologue without significant relationship with the others.

Even the shape of the church, the symbol of the spiritual heart of the neighborhood, contradicts what one would expect from a place of Christian worship. Its shape, squeezed by the heavy, horizontal slab that functions as its roof, progressively decreases in size from the roof slab downwards rather than from the ground upwards, as in the case of archetypal religious buildings. By denying verticality it loses its own identity within the neighborhood as well as denying any aspirations towards a spiritual or divine dimension.

The historic memory of the Roman past of the *borgata* has been lost. For its contemporary inhabitants it never even existed as a socio-cultural memory. Because the materials La Rustica is made of – their forms, surfaces, and colors – stimulate neither memories nor care, nor participation, nor love, next to the problem of rehabilitating the physical integrity of La Rustica there is the need to rehabilitate its psycho-existential integrity by paying attention to the emotional involvement between people and place.

Largo Corelli: A Proposal

If any form in architecture or planning is the image of an intention, what intention is manifest nowadays in the urban design of La Rustica? What intention, then, did we wish to propose for the *borgata* even before thinking of the form that would be able to manifest it? To speak about the intention of a built form doesn't only mean to speak of aims but also of the economic and existential philosophies that underlie those aims. These philosophies are related to the specific place where the built form is located and to its inhabitants.

Given these premises, the main information concerning the neighborhood's problems, the historical memories, and the contemporary needs were solicited from the neighborhood committee, the local cultural association and by a scholar of the history and archeology of the area who lives in the *borgata*.

Having established the need for a "pacemaker" and having adopted it as a condition for any acceptable scheme, Bianca developed with Michele Augelli a proposal that had four intentions:

1   to create a circumscribed area for pedestrian movement and use that would take into consideration users of different ages: children up to six years old, children older than six, teenagers, elderly and generic users;

2   to create a "unity" which visually as well as tactilely would bring together the heterogeneous existing environment;

3   to create an environmental identity that would give dignity to the area with the uncovering and rehabilitation of the historical roots that link La Rustica to its Roman past and of the roots that link the neighborhood to the historical background of its contemporary inhabitants;

4   to introduce the dynamic of verticality, completely absent in the neighborhood at present.

These intentions were manifested in the following design choices.

The pedestrian area, profiting from that part of the road now no longer in use thanks to the creation of the "pacemaker," is very generous and varied. It is articulated in plan and elevation, creating spaces at different levels that interconnect without meeting the traffic. To this end a bridge is proposed to connect the newly acquired area with the one on the opposite side of the street where the market is. Although located in two different sections, the different areas maintain a certain degree of continuity thanks to the bridge and also to forms and materials that are carried through from one area to another. This is to fulfill the intention of creating a square-and-path that is composed of a common, but not a monotonous, language, made of recurring elements.

The area for small children, made primarily of patches of grass scattered with natural elements such as logs, stones, and sand is characterized by spontaneous paths of worn earth. From this area, which is not rigidly structured, a linear path corresponding to the acquired part of the road, leads towards the focus of the square-and-path; it is stone paved and has stone walls of different height running along it. These transform into a series of terraces, raised above street level, for meeting, talking, and resting, culminating in a portico and galleria, in the wide area opposite the church. This area is structured along geometric axes that create different perspectives. Here water streams gently out of a cut into a concrete screen into a low pond.

On the other side of the wooden bridge an area for teenagers provides spaces for school groups where musical, artistic, and educational events can take place. This is a green area, and like the one for small children has spontaneous paths; here, though, more structured features are provided. An open air theater invites gathering; a small cultural center, library, and small museum are planned for the future. Finally, at the far end, next to the market, a sports area for teenagers and adults is located, as required by the brief.

In order to create the desired "unity," since streets are defined only as two-dimensional elements, the proposal redefines the area around the square through a system of screens, either built or created with plantings. The built screens also serve to support information carrying panels about the city's events. (A new metro station will provide easy access to the center.)

Recent discoveries and documentation indicate that La Rustica is the site of the ancient Roman city of Caenina, the legendary shepherd settlement, of wooden huts, related to the Ratto della Sabine. Archeological excavations have revealed that next to Caenina was a necropolis of almost 200 tombs, which shows the considerable wealth the inhabitants had accumulated. Another significant historical feature is the nearby underground aqueduct built in 19 BC whose location was once marked by marble blocks called *cippi*, inscribed and decorated, that covered the holes used for inspecting the aqueduct. Still in use today, the aqueduct brings virgin spring water to the Vatican; it runs in the north–south direction parallel to the ancient Roman road called Collatina.

Each of these historical elements is evoked in the new design. Screens made of timber refer to the shepherds' huts, while the arrangement of stones surrounding the opening in the concrete screen through which the water falls are inspired by the necklace, ancient stones found in the most significant tomb of the necropolis, that of a young girl which was furnished with cups, rings, *fibulae* (buckles) and jars. To indicate the location of the aqueduct, under the closed street, a section in scale of the aqueduct is drawn into the paving, marked with of a block of travertine marble used as a small fountain.

The ancient Roman street, the Collatina, is evoked by the location of big slabs of stone across the new pedestrian path. The crossroads created is reminiscent of the ancient one between the Collatina running north/south with the road of the *transumanza* running east/west in that particular area.

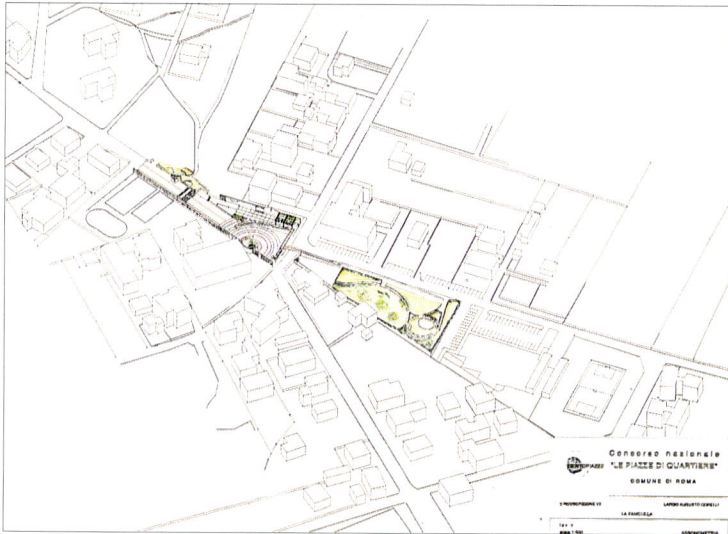

a

Proposal for Largo Corelli
(R. Bianca Lepori and
Michele Augelli)
a. Axonometric
b. Details
c. Diagnosis and proposed
design

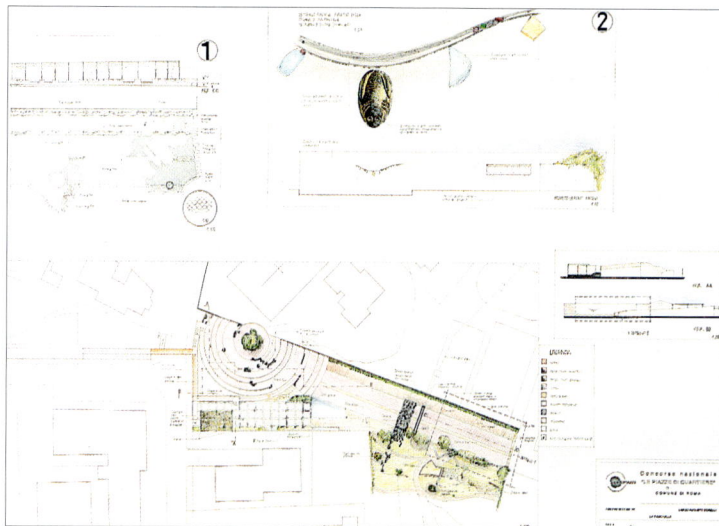

b

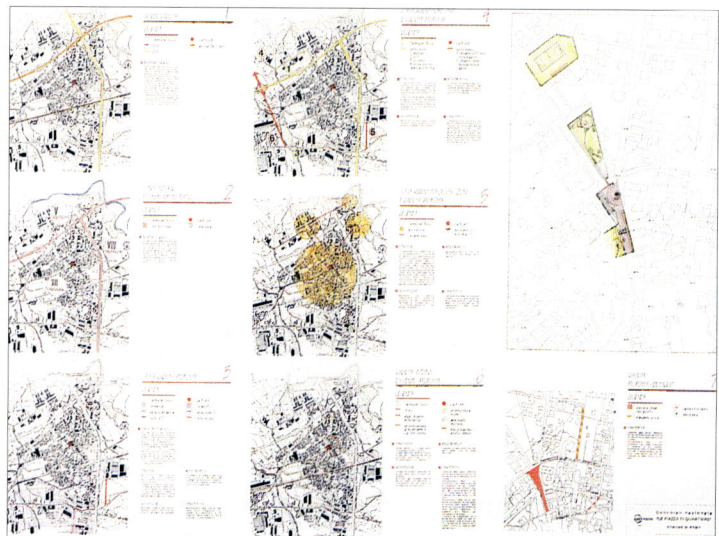

c

Regarding the history of the contemporary inhabitants, the proposal introduces forms and materials that link La Rustica to the Eternal City *and* to the regions of origin of the inhabitants – Puglia, Calabria, and Sicily. The raised square opposite the church suggests the terraces outside the cafés in Sicily where people sit and meet under pergolas. The stones used come from Puglia. The paths will include *sanpietrini* (cobblestones) typical of Rome. The walls will be mainly of terracotta bricks or stone.

Having chosen to approach the brief by diagnosing La Rustica as if it were a human body leads to a proposal that is a way of curing as well as of designing. Furthermore, due to the different levels of discomfort peculiar to the *borgata*, the focus was on healing as well as curing. For this reason the proposal suggested that local masons contribute to its construction.

Space therapy invites designers as well as clients to listen, to speak, and to facilitate the expression of what is already there to be expressed. Space therapy provides a good tool for analysis as well as for design that can be applied to existing circumstances which need to be transformed.

Between Earth and Sky

I had just arrived in Dallas and already there was an invitation for that evening: a cocktail party to celebrate an award to three famous journalists. The party was going to be held in a house built by a well-known architect.

We drove along a rather deserted street until we turned on to a narrower one. The area, dense with trees, looked rather wild despite the many parked cars. I expected to see the famous house standing out, asking to be noticed. Instead a natural rocky mass was there at the end of the street with a delicate translucent door, pale blue-green, wider than it was tall. Was this the house we were meant to go to or yet another place to visit beforehand?

Once I left the naturalness of the outside and entered an unexpected interior, a crowd of people appeared. My first feeling was simply one of being in a wide, modern room of great dignity. A few steps away from the entry door, the space opened up, stretching out primarily toward the right. The clear geometry created an inviting, complex space that asked to be explored.

Small groups of people were conversing a few feet above what I thought was the ground floor, on a wide concrete stair leading to another open space higher up. When I started to climb these stairs, I noticed, by looking down through a glazed parapet, another flight of

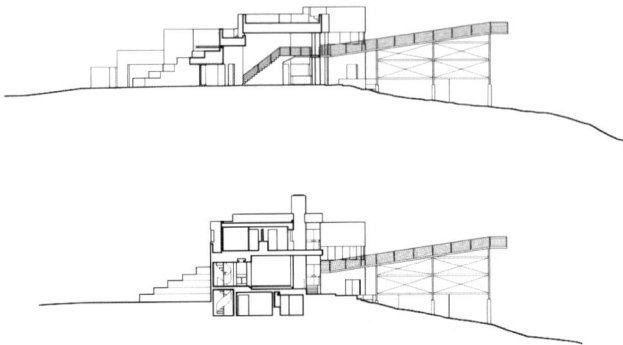

Sections, Turtle Creek House, Dallas
(Antoine Predock)

stairs parallel to the one I was on, going down to a lower level. The entry hall, rather than being on the ground floor as I had imagined, was actually an intermediate one between a lower level and the one above me. This sudden discovery of another floor beneath the entry level increased my sense of distance from the ground.

Once I reached what, from below, had appeared to be just an intermediate landing I found that it expanded towards the left into a vast double-height sitting room with a library alcove in the background. I entered the living room where the tension of the building's structure was definitely relieved. I was no longer pulled in a particular direction even though a horizontal, black-steel structure was inviting me to the left, along the external glazed wall. Horizontal connections are indeed less powerful than diagonal ones that lift you up or pull you down.

Leaving the sitting room to return to the people still visible in the entry hall, I noticed a landing expanding in front of me, on the opposite side of the sitting room. This became a cantilevered platform stretching out above the corridor of the lower level – a true space for pausing and resting outside of the visual tension of the main stair. Standing on this platform and looking down, I discovered that further down to the right, but two flights of stairs up from the lower level corridor, I could see the entrance lobby. Having previously lost any visual connection to the entrance hall, here, in this niche, I could relate to the hall once again. Lifted between earth and sky, the feeling was one of being concealed and in control.

This breathtaking experience continued when, looking up from the platform toward the side opposite the entrance, I saw a black steel staircase winding down to the floor of the lower level. And so I realized that the corridor on the lower level was, in fact, a three-story gallery.

That the platform didn't touch the external wall of the house made me more aware of the wall itself and able to understand the intention of the architect in creating such an affirmative barrier. It reminded me of when I was a child roller-skating downhill with my little brother toward my uncle standing at the foot of the hill on the edge of Lake Como. We knew he was there, with his solid, elastic body and his open arms, waiting to catch us and push us back. He was a barrier offering us both safety and a degree of freedom.

The house, designed by Antoine Predock on Turtle Creek, has a single powerful wall that forms a boundary between the public space of the street and the private

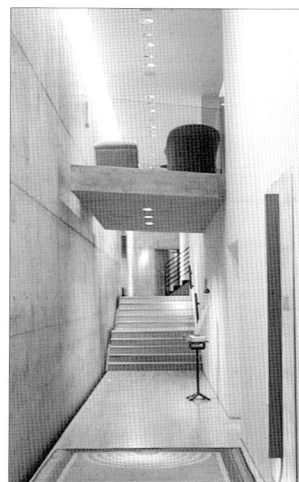

Views of platform from entrance hall and from gallery

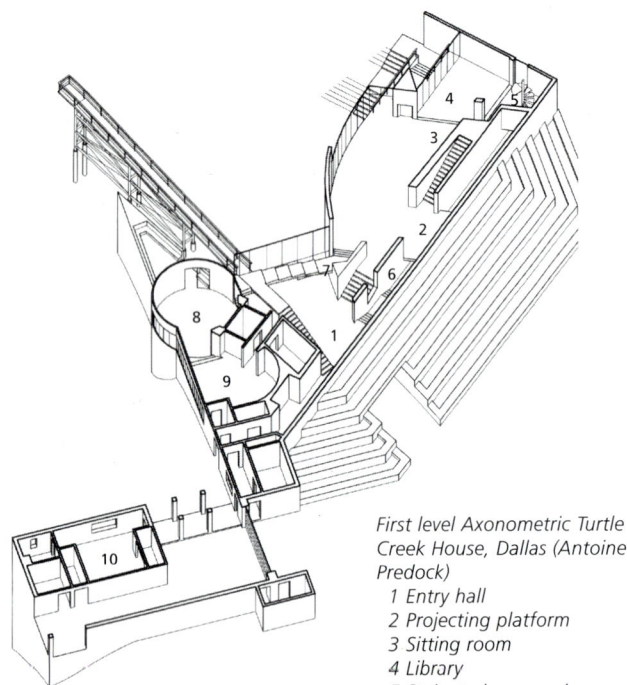

First level Axonometric Turtle Creek House, Dallas (Antoine Predock)

1 Entry hall
2 Projecting platform
3 Sitting room
4 Library
5 Stairs to lower and
   upper levels
6 Steps to lower level
7 Bridge from sitting
   room to dining room
8 Den
9 Kitchen
10 Grandmother's suite

Client's details

domain of the house. Behind this long, straight wall the house opens up toward the woods that are visually absorbed into it through extensive glazing which counterbalances the solidity of the wall-barrier. Between these two external affirmations, the other, internal walls are a means of connection rather than separation. Through a sequence of surprises, they convey transparency, permeability, continuity. Their solidity is an anticipation of what lies behind them.

Designed for a client with a passion for bird watching, the house creates opportunities for this at every level, inside as well as out. Furthermore, the combination of straight and delicately curved lines in its layout as well as the acute angles and the stretching, vaulting spaces evokes the freedom of flight as well as the structure of a bird's wing.

Fragility is a quality of this house, not only because of the transparent walls or the daring steel bridges and stairs. As part of the building structure, maintaining a dialogue with it, responding to it and emphasizing it, pieces of art, delicate colorful misty textiles, little seeds planted within the porousness of the internal concrete walls whisper their own tunes of an equally seductive song.

The lady of the house, the curator of a museum of contemporary art in Dallas, was deeply involved in her home's design and furnishing, and in the choice of the architect. Having found the right site, she visited the offices of several famous American architects to choose the most suitable one. Once she had selected Antoine Predock, the process of designing the house lasted for over two years. She and her husband required large areas to receive people, a master bedroom, two guest rooms and an annex. She also needed space to display her collection of paintings and sculptures and wanted, as did her husband, a view of the woods from every room.

Having described their needs, they let Predock produce the design. It was only when the working drawings were ready that she realized the consequences of not having participated in the design process: the building design didn't specifically suit her needs. "I got the floor plan out and realized we couldn't do furniture arrangements or hang a large painting. I hadn't really put myself in the design. Antoine couldn't see the design through my eyes. The architect needs a client to push and pull. I was not being a good client. I became one. We made some changes" (client in Anderson 1994, p110).

The plan of the sitting room shows an interruption in the glazed wall facing the garden where the wall

Exterior view from the garden, Turtle Creek House, Dallas (Antoine Predock)

Exterior view from the street, Turtle Creek House, Dallas (Antoine Predock)

becomes solid with a curved surface on the outside and a straight one on the inside. On the inside, this portion of the wall stands suspended from the floor, detached from the ceiling and from the wall to the left. It is more a screen than a wall. On the outside its surface is veneered in stainless steel with the effect of being a continuation of the curtain wall, equally reflecting the trees.

Maybe there had been a curtain wall there before the client started her constructive dialogue with Predock. Maybe she felt that yes, the curtain wall did emphasize the dialogue between inside and outside. It was perfect for her bird-watcher husband, but what about wall space to hang her paintings? She also needed to balance their distribution through the sitting room. How to please her without denying the plot already set up for the house? There could not be a solid wall on that side of the building. The function of that curtain wall was the one of seeing through, for people to look at the woods and admire them. Maybe the architect's response was to make the concrete screen a replacement for part of the glazed wall, still dedicated to seeing, on which to admire paintings, or maybe slides or videos, rather than trees? As for the outside, the stainless steel mirror would still safeguard the lightness of the wall, adding a playful ambiguity as well as a contemporary counterpoint to the paleolithic facade as it does now. This way the language of the building remained coherent, its owner satisfied and the building enriched.

References

Anderson, Kurt. Antoine Predock: Sensuous modernism in Dallas. *Architectural Digest*, March 1994.

Borges, Jorgeheis. *Elalph*. Madrid: Emece' Editores, En El Librio de Bolsillo Alianza Editorial, 1985.

Cage, John. *Silence: Lectures and Writings*. Middletown, Conn.: Wesleyan University Press, 1961.

Chevalier, Jean and Alain Gherbrant. *Dizionario dei Simboli*. vol. 1. Milan: BUR Dizionario Rizzoli, 1986. (Passages translated by R. Bianca Lepori.)

Cobb, Noel. *Archetypal Imagination: Glimpses of the Gods in Life and Art*. Hudson, N.Y.: Lindisfarne Press, 1992.

Eliade, Mircea. *Giornale*. Torino: Boringhieri, 1976. (Passages translated by R. Bianca Lepori.)

Hannay, Patrick. Just what the doctors ordered. *Architects Journal*. February 19, 1992

Higgs, Roger. Surgical spirit. *Architects Journal*. February 19, 1992.

King, Stephen. *The Talisman*. London: Penguin, 1985.

Lobell, Mimi. Spatial Archetypes. *Revision*, 1983, 6:2

Tansley, David. *Subtle Body: Essence and Shadow*. London: Thames & Hudson, 1984.

Valéry, Paul. *Eupalinos or The Architect*, trans. by William McCausland Steward. London: Oxford University Press, 1932

Valéry Paul. *L'âme et la danse*. Paris: Gallimard, 1945.

Yoshida, Tetsuro. *The Japanese House and Garden*. London: Architectural Press, 1963.

Chapter 5

Product and Process

To produce, to bring forth into existence, occurs in the biological world, in the industrial world as well as in the worlds of craftsmanship, literature, art, and science. Except for the products of the industrial world, the creations of the other worlds are called into existence through a particular process, a continuous and regular action or succession of actions involving a one-to-one relationship between the creation and its creator. In the biological world and in the one of craftsmanship the process or succession of actions takes place within a body or from a body.

In the human biological world production is the act of giving origin to a living being with the consequence of establishing, between creator and creature, a physical as well as psychological bond. Besides inheriting the genetic characteristics and often the traits of those it evolves from, a creation of a biological production is generally loved by its creator with whom it has an emotional bond as well.

Shaped from raw materials, the objects made in the world of craftsmanship, although inanimate, embody and manifest the amount of participation as well as the skill brought by the maker into the creation itself, through his or her hands, mind and soul. The more intense the participation of those hands and minds in the making and the greater their skill, the more alive the creation. As in biological creation, the product of craftsmanship retains the memory of the one-to-one relationship between creator and creature.

Unless significant financial interests are involved in the craftsmanship or unless unhappy circumstances surround the birth, the first benefit these creations bring to their makers is pleasure and the value of these creations, except for exceptionally expensive works of art, is in the creations themselves and the qualities that emanate from them. The pleasure is the one of expanding, of expressing natural gifts, individual talents, or mastered techniques. This happens with biological and crafted creations and also with works of art and literature that not only please the body through the senses, but also nourish the soul and the mind by generating relationships between the maker and what is made and by manifesting beauty, harmony, and mental brightness. The creature itself profits from these conditions and offers them, transmuted into its own qualities, to the world.

The nourishment derived from the artifacts of industrial production is generally of a different kind. The value of an industrial object is the economic value or profit derived not so much from its production as from its reproduction. It is devalued unless it is repeated a sufficient number of times to become not so much affordable as profitable. The object created is not seen as having value in and of itself but is only a means for yielding pecuniary profit. Since, for the industrial world, to produce and therefore to reproduce is equivalent to giving origin to a pecuniary gain, the "pleasure" of industrial production lies primarily in creating sources of revenue and not in the particular qualities of the objects themselves. Even when useful, harmonious, and beneficial objects are produced, they are still instrumental.

Furthermore, the participation of people in industrial production follows a systematic

Male sexuality – and according to Freud there is no other kind – is built upon a dynamic model in which energy builds up and is released, returning the organism to homeostasis. . . So according to this theory, sexuality is linked to the laws of physics and thus has no freedom and a future that involves only repetition and explosion, never evolution. (Luce Irigaray 1993, p197)

Pro-jacere: to throw
Pro-ducere: to bring
forward

pattern, composed of repetitive actions that speed up the process. The more repetitive the action, the faster and cheaper the production. When the rhythms of industrial production were applied to craftsmanship, as they still are in some countries, the object produced kept the memory of the one-to-one relationship between creator and creation as well as maintaining its own individuality. The fast production in craftsmanship, despite the lack of time for the truly inspired creative participation of the maker, still takes place from the body. The object retains a memory of this participation with the body, thus carrying and stimulating sensual and emotional relationships in the people who are seeing it or using it.

When, with the industrial revolution, machines were introduced to replace people, they relieved people of the burdens of very hard work but also removed them from contact with the objects being produced. Machines also robbed people who were directly involved in production of the opportunity to design or to schedule the process of production. Torn from the creative process, experienced now only as a schedule of duties determined by somebody else's project, these people merely assist the process. They stand or sit in fixed positions next to machines that move as identical parts of an object, which they are only told exists, pass by. They hardly see the raw materials from which the objects are made; they hardly touch their parts; they rarely see the final product which is packed away by the last machine on the assembly line.

The industrial mind that designed this system is the same mind that cures parts of the body without relating the pathology of one part to the rest of the body, that repairs the physical while ignoring the non-physical, the one that brings the world to you on a screen, making you feel that you know that world, that you have experienced it. It is the same mind that can travel anywhere while sitting in an armchair and consumes the places it visits through a camera's eye.

Fast production and fast consumption, absent producer and absent consumer, the industrial mind is also the mind that creates many of the environments we inhabit. The way a built form relates or does not relate to its human and physical environment tells us a great deal about the attitudes that characterized its creation: whether it was developed through a continuous participatory process or whether it was simply pro-jected as pro-duct.

Being the products of a creative act, all built forms are the children of their creators and each creation embodies, as children do, the qualities of its mother and father. However, there are other qualities that any creation also carries: the ones that relate, or do not relate, to its socio-cultural and environmental context. In architecture these qualities speak about the bond between the object of the creative act and its milieu; and this bond, in its turn, speaks of the way its creator has related to the human and physical environment during the process of creation.

We all know about historical centers and vernacular buildings: the organic evolution of their forms and the meaningful and practical use of materials tell us about a principle of continuity that links past to present and present to past, building to land, artifacts to people and vice versa. Respect for this principle brings forth aesthetic qualities that naturally, silently, and softly permeate walls, streets, proportions, perspectives, and details. Thoughtful and careful attitudes have fashioned them: practical and loving intentions have synergistically combined to create something with a dignity of its own, an identity of its own, yet speaking a communal lexicon, blending in with people and environment.

Historical centers and vernacular building are the expression of a process of building as well as of being; they are part of the environment and also part of us. They do not represent one individual ego's affirmations, as in the case of everyday contemporary architecture; in choral harmony within a local context they resonate through time and space. As in an organized body of singers, each of the buildings sings its tune in harmony with the others and, although bases are far more numerous than altos, houses more numerous than churches or mosques, they all relate one to another as in a correspondence of sounds.

Unless they were designed by a famous architect whose singular presence is manifested in the built design itself that then carries the qualities of the father – Eisenman, Piano, Aalto – contemporary built forms do not have a name one can refer to. They could be called anonymous, as the vernacular is, and yet no blending, no choral harmony is present. They are often dissonant with their context, inharmonious sounds which, in combination with others, resonate harshly.

When not made in the image of their fathers and lacking an identity, those discordant but identical buildings are truly fatherless creatures, children of a drive to produce that is seldom followed by the courage to take responsibility for the premises and the consequences of their production. They are like children dropped off by their parents and left behind, children who express indifference or suffer the discomfort of being abandoned, but such buildings also produce comfort or discomfort for their occupants. Having been produced to be inanimate, isolated *objects*, they acquire a life of their own and, paradoxically, become the *subjects* that generate comfort or discomfort. Since no one takes responsibility for their creation, the buildings themselves are forced to take the blame for any negative consequences that occur. What ought to be blamed instead is the attitude behind their design.

It is not simply a matter of focusing on the responsibilities of their parent-creators and thus on the fathering and mothering attitudes of the designer – on his or her ability to attend to technical and practical issues as well as to resonate empathically with the context. Nor is it a matter of moving away from the fathering model toward a mothering one or vice versa. Since what is important here is the way a creation relates to its human and physical environment, it is rather a matter of examining both the masculine *and* the feminine participation in the act of creating.

"First the Building and Then the Site" (collage, Nils-Ole Lund)

Creating, Conceiving

The act of human biological creation offers a useful model for understanding different ways of pursuing the creative process and, more specifically, of understanding how to bring forth living creatures rather than pro-jected objects. Spermatozoa and egg, the two complementary biological elements needed to create a human being, are here seen as complementary energies, attitudes, or qualities that are involved in any creative process.

If both male and female gametes/energies play complex and interdependent roles in the creation of a child, why not consider how similar energies may be inherent in any creative process, including that of design? If activity and receptivity, which the masculine and feminine archetypes refer to, are physically rooted in the nature of the two gametes, why not explore how they conceive a living being together? What is the natural use of their differences? How does each of them contribute to creation and how are they meant to combine?

The point is not to dwell on the traditional propensity of the masculine toward technical and practical issues and the inclination of the feminine toward caring and empathy. Nor will the focus be on the established pairs of opposite qualities that relate to masculine and feminine, such as rational versus emotional, analytic versus holistic, intellectual versus intuitive, light versus dark. Instead, these will be in the background while we review the nature and behavior of the masculine and feminine gametes, spermatozoa and egg, and the way they come together to create a new being.

Living in two different environments, a pressurized room packed with millions – 200 – of similar competitors and a lonely dimly lit alley, one struggling in *vorticoso pullulare*, the other peacefully waiting in self-contained solitude, the two actors of biological creation, have different shapes purposely chosen for their task: one smaller in dimension, slim, equipped with head and fibrillatory tie, the other 75/100 times bigger (2 x 10/150 - 200 x 10), of rounded undifferentiated shape (Quaderni 1992).

As shown in that masterpiece of electronic microscopy, the Swedish documentary by Nielsson about the life of the egg and the spermatozoa, *The Miracle of Life*, spermatozoa are in constant motion, carrying the tension of incompleteness. Their restlessness seems to build up a need for action whereas the egg remains in a sort of restful, meditative phase, waiting for the precise sign which, more than action, will produce recognition and fulfillment.

Within the spermatic liquid, male gametes are not only in continuous motion, they also are of different kinds – more or less strong and handsome, one might say. Only the stronger and the most handsome ones survive the acidity of the female environment which kills most of them. Those that survive propel each other toward the Fallopian tube in the rush to gain access to the egg. It is very moving to observe how spermatozoa literally support each other, how the weaker ones play the role of stepping stones for the ones that are more qualified to fulfill the creative task. None of them works alone: they work in teams, which suggests that the drive toward creation, in nature, is not competitive. The position in which creation is possible is only reached by those spermatozoa that have the qualities to obtain that position. A meritocracy seems to assure that the gametes that reach the eggs are the ones most suitable to participate in creation.

Such seems to be nature's way of ensuring the future quality of its creatures: in order to produce healthy offspring, the gametes most qualified for the job are assembled. This is not a good metaphor however for the production of most building designs. The reason these are often so disastrous may well be that other criteria than merit are adopted in the choice of architect. These criteria do not necessarily ensure that the architects who reach the position where creation takes place are the most suitable.

Once a few spermatozoa reach the egg in the Fallopian tube, they move anticlockwise round and round her without knowing which of them will be accepted. A sort of courtship takes place at this point. The fusion between one of them and the egg does not occur casually but rather through a natural decision. The same Swedish video sheds light on the mechanics of gamete fusion, which starts with the reaction of the egg to the attempts of the spermatozoa to penetrate her *sacco vitellino* (the external skin of the egg). This skin allows passage only to the particular spermatozoon whose enzyme the egg has recognized. Only in this circumstance is the egg fertilized and does gestation begin.

It's as if, in a way, the female cell had not taken, like the male, the last steps that would lead it out of itself into the unknown, the void, the thousand vague possibilities of being and life offered by the outside world. It's as if the female cell remained more directly linked to the infinite Whole that preserves everything and that, for this reason, is linked by an even stronger inertia to its ground and original foundation. For this reason the feminine principle contains, thanks to its form that is so elementary and primitive, a sort of outline of the most intangible harmony, a more stable sphericity, a stronger perfection and achievement, all things that temporarily give it peace. As for its deepest essence, the female cell contains an autonomy which is incompatible with the restlessness and the agitation without respite of the male cell that stretches itself towards extreme limits and divides and scatters all its energy with a progressively increasing violence and outburst towards specialized activities.
(Lou Andreas-Salomé 1984, p14)

Creation at a biological level is a sort of love story: the egg recognizes a particular spermatozoon that she accepts as the one to fertilize her. An enzyme, which the egg and the spermatozoon share, makes fertilization and therefore the process of creation possible. *Recognition* rather than chance or magnetic attraction seems to be at the basis of creation. It is what the gametes have in common that makes their differences productive, that allows their duality to transform into a third being. Rather than being simply a complementary effort between two opposites, biological creation unfolds from a substance that is shared. Without this substance, hundreds of millions of active male gametes and the still egg offering herself every month are simply a drive toward creation without conception.

The genesis of eggs and spermatozoa suggests another analogy. Whereas ovogenesis (production of eggs) starts in the fetus during pregnancy and the first ova dwell in the primordial follicula waiting to be expelled at puberty, spermatogenesis does not start until puberty. Ovogenesis reminds us of what is there waiting for architectural creation to occur – the history of a place, the social context of its people, the tradition. It reminds us of the knowledge that is already available to be drawn upon during the creative process. And spermatogenesis reminds us of what is improvised, what is suddenly invented with little apparent relation to the past.

Let us go back to the analogy between the creative process of conception and the creative process of design. From the outset both processes are complex and it must be remembered that, in either case, conception is only the beginning of a long period of gestation and maturation. Similarly, behind the creation of built forms, there is a long process of gestation, made up of hypotheses, attempts, solutions that seem right at first but are not or cannot be adopted because of budget limitations, planning regulations, or new inputs of information.

Conception between the egg and a spermatozoon is made possible by the specific enzyme that transforms anonymity between the two gametes into recognition. Only then can they come together to create a third cell, different from each of them and yet impregnated with the qualities and the biological aspirations of both. Design, too, is a matter of a certain chemistry being right for the choosing of partners: the right architect for the site and client or the right site and client for the architect. However, it is not only the quality of these relationships that ensures the future stability and strength of the designed product. Of course there must be a sympathetic relationship between architect and site/context/client and a commitment on the architect's part to see the job to a successful fruition and maturation. However, there can also be another kind of chemistry that *transforms* site, materials, architect, and client, from separate anonymous elements into ones with specific identities that combine and manifest their qualities and aspirations in a product that transcends each of them.

This can happen if the architect has the ability to tune in with the complexity of all the parts involved, if s/he filters and re-elaborates the given complexity into the complexity of a new third. This ability to "tune in" is the enzyme of recognition, the one that makes conception possible. It is the substantial element that initiates the natural process of designing from within the real requirements of people, history, and land. There is no way, however, that architects can tune in with the complexity of all the parts involved without the active and continued participation of their clients. The client's vision of what they need or desire, their descriptions of how they live or work are of great importance to the designer who can then be clearer in his or her design intentions.

The relationship between client and architect is indeed a very intimate one. Rather like doctors and counselors, architects have to know the client's habits; they have to

In its relationship with the male principle, the female one behaves as a fragment of the aristocracy of origins, the most noble one that, in the ancient sense of the word, is mistress of her own castle and her own dominion, in opposition to the parvenu rich of the future and certain of being able to control it. The male principle will go much further than the female one. However, it will see, as a price of its conquest, the necessary ideal of an utmost beauty, of a last perfection always rising ahead, out of reach, like the horizon where sky and earth meet that is constantly moving away from the traveler. (Lou Andreas-Salomé 1984, p14)

Working and Reworking Towards an Incubator (R. Bianca Lepori and Francesca Onarati)

find their way into the client's heart and soul to design what is most desired, which often has to be discovered.

The most gratification I ever received from a client was in a phone call. The client said, "You know me more than I know myself." In the conversion of a house for this couple, who were two very different people, I chose to please both of them with the over-all atmosphere of the house and each of them, separately, with the choice of materi-als for two rooms. I chose warm, delicate tiles for her country kitchen overlooking the garden and a high-tech, black-tile and stainless steel bathroom for him upstairs.

Of course we are talking about the privileged situation of the right client for the right architect, when both are engaged in the creative process, each with his or her specific role. Another privileged situation occurs when the clients and the users are different people and yet both engage in the design process. Private clients are usu-ally both client and user but with public buildings, the client is usually the representative of a company or institution, or a committee of representatives, who are primarily involved financially and not as future occupants. If the users join the process, the situation may be quite difficult to handle but very productive for establishing the uniqueness of the result. Once the building is complete, the users will be more likely to feel that it belongs to them and will care for it since they have participated in its creation.

The arbitrary attitude that creates buildings without regard for context or occupants is an arrogant one, closed and defensive because it is ignorant of the reality of the situation, generating buildings that are also closed and defensive for the same rea-sons, afraid to confront their surroundings. The attitude of tuning in with the com-plexity at hand requires that the architect approach the work open and empty, with ideas but ready to absorb what is there, ready to pause and listen. After having paused and listened, action spontaneously unfolds as a continuous process. Starting from the first diagrammatic sketch, made to raise questions more than with the intention of being a definite proposal, answers and more information lead toward each subsequent proposal that uncovers additional problems and requirements. In this way the dis-cussion and the exploration move deeper and deeper and proposals are laid down decisively, charged with the implicit authority derived from the natural process of their becoming. There may be conflicts, complications and delays but the process leads itself toward an unfolding with the architect as director.

Ejaculating without Conceiving

Going back to the biological analogy, there is one aspect of the process of biologi-cal creation that can be carried out at will, that does not require any of the other stages in order to take place. Ejaculation, in its positive sense, is an intimate part of the cre-ative process in conception and in design. It is the force that actively approaches the topics at hand, producing motion and action, always with dynamic energy, sometimes with enthusiasm. It is the energetic potential that, different from passivity, faces cir-cumstances and deals with them. It may be an impetuous action or the climax of a long period of reflection.

To ejaculate is not to conceive and ejaculation in itself is no guarantee of conception in biology or in design. In the design field, however, when ejaculation begins a process of working and reworking of ideas to reach a design solution, it can indeed lead to conception. However, when it is only the release of an urge to produce, when there is no enzyme of recognition and no engagement with people or context, what is pro-duced is a self-serving solution without commitment to the creative process. Whereas nature has designed conception to be the outcome of an inside/out as well as out-side/in recognition, of a courtship as well as a mating, people can create without being

The male cell, despite its small shape, or better yet because of its small shape that in any case must fulfil its purpose, appears as the natural cell of progress, the cell of dissatisfaction, the one that always gives itself new tasks and undertakes new works. The male cell is like an infinitely progressing line whose terminating point is unknown. (Lou Andreas-Salomé 1984, p13)

substantially engaged. Just as we can produce for the sake of production alone without any concern for the reasons, let alone the consequences, of our actions, so architects and designers can create in isolation, without concern for site or socio-cultural context. Then they give expression only to their own personal talents and drives and offer their products to the world that becomes simply a shelf on which these sit, wholly unrelated.

In order to complete the drive toward creation the semen must be expelled for its gametes to fulfill their task, but to achieve conception, they combine with the egg, they work in concert with something outside themselves. In design, however, ejaculation can lead to creation without a similar combining, occurring only for its own sake, or as a consequence of the conditions one is forced to work in. This is detrimental because it follows the same pattern of impersonal industrial production, fulfilling its own purposes rather than the purposes of the people the creation is meant to serve. The mind and the hand that create with this attitude project their own drives, knowledge, and desires, upon the world without entering the context or engaging with the people their work is for.

Like the lens of a slide projector, this mind imposes the figures already stored and waiting in its carousel. These are static pictures that can only change among themselves, repeating the same familiar images that vary only in scale according to the distance of the lens from the screen. Following the projector metaphor, ejaculation in design is the generation of forms from a single point which, for geometrical reasons, can only produce surfaces, two-dimensional figures without life. It is only through the interconnections of many generating points, and many points of view, that the life of three dimensions is generated.

Ejaculation in design, as well as being a common attitude, is often a necessity. When deadlines must be met, when funds will run out unless a proposal is completed by a certain time and when there is not enough time for confrontation and resolution or even for reflection, abrupt projection may unavoidably occur. The sudden release of the urge to create, like an eruptive production of goods and services, relieves individual or collective tensions, including the one of meeting a deadline. The tensions of what has not yet been solved or properly solved are transferred to the proposal; hopefully they will be relieved later when, after the deadline is met, more careful detailing, elaboration, or modification can take place.

In the creative process women as well as men ejaculate. Furthermore, since this drive comes spontaneously out of a natural need, neither men nor women are aware of the damages that can result if the first response to a design problem is retained without exploration of context and needs. Then design proposals become arbitrary decisions dictated by personal choices of aesthetics and style as well as by ignorance or nothing at all. In spite of the possible quality of the formal choices made or the evident skill of the projecting egos, the damage produced is often two-fold: lack of relationship to the site and the people living in it and a lost opportunity for true improvement and transformation. The damage is certainly not intentional, deriving primarily from a superficial approach to design that generates solutions that are not appropriate for the context or the occupants.

It might be interesting to see how this drive operated in one design proposal for Largo Corelli, the square that was analyzed in the previous chapter. It is also interesting that such a drive was rewarded by the committee appointed to select the best projects, to the point of honoring this proposal with the first prize. The proposal, called "Simpler Scenarios," is, in the designer's words, "the attempt to give to Largo Corelli the character of public space that now is lacking."

a

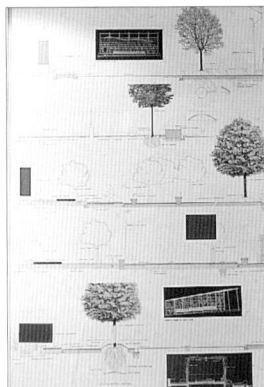

b

Winning proposal for Largo Corelli, La Rustica, Rome
a. Layout
b. Details

A path between the motorway and the railway through gardens and a square-street, of great simplicity, strong in its materials, a street on which it would be possible for the social community of the Roman periphery to structure itself.

Together with this boulevard are other small interventions: pergolas and hedges, located between public and private spaces, the rehabilitation of parts of some streets, the creation of sidewalks, often completely lacking in the area.

Within the square the qualities of existing public and private paving will be used to rehabilitate the space as a dynamic unity of fluxes. A level between the asphalt and the new paving will be in stabilized earth with rows of maples of two kinds, of monumental height (7–8 m) in order to give immediately a strong signal, an answer to the immediate need of strong signals for the entire area.

Little bushes of arboreal essence play the role of counterpoint to the dimensions of the boulevard, in order to integrate the function of transition to the one of parking.

Between the services, a court for playing boules is provided.

It is not appropriate to heal a neighborhood with a type that has been the archetype of the big urban clearance-demolitions. Didn't Haussmann destroy the ancient texture of Paris in order to build a boulevard? A boulevard is a big traffic axis, precisely what is not needed in a small neighborhood such as La Rustica. A boulevard has no relationship to the existing urban texture of the neighborhood, nor with the one of Rome or Italy. The proposed boulevard only increases the original wound and tears apart the texture of La Rustica rather than strengthening it. A boulevard requires wide spaces, with a generosity of green, and shops but at La Rustica there are very few shops and even fewer bars. Its inhabitants need convergence not more separation; they need to find unity in a recreated texture.

What else characterizes a boulevard? Width, wide paving, cafés, restaurants, jugglers, clowns, musicians, and little entertaining events. At La Rustica right now the only form of entertainment is the one offered by gypsy children climbing up the trees! As for the court to play boules, the neighbors felt offended: there are already three of them at La Rustica and a fourth one is certainly not needed.

It is not with *passatempi di paese* (village recreation) that dignity can be given to a neighborhood of living people, of different ages, who need help in finding a way of contributing to Rome the traditions they have brought from Southern Italy. Whose needs was the architect considering when he proposed a boulevard? Did he tune in with anyone who lives there? Was he even aware of the meanings of what he proposed?

Simpler scenarios could signify squalid ones, and those we already have. We want a place, we want something that gives value to our neighborhood. We want to have the pleasure of going out in the street, to let our children run, to have a place that unifies us: a square, precisely the square you have also felt the need for, but that the winning project doesn't give us. We want a square, not a junction.

We would like to know from what point of view this project can be considered "a model for the healing of the *borgata*." As for us, it is only a waste of money that doesn't heal anything because our problems will remain. These are the ones that we have already written about in a previous letter to the administration and that the winning project does not give any consideration to.

The project doesn't take into consideration the new railway station either, as it doesn't take into any consideration the speed of the traffic going through the neighborhood. It doesn't pay any attention to our history either; therefore it is only an alien and incompetent prevarication.

Once again professionals, with the sponsorship of politicians, have thrown from their positions high up in the nowhere of their incompetent knowledge solutions that do not have anything to do with the reality to which they are meant to apply.[1]

The word "project," which relates to production in general and to architecture in particular, implicitly gives permission for proposals like this one to pass for solutions. Projects, as pro-jections, are abstract hypotheses which are, by definition, separate from the context. As such, they become arbitrary answers whose lexicon can be accepted or rejected by judges who are as removed from the reality in question as the designer is.

Marketplace and Complexity

If we look at our land, at the periphery of our cities as well as at most of our shop windows, we witness the outcome of so many urges to produce regardless of needs, context, or people. The purpose and motivating force of production has become primarily the production – or the saving – of money. The focus is on the economic side of the objects produced; the goods as well as the buildings become instrumental in the creation of what is seen as the true product: the profit or the saving one gets.

This being the case and time having become money as well, no wonder no consideration is given to carefully thought out solutions. Nor is it surprising that the *rethinking* and the *reinventing* of spaces and places as well as tools, furniture, and life patterns are rarely undertaken in designing or in evaluating a design. Production is mainly re-production or repetition in copies that are never precisely alike, that are different enough to meet the need for what is new, but never new enough to make people reconsider their habits and patterns. Creations are never creative enough.

Re-production and replication also characterize the production of culture and education. The word "educate" comes from the Latin word *educere* which means "to bring out," but those who are meant to educate keep "filling up" students with notions and abstract theories that produce mental attitudes devoted to repetitive, abstract, and impersonal patterns. It is the academy that teaches how to pro-ject, how to impose on the world the notions one has in-gested.

"Yes, I studied architecture in Cairo, but it took me ten years to get rid of what I had learned there." This was the answer of Hassan Fathy to the Italian journalist who interviewed him on the occasion of his receiving a new award and who probably wanted to attribute the peculiarity of Fathy's way of designing to his academic training.

From primary school onwards, every effort is given to learning to adapt, to doing what is expected by others and to reducing the differences that make people and places special. You are taught to silence your own voice. On a personal level unlearning means having to reprogram oneself, to get rid of the notions one has been filled with and to find one's own voice again. At a socio-economic level, this means slowing down the time of production and creating higher costs that lower the profit. Until caring and learning about a situation, a place, and people are considered an "investment" of another kind and until places and people are viewed as also "profiting" from the quality of a product, this reprograming will not happen.

The rate of speed that governs our economic, social, and personal lives is indeed conspiring not only against caring, depth, and rooting, but also against an inventive, or reinventive, approach to production. On the one hand time is money; on the other there is no time to pause, to listen and to be creative from within. Yet the speed we seem to be victims of is also taking us toward dimensions never known before: it is a necessary step along the path from the simple to the complex. The history of the cosmos, says Hubert Reeves, is the history of a waking up of matter. "At the beginning there is only a small number of particles, simple and without structure. Like balls on the green carpet of a billiard table, these particles are satisfied with wandering

---

Fast movement characterizes the spermatozoa but their mobility should not be mistaken for an ability to fertilize. On the contrary, it seems that spermatozoa that remain still maintain this ability for a few days. Slow movement characterizes the egg, whose vital cycle is always accomplished, unless external factors interfere.

Many buildings are built without belief. They are built merely for profit. They are built to make things more convenient, more modern. But they don't have the belief in the back of them which has to do with the establishment of a new institution. The same kind of belief that made the first monastery, that made the first schools, that made the first bureau of health. That's the kind of belief which, when established, becomes an inseparable way of life.
(Louis Kahn in Wurman 1986, p11)

and colliding. Afterwards, by successive stages, they combine and associate. Their architecture becomes more elaborate. Matter becomes complex and thus capable of performing specific activities" (Reeves 1988, pp18–19).

Solutions like the boulevard proposed for Largo Corelli that do not explore contextual complexity remain at a primitive stage of expression, the one of particles satisfied with being scattered on a billiard table. The overly simplistic association of elements, unrelated in their deepest core and pro-jected from private or polit-ical egos on to the land and into the city, increases the complication without acting upon the complexity of the existing reality, adding instead arbitrary elements of confusion.

Each second the universe is preparing something new; it is gradually stepping up towards greater com-plexity. To acknowledge this complexity may be our task today. And yet in our own making we may be asked to go further: to master the act of creating by combin-ing places, spaces, forms, materials, and people, keep-ing the complexity of each in mind while also aiming to manifest the whole that they, and we, aspire to.

From the Community

On almost every block there is an empty lot, sometimes strewn with trash, sometimes occupied by the shell of an abandoned car and sometimes home to a well-tended community garden. The sidewalks are so bro-ken and the blocks of paving so jagged and uneven that a mother is pushing her baby carriage in the street. On every block there are also several well-maintained brick apartment buildings and clapboard houses. A 24-hour grocery store is on the corner, next to a laundromat and further down the street is a storefront church.

For many years, planners in the New York City Department of Planning saw only the empty lots and abandoned buildings in this 35-block section of the South Bronx called Melrose Commons. They underes-timated and, more significantly, ignored how much life and work continues in Melrose and how much the res-idents and businesses wish to stay despite the vacant land and the serious lack of city services to repair the sidewalks and collect the trash. They did not see what was there but only what they wished to see; they did not give the neighborhood an opportunity to speak, thus giving themselves no opportunity to listen.

It was only in November 1992, after nearly a decade of work, that the planners presented what they consid-ered their final urban renewal plan to the community for

a

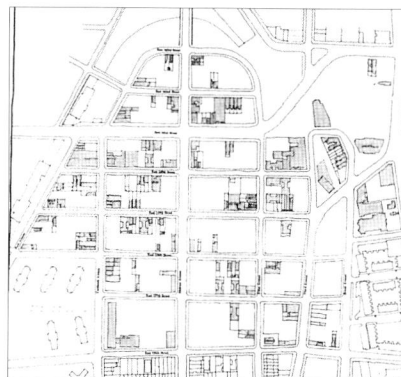

b

Melrose Commons, Bronx, New York
a. Aerial view
b. Vacant land and remaining buildings

the first time. This plan required the displacement of all the existing residents and businesses, the creation of 250,000 square feet of new commercial space, 2,600 units of new middle-income housing, a centrally located four-acre park and the re-alignment of the street system in part of the area. The city's intention was to create a new middle-class community based on home-ownership, completely ignoring the needs of the existing population of families with a median income of $12,000. The plan included no opportunities for expansion of existing businesses and no services such as health-care, senior centers, youth centers, or libraries. The proposed re-alignment of streets conflicted with the streets that were actually used. Voicing these objections, community residents attending the meeting said "no," forcefully, and formed their own planning group which they called "Nos Quedamos" ("We stay").

The group canvassed the neighborhood thoroughly, determining that many other residents shared their opposition to the city's plan and discovering that the population was in fact 6,000, almost three times the city's figure (Potteiger and Purinton 1998). Six months after the city's presentation of its plan, Nos Quedamos completed an alternative proposal with the input of city agencies and architects working *pro bono*. Instead of a single type of housing for middle-income families, their proposal includes 1,700 new units that are a mixture of two- and three-family houses on the side streets and six- to eight-story apartment buildings with stores on the ground floor on the commercial streets, in keeping with what the neighborhood used to be. Rather than tearing down the existing buildings, these are integrated into the new fabric, creating a mixture of new and old and a variety of development sites.

Instead of a single four-acre park, which would destroy existing buildings and would be hard to maintain and keep safe, Nos Quedamos proposed open spaces of different sizes and purposes: a one-acre park, community gardens and pedestrian mews in the middle of residential blocks. Instead of a physically and socially homogeneous community built on the image and exclusions of the suburban model, Nos Quedamos imagines a varied, inclusive, and denser neighborhood on the urban model, with people of different incomes and ethnicities living in different kinds of households and different types of housing, with a mixture of commercial, residential, and service uses, often on the same block.

The ground floor meeting room of 811 Courtland Street in Melrose was full of people and lively talk and the smell of coffee and doughnuts. Plans of the neighborhood, which indicated that 60 percent of the area is vacant lots, covered one wall; other plans and drawings lay on the table. As more people entered, they were warmly greeted and often embraced – professional, community resident and visitor alike. This building is the home of Dolores Lisanti who has given time and money and one floor of her house to Nos Quedamos to help save her home and her community.

Every Tuesday for two years design workshops and meetings took place here or in a larger venue in the neighborhood as Nos Quedamos developed, modified, and negotiated their plans for the neighborhood's future.

In the warmth and familiarity of the meeting room in Dolores's home, residents young and old could feel that their ideas were not only welcome but might very well be adopted. Albert Messiah came to the storefront meetings and workshops for many months before he made a sketch of housing around a tree and a courtyard. This sketch stimulated the plan for a pattern of midblock pedestrian mews.

A group of single mothers who live on the same floor in public housing nearby attended a design workshop and described how they are able to share space and child-care because of the proximity of their apartments, the hallway they share and the relationships they have developed. Drawing upon their experience, they proposed a form

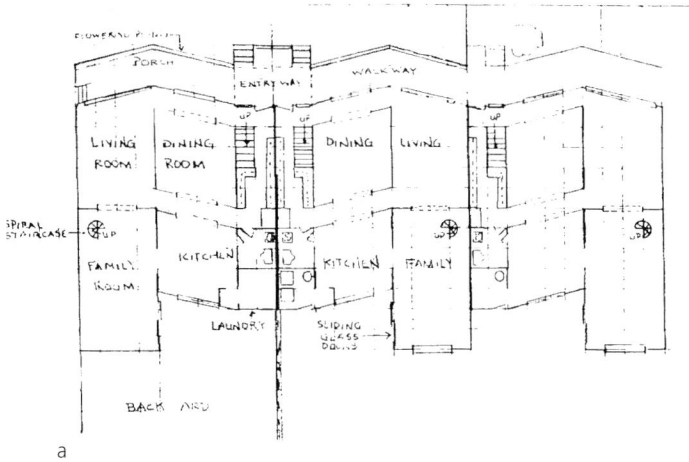

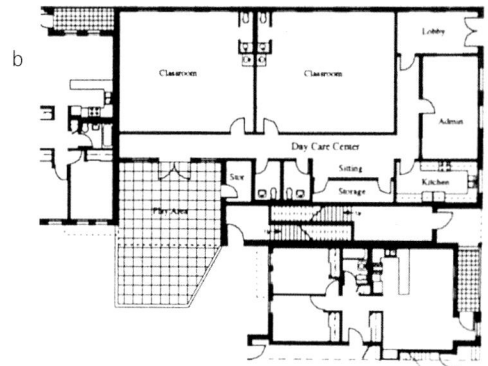

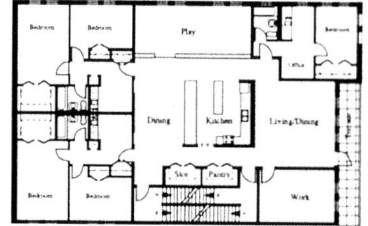

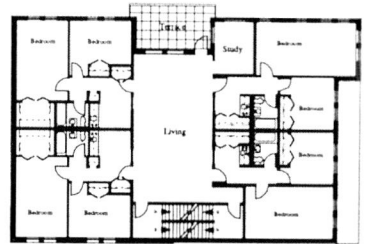

Proposal for Collective Living, Melrose Commons
a. Community residents' plan
b. Housing prototype by Magnusson Architects
(from design study funded by New York State Council on the Arts)

Plaza de Los Angeles, Melrose Commons (Larsen Shein Ginsburg Magnusson Architects)
a. Floor plans
b. Elevation

of collective housing for single mothers and their children in which dining, living, and kitchen areas would be shared. Their ideas became the basis for a design prototype which can be used in the future to build cooperative housing for single-parent families with children.

The process of realizing the community's vision for Melrose has been long, energetic but often discouraging. Nos Quedamos pursued its collaborative design, fundraising, and lobbying activities despite the changes in the city's and state's political climate and the many vicissitudes of politics, financing, and development. In November 1999, seven years after the city's original presentation, ground was broken for construction of the first new housing units on four different sites. Called Plaza de Los Angeles, partly because they are located between two nineteenth-century churches, the units are three-family homes. The owners can live in one unit and receive income from the rental of the other two, which provide housing to those with less income; or those who have a preference for renting can find accommodation. As predicted by Nos Quedamos, many of the houses are being bought by two-generation families who can now live together in the house they own while also having the privacy of separate units, keeping one for rental.

Each house has a small backyard with two parking spaces in the rear since participants in the design workshops were adamant that cars parked in front of the house would obscure residents' view of the street, making it less safe both for people and for the cars of visitors parked there. The kitchens are completely open to the living room, divided only by a counter, offering light and flexibility. This idea too came from the workshops: mothers complained that when they came home from work and started preparing dinner, they had no chance to see their children. Now as they cook, children can sit at the counter or play in the living room, easily visible from the kitchen. Local residents also complained of apartment layouts that allowed a pizza delivery man to survey the living room and "see all my stuff" while standing in the doorway. In the new housing a vestibule prevents this situation from arising.

The houses are solidly made of brick with additional construction features requested by the community. The bearing walls are 8-inch concrete block, not the usual wood-framing and sheetrock, to prevent problems with vermin and sewer pipes that are wider than the standard. As construction proceeds, members of the community observe with care what is being done and the construction company, Procida Realty and Construction Corporation, works closely with Nos Quedamos.

The imagination, determination, and unflagging optimism of the many people involved in this continuing effort have fulfilled the early rallying cry of "We stay!" making it a statement of fact. Over the years Yolanda Garcia, the Executive Director of Nos Quedamos, has learned the architectural and planning terminology to enable her to present the group's proposals to many professional and political audiences without ever losing the eloquence and emotion of her description of the history, intentions, and collaborative process of Nos Quedamos. Petr Stand, the architect from the firm Larsen Shein Ginsburg Magnusson who has worked with the group from the beginning, joins Yolanda and others every Tuesday and many other days and evenings to meet, to walk the neighborhood, to listen, and to help make this community's vision a reality.

From the Academy

The site for the studio project, the Grail community in Cornwall-on-Hudson, was a two-hour drive from the New Jersey Institute of Technology in Newark. Despite this distance, numerous snowstorms and very busy schedules, Leslie Weisman and her students often met weekly with their clients, members of the Grail community, an international, intergenerational movement of women working for peace, justice, and ecological change.[2]

Unlike most architectural studios, the students themselves determined what the studio should accomplish after collecting substantial amounts of information from and with the clients. From this process, in which seven teams of two students and one Grail staff member worked together, several related projects emerged: planning sustainable site development; modifying three existing buildings; and designing new housing. Given the choice of working individually to design a particular project or in teams on what became five projects, students unanimously chose the latter course. Input was also sought from professionals in several other disciplines as well as from the town historian in Cornwall, a member of the local planning board, neighbors of the community and Grail members living in other locations who were potential residents of the new housing.

At the end of the studio students presented the Grail community with a series of design prototypes for three kinds of sustainable collective housing and a comprehensive master plan for specific improvements to all the buildings and grounds. The products from this studio, the master plan and housing prototypes, have enabled the clients to truly see and discuss the various possible alternatives and will help them to reach agreement more easily on a final architectural program for their new housing (Weisman 1999).

Finding appropriate clients with suitable projects is crucial to this kind of studio project since their willingness and ability to participate is key to the success of the studio. The difficulty of finding such clients is greatly reduced when an effective mechanism for matching clients with instructors and students is available. This is one of the purposes of the City Design Center at the University of Illinois at Chicago, established by faculty from architecture, urban planning, art history, and art and design who are concerned with the design quality of the built urban environment and wish to share their design resources with the Chicago community. Under the co-directorship of Roberta Feldman of the School of Architecture and George C. Hemmens of the Urban Planning Program, the center brings faculty and students together to work cooperatively with local residents and organizations on design, research, and public education projects.

In one case, the Shriman Affordable Housing Campaign requested assistance in designing exemplary models of senior housing (Feldman and Hemmens 1998, p17). In response, the center arranged for an architectural studio to focus on senior housing; the studio was to be conducted in a participatory manner with campaign members working as full collaborators with the students to develop alternative senior housing schemes for a city-owned site. The group of clients not only worked closely with the students and the studio instructors, Roberta Feldman and John Macsai, to develop the architectural program and alternative schemes but also attended lectures, joined site visits and had access to course readings. Campaign members, faculty, practicing architects as well as public officials reviewed the students' projects. Since the completion of the studio, the site has been donated by the city, and an architectural firm has been hired; their design has been influenced by some of the research and ideas generated by the studio.

Equally important, however, is the interest and enthusiasm that participation in the studio generated among members of the Shriman Affordable Housing Campaign, giving them both energy and actual images of possible housing to pursue their efforts in raising money and in gaining support from local officials. During the course of the studio campaign members learned architectural terminology that aided their lobbying for the project and became very determined and specific about what they wanted. The design review was a public and celebratory event attended by politicians who could then *see* and talk about what was possible (Feldman 1998).

Students in Darlene Brady's "Urban Issues Studio" at the University of Illinois at Urbana-Champaign also generated architectural proposals for an urban setting which were displayed for public view, discussion, and possible application. The forum for display was an exhibit in the neighborhood where the project took place – a historic business district in Cincinnati, Ohio, called the Northside – as well as an exhibit in Chicago. Some of the proposals for facade upgrades which students developed in the studio guided storeowners in their renovations.

Students began the studio with nearly two months of readings and discussions on the topics of streetscapes, tectonic color studies and by learning a range of computer applications to enable them to complete the task at hand (digital photography, photo-scanning, Pagemaker, CADD with 3-D modeling and animation). The color studies, using manipulation of digital photographs of windows, masonry, and architectural elements, give students a way of looking at and understanding architecture through an analysis of color harmonies. The color studies became both a visual vocabulary and a source of ideas for the subsequent architectural projects.[3]

Darlene and her students then visited the Northside as well as similar neighborhoods in Cincinnati, spending several days documenting their observations with notes and digital photography, collecting information on those buildings selected for adaptive reuse, and talking to business owners and others in the Northside. Using information from the site visit, additional material from the city government and the principles derived from their tectonic color studies, students proposed architectural facade upgrades for a series of buildings and subsequently, in groups, adaptive reuse projects for particular buildings. Students themselves chose the buildings they worked on and developed the programs for their reuse as commercial establishments. Conversations with people in the neighborhood regarding what they wanted, their own insights about possible uses for the storefronts as well as ideas from their color studies all served to stimulate the students' design ideas.

The team that designed Triumph were intrigued by the existing three-sided facade of the building since they had already been working with a three-color harmony. They were further inspired by the idea of multiplicity to propose different types of use – gallery and sandwich shop – and to imagine variations in use over the course of the day and evening and in different kinds of weather (the indoor seating is supplemented by a patio).

Darlene teaches students how to observe, document, and understand what already exists. With the principles of tectonic color studies, they learn a means of seeing and understanding the existing architecture and of finding inspiration in it, not to copy but to analyze, interpret, and apply. In the existing world of everyday buildings and daily life, students discover opportunities for transforming both the environment and the patterns of use it supports. Significantly, the computer serves as an essential tool in this process. Unlike many computer-based studios that emphasize image, final product, and an imaginary world, Darlene's studios employ computer technology as part of a process of exploring design ideas and their relationship to form, materiality, and use as they occur, or could occur, in the world we all inhabit – not in an imagined cyberspace.

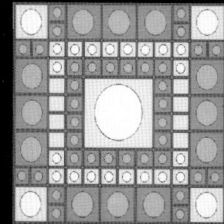

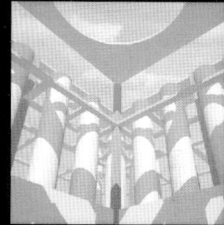

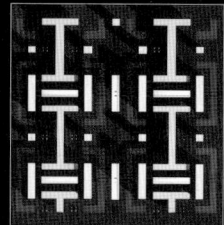

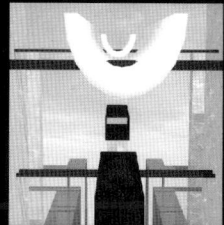

Tri-Building Gallery and Sandwich Shop (Kathryn Culley and Kevin Teague for Urban Issues Studio, Professor Darlene A. Brady, University of Illinois, Urbana-Champaign)

a

b

c

d

Lambeth Community Care Centre, London (Edward Cullinan Architects)
a. Front and entrance
b. Garden view of patio and verandah on second level
c. Bridge to garden, conservatory lounge
d. Sketch (Edward Cullinan)

With Belief

It's a warm Saturday afternoon in June. There is a smell of roses and grass. Children run up and down the hilly lawn; people of all ages stroll along the winding paths or pause in the shadowy groves. Others sit on garden benches or beneath parasols on the patio enjoying tea and cake. Near the small green house volunteers are selling plants of all kinds – tomato, herbs, black-eyed Susans. Inside, the sitting room is empty but upstairs patients in bed can easily see the garden and the bright blue sky. It is the annual garden party and plant sale at Lambeth Community Care Centre in central London.

The center is a new kind of building and special kind of place. By combining rehabilitative day care with overnight nursing care, it is a place for those who are dying, for those who are very ill, and for those who are in need of a short stay or a visit of a few hours. With its close relationship to the community and its interest in health education, it is also a place for visitors and for staff, patients, ex-patients, and local residents young and old to attend parties, fund raisers, and other social and educational events.

There is both an elegance and an informality to the design of the Lambeth center. The quality of materials and construction, the richness of detail, the abundance of glass and light, and the views of a magnificent garden create a feeling of luxury, particularly on the upper floor where patients in light and airy wards look out to a generous veranda and the lush garden beyond. The coziness of the sitting room, the therapy rooms with glass doors, and the seating nooks in the corridor on the ground floor suggest a homey, well-used place where everyone is welcome. It is a beautiful and well-loved building.

Behind Lambeth Community Care Centre lies a story of vision, determination and collaboration. In 1974, Lambeth General Hospital, a 400-bed acute care hospital built in 1880, was closed. Serious cases would now be treated at the near-by St. Thomas's. The local Community Health Council agreed to the closure on condition that the site would be retained for local community health service use (Wilce 1988). Through intensive outreach to local groups of all kinds, to general practitioners, district nurses, home health and social services, the Community Health Council (CHC) developed a vision of an experimental community hospital that would combine in-patient care to infirm elderly and to people recovering from major operations who could not look after themselves with out-patient physical and other therapies close to patients' homes.

Once the idea was clear, a project team consisting of GPs (family doctors), the CHC secretary, CHC members, representatives of community nursing services, occupational therapists, and a representative from St. Thomas's planning department, began to work on plans in more detail, locate funding and negotiate with other groups, including the architects. Only after a dozen meetings with the project team was the firm of Edward Cullinan Architects formally appointed to design the centre.

The architects' first proposal was for a symmetrical, two-story building in red and yellow brick with a garden behind, a central conservatory around the main staircase projecting into the back, and a causeway on the second level across to the garden. The south-facing wards would open on to terraces that looked out to the garden. The terraces, the conservatory, and the route to the garden were all approved (and subsequently built), but the project team was highly critical of the separation of functions produced by the symmetry of the first scheme, the narrow internal corridors and the long trips to the bathrooms. They envisioned a more inviting route for circulation that would encourage patients to move around and to interact with others. In immediate response to these criticisms, Ted Cullinan redrew the plan, grouping functions and generating the asymmetrical layout characteristic of the centre as built.

Over the next seven months, many other changes and refinements were made with additional input sought from each health specialist who would occupy the building and from the works officer; space was substantially reduced to achieve a required reduction in cost. The corridors became more inviting with three small waiting areas, on the ground floor adjacent to the therapy rooms, with seating nooks built into two corners. On the floor above where the wards are, service spaces, including WCs, alternate with window seating that looks out on to the street. A very heated disagreement occurred over the design of the garden. Several project team members were avid gardeners and envisioned a more varied and elaborate garden than the flat lawns Cullinan had proposed. The result is a rolling landscape created by the debris from the old Lambeth Hospital, with private groves and open lawns, dense planting and winding paths.

The process of creating the Lambeth center was one of intensive collaboration between two independent and strong-minded parties. The client was a team of well-informed and highly committed professionals with very clear ideas; the architectural firm was committed both

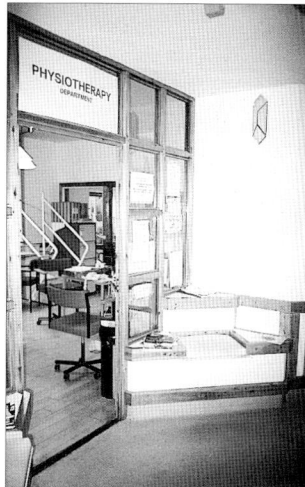

Entry and waiting area for treatment room on ground floor

Window seats on upper level

For whereas I am totally committed to making architecture with *and for people,* I am convinced *that if architects bring no understanding, no commitment, no ego even, and only their obedience to that discussion, there will never be any risk,* but neither will there ever be any architecture again. (Edward Cullinan in Powell 1995, p151*)*

Plans, Lambeth Community
Care Center, London (Edward
Cullinan Architects)
a. Lower level
1 Draft lobby 2 Reception,
records, general
administration 3 Community
worker 4 Administrator and
evaluator 5 Staff lobby and
stairs to staff room 6 Female
changing room 7 Male
changing room 8 Cleaner's
store 9 Store for wheelchairs
and frames 10 Client's WC
11 Cloakroom 12 Servery
13 Dining room 14 Sitting
room 15 Lower conservatory
16 Back gate 17 Seminar
room
18 Occupational therapy
19 Assessment kitchen
20 Assessment bedroom
21 Physiotherapy
22 Passive physiotherapy
23 Workshop with kiln
24 Physiotherapy store
25 Bathroom 26 Delivery and
disposal lobby and staff stairs
to sitting room 27 Dirty
utility and laundry 28 Clean
utility and tratment room
29 Hairdresser
30 Chiropodist/consulting
room 31 Staff office
32 Speech therapy/consulting
room 33 Social worker
34 Dentist 35 Lift

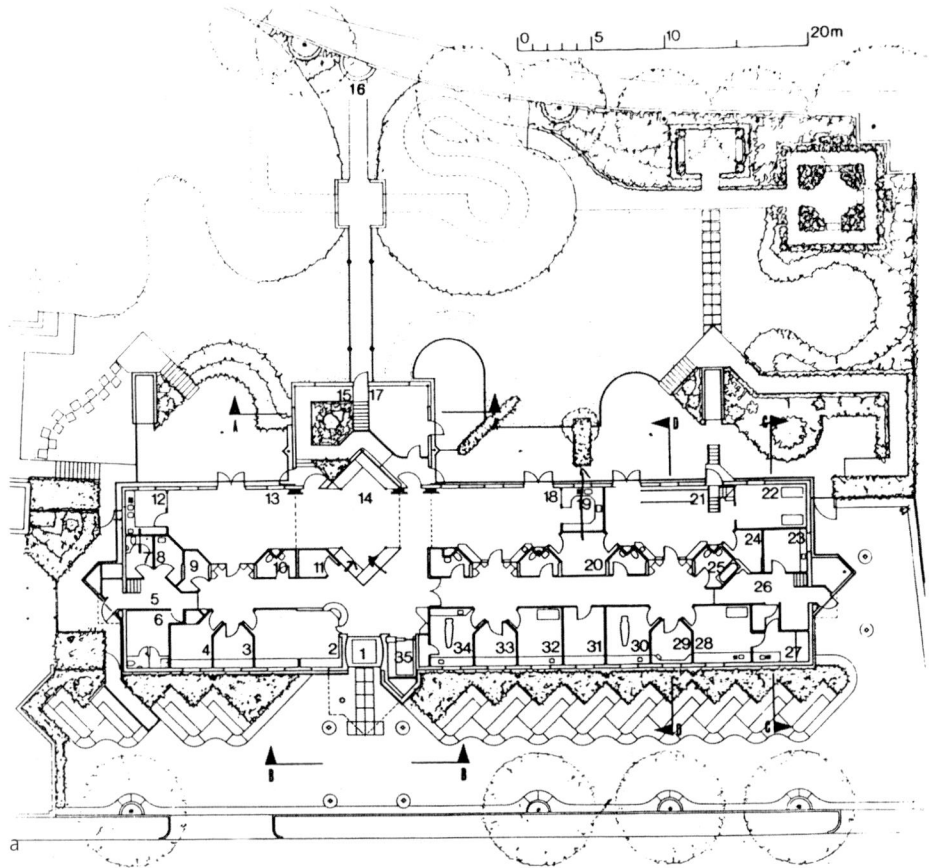

b. Upper level
36 Nurses' station 37 Clean
utility 38 Sister's office
39 Dirty utility 40 Bathroom
41 Client's WC 42 Cleaner's
room 43 Boiler room
44 Staff room with
kitchenette 45 Four bed ward
46 Single bed room 47 Upper
terrace 48 Upper
conservatory and sun room
49 Bridge 50 Belvedere
51 Sitting and dining room
with alcove for relatives
staying overnight 52 Servery
53 Shower 54 Store

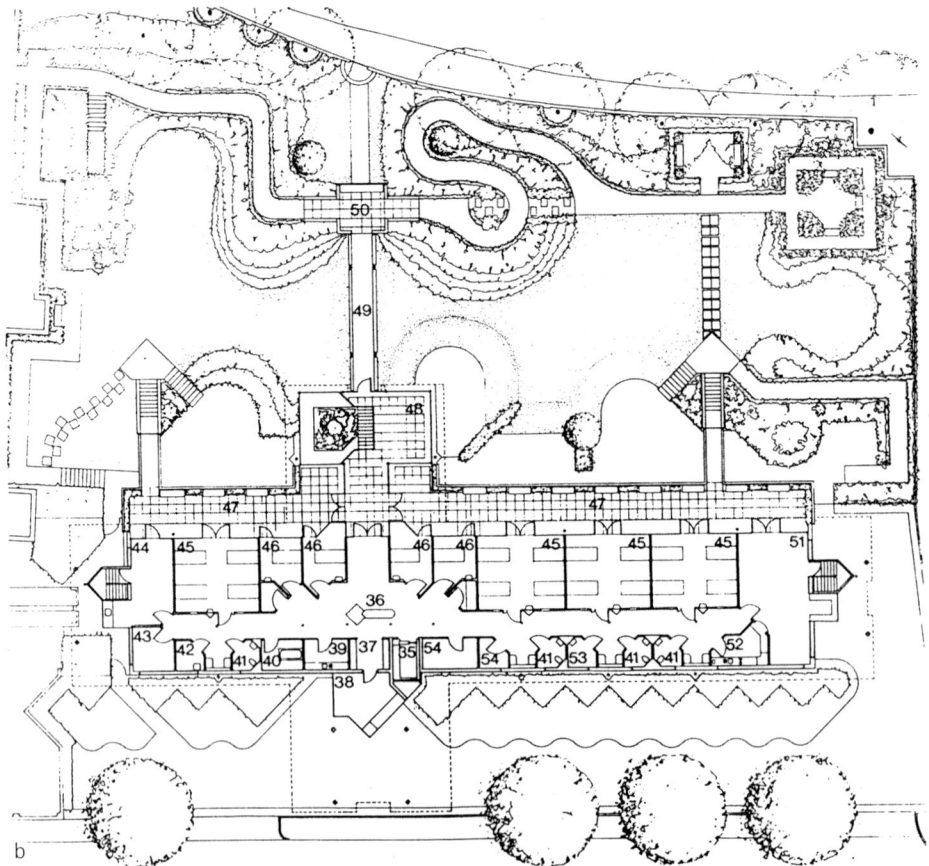

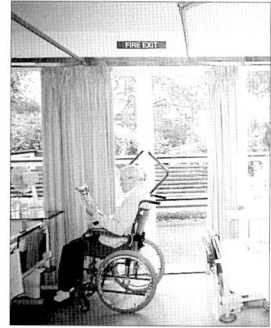

Ward, view to verandah

to working with the client and to employing their own expertise to its fullest. The first of nine proposals was made by the architects in September 1981; over 30 meetings were held with the client before the scheme was finalized in July 1982 and more than 300 meetings took place in all (Lubbock 1985). This process increased the cost of the project: one half percent went to the architects for meetings.

There is no doubt that the final design benefited from the contributions of each party *and* from the negotiations between them. The project team presented the brief and the purpose, philosophy, and anticipated operations of the building in detail and responded to each proposal with a mixture of acceptance and explicit criticism. It was they who imagined the corridors as places of interaction, who rejected extreme symmetry, who emphasized a zoning of functions and who insisted on a varied garden (Lubbock 1985). The architects listened, rejected some of the team's ideas while accepting others, made their own proposals and responded to strong criticisms with alternative proposals. It was the architects' imagination that generated the theme of a "country house party" and the ideas for the ward verandas, the conservatory stairwell, its relation to the garden and the sitting room. The elaboration of construction details and the way the pitched steel roof rises up over the wards to a clerestory allowing for ventilation and even more light to enter the wards emerged from the architects' expertise and care.

The clients and the architects pursued the planning and design of Lambeth Community Care Centre with strongly held beliefs about the purpose and desired character of the building. Those beliefs made all the difference to the process and the product.

> Today, building needs an atmosphere of belief for the architect to work in. Belief can come from recognizing that new institutions want to emerge and be given expression in space. New beliefs come with new institutions that need to be expressed as new spaces and new relationships. The architectural realizations sensitive to the institution's particular form would set a new precedent, a new beginning. I do not believe that beauty can be deliberately created. Beauty evolves out of a will to be. . . (Louis Kahn in Wurman 1986, p257).

Notes

1 Letter written by R. Bianca Lepori to the municipality of Rome at the request of La Rustica cultural association.
2 Please refer to Leslie Weisman's essay, "Redesigning Architectural Education" for a comprehensive description of the many educational goals and strategies of this studio and its underlying philosophy.
3 For a more complete description of tectonic color and the studies Brady assigns, please see her essay "Poetics, Color and Kinetics" and her forthcoming book and CD, *Architectonic Color: Its Virtual and Physical Reality*.

References

Andreas-Salomé, Lou. *Eros*. Paris: Les Editions de minuit, 1984. (Translations by R. Bianca Lepori.)

Brady, Darlene. Poetics, color and kinetics: content and computing. In G.E. Lasker and G. Andohian (eds) *Advances in Systems Research and Cybernetics*. Vol. II. Windsor, Ontario: International Institute for Advanced Studies in Systems Research, 1998.

Buchanan, Peter. A critical condition. *Architects Journal* Special Issue: Lambeth Community Care Centre. vol.16, 1985.

Feldman, Roberta and George C. Hemmens. *City Design Center: Projects 1995–1997*. Chicago, Ill.: College of Architecture and the Arts, The University of Illinois at Chicago, 1998.

Feldman, Roberta. Presentation. Sheltering Ourselves: Seventh Conference on Women & Community Development. Cincinnati, Ohio: The Women's Research & Development Center, October 1998.

Friedman, Dan. We stay! We build! *New Bronx Times*, January 21, 1999.

Higgs, Roger. Example of intermediate care: the new Lambeth Community Care Centre. *British Medical Journal*, November 16, 1985: 1395–1397.

Irigaray, Luce. *Sexes and Genealogies*. New York: Columbia University Press, 1993.

Lubbock, Jules. A patient revolution. *Architects Journal* Special Issue: Lambeth Community Care Centre. vol. 16, 1985.

Potteiger, Matthew and Jamie Purinton. *Landscape Narratives: Design Practices for Telling Stories*. New York: John Wiley, 1998.

Powell, Kenneth. *Edward Cullinan Architects*. London: Academy Editions, 1995.

Quaderni, Ermes Luparia. Text of a course of lectures on prenatal anthropology, Istituto Superiore di Medicina Olistica, Urbino University, Urbino, 1992. (Passage translated by Bianca Lepori.)

Reeves, Hubert. *Patience dans l'azur: L'evolution cosmiques*. Paris Editions du Seuil, 1998 (Passage translated by R. Bianca Lepori.)

Robbins, Edward. *Why Architects Draw*. Cambridge, Mass.: MIT Press, 1994.

Weisman, Leslie Kanes. Designing for difference: The service learning studio. In Sherry Ahrentzen and Janetta McCoy (eds) *Doing Diversity: A Compendium of Architectural Courses Addressing Diversity Issues in Architecture*. Washington, D.C.: Association of Collegiate Schools of Architecture, 1996.

Weisman, Leslie Kanes. Redesigning architectural education: New models for a new century. In Joan Rothschild (ed) *Design and Feminism: Re-visioning Spaces, Places and Everyday Things*. New Brunswick: Rutgers University Press, 1999.

Wilce, Gillian. *A Place Like Home: A Radical Experiment in Health Care*. London: Bedford Square Press, 1988.

Wurman, Richard Saul. *What Will Be Has Always Been: The Words of Louis I. Kahn*. New York: Access Press, 1986.

Chapter 6

Balancing Opposites

They are tall, flat, and achingly bland. Sometimes made of brick, often of concrete and glass, they are endless, repetitive rectangles. Not a single curved line, no ornament and little color or liveliness of texture, of light and shadow soften their sterile appearance. Inside are more boxes – boxes for living or, in a different location and with more glass, boxes for working. You cannot tell front from back, top from bottom, one from another. You cannot tell what city or country you are in: with some differences, possibly balconies on the boxes for living, the buildings could be in New York, Paris, Seoul, or Brazilia. Sometimes the buildings are short, even just two or three stories, but the smaller size gives no relief from their dreary anonymity.

How perfect the buildings are. They record with utmost accuracy the dominant values of the industrialized societies that produce them. All of them proclaim the relentlessness of the forces of production and standardization while the office buildings and luxury towers display the pursuit of profit and the accumulation of wealth. In their severity and rationality, in their rejection of the particularities of site, climate, and local culture, they are the built realization of the Cartesian mind that values abstraction, that is separated as much as possible from body, matter, and feeling.

The boxes for living for those with little money were built with good intentions to house large numbers of people in safe and sanitary conditions. For many different reasons these buildings prove to be difficult places for families with children to live. Often, however, all blame is placed on the buildings and authorities in the U.S. England, Holland and elsewhere destroy them with dynamite.

Fortunately, through redesign and new construction in London, Amsterdam, Newark, Boston and many other cities the anonymous boxes for living are being replaced, or supplemented, with greater articulation of individual dwellings, with private outdoor space, with closer connections to the ground and to services. It is the need for this alternative that Nancy Wolf depicts at the lower level of *Implosion*. Above stands the world of abstraction, of disembodied intellect and dematerialized architecture; the buildings below suggest an architecture that is more human-scale, sensory-rich and site-responsive, that chooses embodiment over abstraction.

Such changes in housing design come from a recognition of the sensual pleasures we derive from the material world and from an understanding of the ways that people actually inhabit space and of need for a closer relationship to spaces outside the dwelling. We see evidence of this change, for example, in the work of California architects Ena Dubnoff, Michael Pyatok and others (Jones et al 1997) as well as in Itsuko Hasegawa's design of Cona Village where the private outdoor spaces, the curves of the bridges linking different blocks, a small artificial river and the perforated metal intended to give a magical appearance of clouds all enrich this low-cost housing development.

The other bland boxes for the rich and the poor, for living and working, will continue to be built. It is not a question of either/or but of offering more alternatives, of

"Implosion" (gouache and colored pencil on paper, Nancy Wolf)

seeking a greater degree of balance. The search for a greater balance between what appear to be opposites applies to what we believe *and* to what we build. Why should we forever choose between mind and body, objective and subjective, rational and emotional? These dichotomies oppose an abstract realm detached from the body and the world to an embodied realm closely engaged with them. Why not recognize the value of both realms and of the connections between them?

Objective and Subjective

The architectural drawings on the wall are beautifully made and beautiful to look at. The black lines on white paper are very finely drawn, so fine that it is hard to tell where the walls are. No poché, no density of material is shown. No people and no furniture are represented so it is hard to get a sense of scale. Nor is there any written explanation of the use of the spaces. There is a cryptic text, including a number of evocative phrases that add yet more mystery to the project. A Cartesian mind was busily at work here, disdaining the material and sensual qualities of the world and the everyday activities of life.

The architect who made the drawings is certainly not alone in having this feeling of disdain; the drawings reflect a widespread Western attitude. It is possible that Western civilization has devalued earth and body, indeed all matter, throughout its history (Wilshire 1989, p94). It was in the seventeenth century, however, that René Descartes articulated the mutual exclusivity of mind and body and posed the possibility that the mind could transcend the body and bodily experience to attain knowledge uncontaminated by bodily sensations. His *Meditations* are largely suggestions for how to do this – to overcome the distractions, seductions, and errors of the corporeal (Bordo 1987, p94).

Since then the ideal model of knowledge in the West has been a male self who is detached from the material world – both from his own body and from his surroundings – who seeks to know that world from a rational and detached perspective (Brodribb 1992). In adopting this view, we attempt to sever ourselves from the world and from our own bodies, both of which are denigrated as "merely" physical. What is sought is a mind that is apparently "free" of both.

This requires that the best knowledge be abstract (or at least be presented as abstract): that is, removed from the single individual, from direct connection with specific concrete events of daily life and embodied experience and therefore deemed "objective." Once a wish, desire, or experience is measured across many people, as in surveys, the details and particularities of individual subjectivities are merged. "It" has been converted from particular individual experiences grounded in particular concrete details to a more generalized presentation from which, it is believed, all subjectivity has been removed and certain, possibly useful details, lost.

The "objectifing" of the "subjective" occurs not only in scientific research but in government reports, in academic texts, in statements made by journalists and politicians, in oral presentations by architects and in the kinds of drawing architects present. Objectivity does not always depend on the accumulation of thorough research: it may simply require a certain kind of appearance, a dispassionate and apparently neutral voice of authority, where content, specialized language, the detached tone and professional status of the speaker all help make it seem "objective."

Following Descartes, the mind that is separated from the body and elevated above it is only a certain *kind* of mind. It is rational and logical, not intuitive or emotional. It is often characterized as masculine while emotional aspects of the mind, subjectivity, and the body are treated as feminine. In Jungian terms this rational, logical mind

An older sense of participation in a world of meaning is traded for a mental world that, however dry and abstract, has the virtue of independence. To know is no longer erotic, no longer relational but becomes instead a means of escape from enmeshment in material existence. (Susan Griffin 1995, p86)

is the animus, distinguished from the anima which is associated with fantasy, emotion, and image.

Descartes's separation of a rational mind from the body and his prescription for reaching a form of objective knowledge served an essential purpose in Western culture: it removed the constraints of religious beliefs in the soul and God from the development of science. The physical world, separated from a mental or spiritual world, became amenable to investigation and measurement. The progress in science, technology, and consequently in the quality of daily life has been enormous and continues today.

At the same time the continuing power of the oppositional and evaluative dualism of mind and body, rational and emotional, objective and subjective is now a serious limitation to thought, design and the quality of everyday life. We devalue both our bodies and the material world, treating them as "merely" physical. Similarly, emotions, dreams, fantasies and all of symbolic life are "merely" subjective. What is valued is the rational mind, an intellectual domain somehow deemed independent of body, subjectivity, and physicality and so abstracted from concrete events and circumstances, indeed from all of daily life. A kind of nether realm. What pertains to the mind, what is abstract, is more important than what pertains to the body, what is enacted, what is experienced. With these values entrenched, no wonder people and furniture or an expression of materiality and color are absent from architectural drawings, no wonder there is more interest in form than use.

In repressing "subjective" knowledge, we repress fears, desires, dreams, fantasies – the stories and images that shape and animate our lives and our surroundings, sometimes called the "imaginal." The imaginal is not only present in private dreams and fears but in commonly shared understandings and descriptions, even in the objectified knowledge we assume is so free of such content. The two domains of the material and the imaginal, both of which we neglect in favor of the rational, are closely and intimately intertwined. The material world embodies hopes, fears, desires. As Nancy Wolf's drawings depict so well, it is this relationship between material and imaginal that is manipulated in the design of buildings and cities. In architecture we are having and pursuing dreams, much as any visionary thinker or artist does, albeit in a very different manner. Striving for objectivity and rationality and attempting to repress dreams altogether, we forget the power of dreams in making the world. We forget our own magic because we are enthralled by what is "rational."

The Western worldview that privileges objective over subjective and idealizes a disembodied rationality began to have its impact on architecture during the eighteenth century with the highly influential work of Durand who rejected the symbolic meanings of geometry and the poetic qualities of architecture (Pérez-Gómez 1983). The techniques of drawing he promoted were devoid of earlier symbolic meanings and representations of materiality. It was Durand who furthered the grid as a key instrument of design, rejected the value of perspectives or drawings in watercolor, and held that only plans, sections, and elevations drawn with thin, precise lines were necessary to convey the idea for a building (ibid., 1996).

As conceptions of space that are then represented, architectural drawings are necessarily more abstract than lived experience and so architects' involvement with space, as they conceive and represent it, is quite distant from occupants' experience of space as they live it. Drawings of the modern period, beginning with Durand, increased the abstraction of space and architects' conception of spaces became more removed from occupants' experiences. The drawing that comes closest to representing an occupant's experience within a space, the perspective drawing, was rejected by Durand in favor

The essence of the problem is . . . that one-sided overdependence on the intellect underlying Western culture. Intellect is valued far above emotion; rationality the essence and ultimate form of humanity. Rationalism has played a decisive role in industrial society, but it has also led us to disdain and devalue the importance of consciousness, spiritual phenomena and emotion. (Kisho Kurokawa 1998, p299)

of plan, section, and elevation which are not views we ever experience. These drawings, compared to perspective drawings and drawings in watercolor, encouraged architects to conceive of space in highly abstract terms and to pay less attention to materiality and embodiment. The space in these drawings became even more removed from people's experience of space, increasing the difference between the architect's space and the occupant's space.

Today this difference between architect's space and user's space is increased by the very evocative deconstructivist drawings of buildings as flying fragments. Lynda Schneekloth, at the State University of New York at Buffalo, describes studios where the exploration and graphic depiction of an idea replaces the realization of that idea in a building, at a particular place, to be occupied by people. She notes that, as a result, "the students' drawings float. Their projects are not tied to the earth. Architecture becomes a thing in and of itself." While color may well be used, it is more a graphic device used in the interests of the drawing than a depiction of materiality or the anticipated experiential qualities of the space. Computer programs offer yet more opportunities to generate unusual shapes, sometimes apparently in motion and in striking colors, ever more removed from actual places, experiences, and activities.

The ideal of a mind that transcends bodies and matter is the Cartesian *dream*. It took several hundred years but now many parts of the built landscape are a reflection of that dream, making the inhabited world in the image of a disembodied mind. Following Durand, the representation of space in highly geometric and abstract terms eventually encouraged the creation of buildings that are abstract, devoid of detail and a sense of materiality. A style of drawing became a style of building.

Somber, anonymous buildings whose only ornamentation is a regular grid of windows and, more recently, strangely shaped structures modeled by computer programs help create what appears to be an abstract, uninhabited world. The choice and manipulation of materials as well as the inattention to human scale or human needs contribute to that image. Often attempts are made to reduce the material appearance of the building as much as possible: with large expanses of glass in certain weather conditions the building surface seems to blend into the sky. Stark simplicity, flatness, transparency, and weightlessness all reduce the appearance of physicality. Interiors where all environmental conditions are controlled by a central computer and the windows cannot be opened nor the lights turned off or adjusted manually complete the picture.

A desire for transcendence is apparent in theoretical discussions of architecture as well; even the "body" remains highly abstract without reference to lived bodies, their actions or their experiences. Just as Descartes prescribed a transcendence of the body to achieve a purer knowledge, so contemporary architectural theorists attempt its transcendence, perhaps to achieve a similar purpose by ignoring it or treating it only as an idea and by employing a language of abstraction that obscures all links to embodied experience or materiality.[1] And those who design buildings without attention to inhabitation are attempting a similar transcendence – of idea over body, or more precisely of idea over the bodies of others.

To restore importance to lived bodies, to materiality, and to experience depends upon a reconciliation of mental/physical, reason/emotion, objective/subjective. Where we now see oppositions we can see complementarity and interdependence. Key to this change is a recognition of the integration of mind and body. Leading neurological researchers are pursuing studies that demonstrate not just that the mind is embodied but are exploring how this is so (see Edelman 1992). At times we may focus on what is more mental than physical and at other times the reverse will be true but nevertheless mental and physical are unavoidably linked. Processes in the brain cause

Battery Park City, New York

particular states of consciousness but that does not mean that consciousness is separate from the brain; it is instead a *feature* of the brain (Searle 1997, p8).

The metaphor of something that has two sides is often invoked to capture the uniting or "intertwining" of these two properties of the physical and the mental. Maurice Merleau-Ponty's concept of the "lived body" posits this doubleness: "We say therefore that our body is a being of two leaves, from one side a thing among things and otherwise what sees them and touches; we say. . . that it unites these two properties within itself. . . " (Merleau-Ponty 1968, p137).

In architecture recognizing the intertwining of mind and body, of body and world restores value both to the body's needs and experience *and* to the spatial and material qualities of the world. Architecture then arises not from highly intellectual ideas severed from human experience but from ideas closely connected to it. Then design reflects not the ideal of a disembodied mind but the ideal of embodied experience. Then color, texture, human scale, light, and shadow animate architecture. A more sensuous, embodied approach to design starts *from* the body, and relishes the role of architecture in meeting people's needs and enhancing daily life. The world is considered a source of nurture and stimulation; the possibilities for design to evoke sensory and kinesthetic experiences are seized.

Itsuko Hasegawa and Steven Holl pursue this approach. Hasegawa pays careful attention to the needs of clients and users, helping to develop the program for a project, finding innovative design responses in choice of site, in building, room and furniture design, and in the selection of materials. For her, needs do not translate into simple functional requirements but into ingenious manipulations of site, program, materials, space, and light. Each of these architects pursues thoughtful and detailed research prior to and during design. While they design so fully for subjectivity, they utilize a range of what are traditionally considered objective methods. And their buildings, while sensorially stimulating, also make programatic and spatial sense.

Significantly, Steven Holl uses small perspective drawings, in watercolor, as a first step in the design process and as a means of presenting ideas to clients. These drawings anticipate the experience of being in the space; they bridge the division between space as conceived and space as lived; they give significance both to the materiality of the world and to our experience of that world. Holl's watercolors of his proposed design for the Kiasma Museum of Contemporary Art in Helsinki were

. . . our life, this "intertwining," is a network of reciprocities (I only know myself through the "other"); moreover, reality is not reducible to the conventional poles of objectivity and subjectivity, it is a gift to a non-dualistic, embodied consciousness – the whole, experiencing the human body as a synesthetic receptor. (Alberto Pérez-Gómez 1996, p9)

Architecture, perhaps more than any other form of communication, possesses the power of uniting intellectual and intuitive expression. Fusing the objective with the subjective, architecture can stitch our daily lives together by a single thread of intensity. (Steven Holl 1996, p23)

Interior perspective, Kiasma Museum of Contemporary Art, Helsinki (watercolor, Steven Holl)

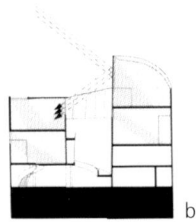

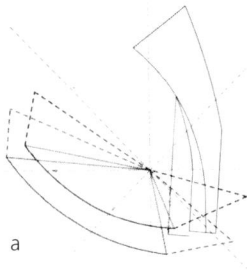

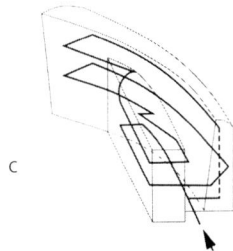

*Kiasma Museum of
Contemporary Art, Helsinki
(Steven Holl Architects)
a. Sun path reversal
b. Light-catching section
c. Circuit diagram*

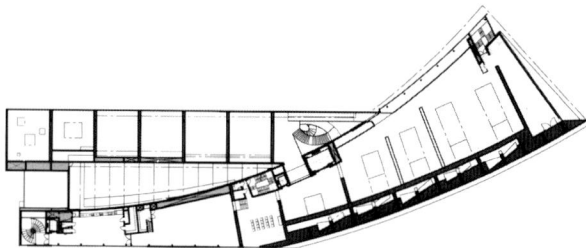

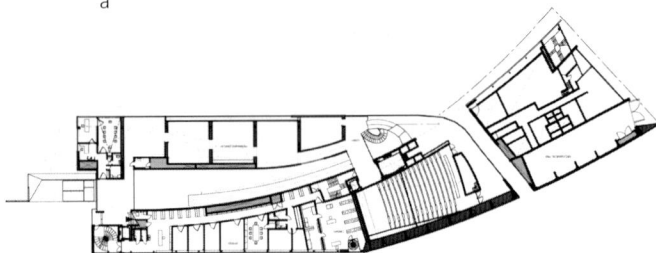

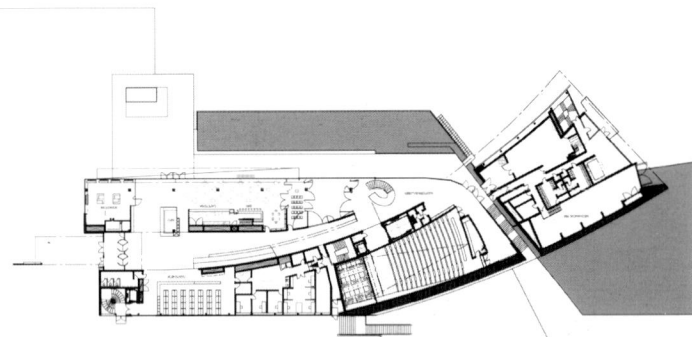

*Selected plans, Kiasma Museum of Contemporary Art, Helsinki
(Steven Holl Architects)
a. First floor
b. Second floor
c. Fifth floor*

a significant factor in the jury's selection of his design.

Each entry to the competition for the museum had to have a code name. Holl chose "chiasma" which means a crossing of lines as in the letter X. The building is a crossing in several senses. According to Holl, the initial idea came from studying the site and choosing to recognize the crossing of a "line of culture" extending from Alvar Aalto's Finlandia Hall with a "line of nature" extending from Töölö Bay. It also came from understanding the natural condition of low horizontal light in Finland (Holl in Futagawa 1996).

Working on the initial concept and testing it against many other schemes for six months resulted in a building of complex geometry: the intertwining of two volumes, one dramatically curved and one orthogonal with the entry hall and central circulation space, or atrium, located between them. During the development of the scheme, internal perspectives depicting spatial experiences were made in parallel with the elaboration of the external concept. Careful research on many issues shaped the building's design internally and externally. The primary curvature of the building is a reversal of the sun's path between 11 a.m. and 6 p.m. when the museum is open. The curved section captures the horizontal sunlight typical of northern latitudes, which only reaches 51 degrees maximum in Helsinki, and diffuses it through the atrium and through openings carefully oriented to allow natural light to enter the exhibition spaces. A central circulation ramp connects the 25 galleries in a processional movement; stairs and elevators provide alternative routes and shortcuts, giving visitors a choice of paths to follow.

Analyzing the size of the human body, and measuring the best gallery spaces in Manhattan, suggested to Holl that the best size of a gallery would be 9 m x 9 m x 4.5 meters (Holl 1996) and so he set the structural grid for the galleries at 9 meters. In keeping with the original watercolor sketches, the entry hall and many of the galleries are sculpted spaces, with a curved wall, and on the top level a curved ceiling. All of the surfaces were kept as neutral and undisturbed as possible, without visible fixtures, or vents, or smoke-detectors (the exception being exit signs for emergency purposes). Holl designed the lighting fixtures, bathroom fixtures, door handles, and cafe furniture.

Careful attention was given to fulfilling the program while also creating a variety of spatial and sensory experiences indoors and out. All the galleries are on the upper levels with the café, museum shop, and auditorium on the ground level, opening out on to a terrace and the street, so they can be used when the galleries are closed. At many places in the building large windows and even an outdoor deck on the top level give views to the city. These openings offer views into the building from the city as well.

Visitors actively engage with the building, as they move through it in different ways, as they look up at the sculptured ceilings, down into and across the atrium, and out to the city and as they touch the plaster walls. The museum succeeds in achieving the balance between sensation and thought which Holl seeks – the same kind of balance that is evident in his design process. "When the intellectual realm, the realm of ideas, is in balance with the experiential realm, the realm of phenomena, form is animated with meaning. In this balance, architecture has both intellectual and physical intensity with the potential to touch mind, eye and soul" (Holl 1993, p26).

Separated and Connected

I am sitting on a white, plastic swivel chair at a gray formica desk, writing with a black roller ball pen on white paper with blue lines. On my desk is a cup of tea, several pens and pencils, books, a few stones from the beach and a black cat who is watching me. Bianca sits across the room from me on a small, beige couch, her feet propped up on a wooden coffee table painted burgundy red. She is writing with a blue ballpoint pen on unlined white paper on her lap.

The world is given to us, through perception, as a multitude of visibly and tactilely separate items. Their physical boundaries, apparent to sight and touch, delimit them from each other. To survive and to thrive in the world, humans depend upon physical, perceptual distinctions. Our ways of naming and categorizing further reinforce the separateness of phenomena.

We depend upon the social and symbolic categories that language and culture provide. So people do not see only separate objects; we also "see" the categories to which they are assigned. These categories, in any culture and at any period in time, are containers that divide up the world as much as the buildings and rooms we physically inhabit. They can simply be the names of physical objects at a "basic" level of categorization such as "chair" or "cat" and they can be more abstract kinds of classification such as sacred and profane, culture and nature, body and mind.

While our manner of seeing is fixed by the nature of human vision, our manner of separating and connecting is shaped by language, culture, and history. What

a

b

c

d

Kiasma Museum of Contemporary Art, Helsinki (Steven Holl Architects)
a. Entrance hall and atrium
b. Looking into atrium
c. Looking into atrium
d. Looking out toward city, above entrance

is separated from what and, once separated, what kind of relationships are envisioned, are consequences of this context and therefore change over time. In Western culture mutually exclusive and even oppositional categories have long been preferred to connections, overlaps, and interdependence. We are forever distinguishing one thing from another and making the distinction sharp and clear, breaking the world apart into pieces and assuming independence where we might see relationship.

The model of separation and isolation among parts permeates so many aspects of modern life. We create and negotiate a multitude of divisions, between objective and subjective, between form and use, between people and places, between public and private, between expert and non-expert. Too often we conceive and design buildings as objects, separated from context and use. All over the world, buildings and cities are created that have no connection to their geographical or cultural location.

This tradition of separation and independence between individual parts is characteristic of a mechanistic worldview, arising from the seventeenth-century revolution in science and philosophy. The metaphor of the world and the body as machines became a powerful organizer of ideas and assumptions. This model frames physical (and subsequently social and psychological) phenomena as composed of separate and isolated parts, following repeated, predictable and controllable actions. The mechanistic paradigm allowed physics and mathematics to be used to understand the world, allowed predictions to be made and made it possible to manipulate the physical world in extremely useful ways (Sheldrake 1988). And so this paradigm has been an eminently valuable guide to perception yet we have treated it as much more – as an accurate reflection of what actually exists (Bohm 1980, p7). And so we are "led to the illusion that the world is actually constituted of separate fragments and . . . this will cause us to act in such a way that we do in fact produce the very fragmentation implied in our attitude to the theory" (ibid., p29).

One way we do this is to build environments that embody separateness at many different levels. In the United States we build communities where each dwelling is as physically and socially distinct as possible from every other dwelling so that virtually no overlap in space or in activities among households will occur (Franck 1994a). We organize the built landscape into discrete, separate and highly bounded types of places, devoted to single, highly homogeneous uses. We adopt zoning laws that separate all commercial and wage work land uses from residential uses, that divide single family homes from multi-family buildings and that create neighborhoods populated only by households of the same income. The distinction and separation between uses and the construction of specialized kinds of places to house the use and the users began with the increasing specialization of interior spaces in the eighteenth and nineteenth centuries and has increased in the West ever since, creating a segmentation of contemporary life (Tuan 1982).

Because buildings actually *are*, in a visual and tactile sense, *objects*, distinct from their surroundings and from the bodies that occupy them, it is tempting to conceive of them as autonomous, disconnected from their use and their surroundings. It becomes even more tempting to create built form as an independent object, not only autonomous but even dismissive of its use and its surroundings. Then the built artifact can be made as fully separate from its surroundings, stylistically and urbanistically, as possible. As computers allow architects to create more and more fluid forms, there is greater and greater opportunity for the distinctiveness and peculiarity of each building; they may have even less connection to their neighbors or to their use.

The chair, the desk, the couch, pens and paper, Bianca and I are, indeed, separate physical objects. However, at other levels not seen by the naked eye, at the levels of atoms

The party wall, as a traditional element of urban housing, plays a dual role. In keeping with its name, it is shared, but, paradoxically, it also separates: that is, while the wall belongs to the configuration of both dwellings, it is the element that prevents the dwellings from belonging to each other. Architecture can bridge this dichotomy. (Jill Stoner 1989, p127)

and subatomic particles, we are all part of one pattern of energy. And, at an observ-able level, Bianca and I are also a pattern: we are partners in the writing of this book. We wouldn't be writing this book or doing so in this manner without the presence and influence of the other.

The physicist David Bohm described reality as consisting of two levels: the expli-cate and the implicate. The explicate order, the one we inhabit, is where things appear to be separate. In the implicate order, at the subatomic level, all is interconnected in a seamless whole, a continuum of energy. What looks separate at our level of per-ception, the explicate level, are aspects of one cosmic unity. Another way of describ-ing what is simultaneously separate and related is given by Fritjof Capra: " . . . there is a reality but there are no things, no trees, no birds. These patterns are what we create. As we focus on a particular pattern and then cut it out from the rest, it becomes an object" (Capra 1992 p124). The rose, the boat, the butterfly in Ellen Wiener's prints are, indeed, such objects.

Once the object is "cut out," it may be viewed more or less independently from other objects. It is precisely because reality is whole that it appears to be fragmented when we choose to see it so (Sheldrake 1988). We have the *choice* to see con-nections where once we saw only separations, to embrace the idea of being as being-in-relationship and to design and build accordingly. One small but telling example is given in Jill Stoner's proposal for sharing space. Within the party wall that separates one apartment from another, she finds precedents in plumbing, the chimney flue and the light shaft for sharing across the wall and mines these precedents for designing a shared workplace, kitchen or gallery. The potential for closer spatial and social rela-tionships among households is being seized in many different types of collective and shared housing, including cohousing (Franck and Ahrentzen 1989).

Being on the earth, at a particular site, near other buildings, a building necessari-ly has particular physical, spatial and social relationships with its surroundings – with earth, sky and neighbors – and with its occupants. Even those people who simply pass by may remember what was there before, welcome or reject a new presence, and develop new associations. Those who enter and occupy a new building or a newly converted one may modify and adapt it and develop strong feelings of attachment to it over time. As we live or work in it or visit it, it becomes part of our routine. As we enjoy its pleasures and become annoyed by its deficiencies, it takes a place in our lives. We are in it and it is in us.

And so a building is part of a dense network of relationships, part of a field of energy to which it contributes: it is never alone. At the same time, however, the build-ing is also separate, an object that the architect envisions and designs, we hope while being well aware of the relationships that will be created and those that will be changed by its insertion into an existing physical and social fabric. Its insertion may reweave or mend that fabric, bring benefits to its surroundings. It is with the idea of mending that Bianca approached the planning and design of the square for La Rustica. Similarly, the plan developed by Nos Quedamos for the redevelopment of their neighborhood in the Bronx retains the existing residential and commercial buildings, fitting the new construction around them.

When what exists is both very old and well loved, the addition of the new, of what is therefore necessarily separate, is extremely difficult, particularly when imitation of the old is excluded as an approach. In 1978 the parish church of St. Mary's in Barnes, south London, was half destroyed by fire. This ancient village church, with its sev-enteenth-century brick tower, had been partially hidden by a Victorian rebuilding in the 1900s designed by a little known Victorian architect, Charles Innes, who added a

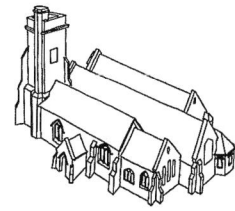

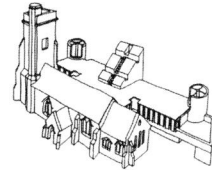

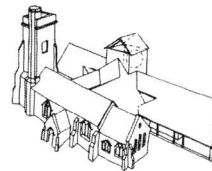

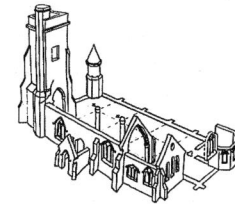

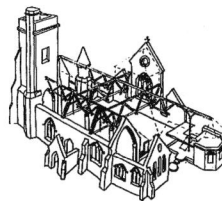

Transformation of St. Mary's, Barnes, London (rebuilding by Edward Cullinan Architects) From above: axonometric before the fire; axonometric of first scheme; axonometric of second scheme; old elements; new elements; as built.

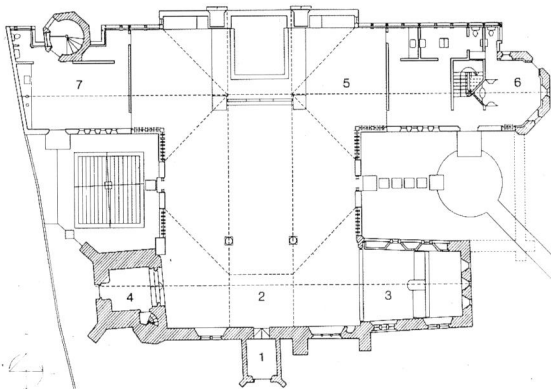

Ground floor plan. Retained structure is hatched.
1 South porch 2 Narthex 3 Langdon chapel 4 Ringing
chamber 5 East transept 6 Clergy vestry
7 Coffee room

Retained structure and new building

View of pulpit toward narthex and door to
ringing chamber
(Note new columns, new roof and existing
walls, window, door way.)

new church alongside the old one (Powell 1995, p19).

While some felt the twentieth-century rebuilding after the fire should be a literal reconstruction of what had burned down, others felt that the Victorian additions could be sacrificed to create a lighter and more spacious setting. There was also interest in making the church more responsive to the new liturgy of the Second Vatican Council, with a closer relationship between priest and congregation, with a clearly visible altar, space for the congregation to gather around it, and additional support spaces.

The first proposal Edward Cullinan made was for a new square church, on the site of the Victorian additions, with a striking roof line created in part by large solar collectors. This proposal was roundly rejected and a more contextual but still radical approach was adopted: to rebuild within the gutted walls, but with contemporary materials and a contemporary look. The large new roof resting on two new columns covers the new spaces as well as the old church. Its height and exposed trusses of colored steel and wood create an airy barn-like space. The trusses, the roof, the new tower and walls, and the light-colored wooden seating, all designed by Cullinan, are clearly contemporary but they sit well with the Gothic Revival fragments and with the original east window. The medieval church can now be seen as a nave, chancel and altar for small congregations or as the narthex to a much larger church (Cullinan in ibid., p89).

Since the completion of the church in 1984, the congregation has grown and, because of its excellent acoustics, the building is also used for concerts. The church is connected at many different levels to the past and to the present. The new parts are connected to the old forming an integrated whole while, at the same time, the new and the old retain their own identities.

The importance of separation and connection in the practice of architecture and in architectural education is captured in Sherry Ahrentzen and Linda Groat's metaphor for conceptualizing architecture as a "tapestry of cultural invention" (1992, p14). Such a model acknowledges the relationship of architecture to other fields, the multiplicity of viewpoints, participants, and creations it embraces, and the responsibility of the architect to the culture at large while, as in a tapestry, the separateness of the contributing entities is still apparent.

Static and Changing

On the shiny pages of the architecture magazine the building's exterior is bright and clean and the interi-

or calm and quiet. Everything is new and perfect; even the sky is clear and blue. There are no people, no signs of human habitation. The building, just completed, has not yet been occupied or perhaps all the furniture has been removed for this picture. Either way, there is no sign the building has been touched by people or by time.

Over and over again, through the years we will see these same photographs in architecture books and magazines. Even as the building is occupied, even as it is used and ages, we will still see it portrayed as spanking new. The good building is the new building. The best building is the one that appears to be unoccupied.

Just as buildings are portrayed and treated as objects, independent of context and inhabitation, so too are they frequently designed and celebrated as frozen in time. How they may change or be changed is far less important than their first, pristine appearance, before they have been sullied by time, weather, or use. How strange. It is precisely and momentously the life, over time, the memories, associations, and experiences which accrue to the built landscape that endear them to their occupants. However, because the building's image takes precedence over all else, there is very little collection or dissemination of information on how well buildings meet occupants' needs, how certain material, structural or spatial choices were successful and others were not, how changes have been incorporated. The photographs, taken when it was new, perpetuate the fiction of a static, uninhabited object.

Like the building, the body is treated as an object, and so it too is almost immobile. The ideal citizen is one who is still or follows only predictable and routine patterns of movement. In work or school, unless the task at hand requires changes of position, we are expected to remain in the same, usually upright, sitting position. In meetings, conferences, reviews, and classes we remain still, passive, our feelings deadened by our immobility. The good body is a still body; it can be dominated, controlled. So, when the architect does consider the body, it is often motionless or follows a limited range of predicted postures and movements pertinent to the tasks expected in that type of room or buildings. So much space for so many people standing, for so many sitting at tables, for so many sitting in rows of seats, for so many to enter or exit. It is a neutral and universalized body controlled by the social and physical context.

The building, its images captured on the magazine's pages, is not only an object. It is also a complex pattern of energy that changes over time. The form of the building, its objecthood, is only one element of a mutable web of elements that also include use and meaning (Franck 1994b). It is the looseness of the connections among these elements and their potential for change that makes the built setting itself a *process*. The use of a building may change with very little alteration in form.

The Limelight in New York City is a disco in a former church. The pews and other furniture and ornaments have been removed but the building is otherwise unchanged. In Newark a church's interior has been radically altered to accommodate a restaurant and offices but the outside is still recognizable as a church. Transformation occurs in the other direction as well. Large interior spaces in all kinds of buildings in the U.S. including movie theaters, bowling alleys, and warehouses are being used for community mosques (Wright 1999). Schools are transformed into housing, fire stations into restaurants, factory buildings into lofts, mills into shopping malls.

With or without changes in use, physical aspects of a building necessarily change over time. Materials, structure, and contents all age; many intentional replacements, modifications and transformations are made. A building can be considered as composed of six components that vary dramatically in their longevity: site (permanent);

. . . greater sensitivity to the latent *potential of situations might encourage us to think about things not just as they are, but where they are going, what they will become.* (Danah Zohar and Ian Marshall 1993, p24)

structure (30 to 300 years); skin (20 years); services (7 to 15 years); space plan (3 to 30 years); and the building's contents (Brand 1994).

If the building is conceived as a process, attention can be given to its potential for transformation from the beginning. Architects can raise questions with clients about possible future changes in needs and activities and, when desirable, incorporate opportunities for modification into their design. The goal for the architect is not to achieve a perfect and pristine state of objecthood but to participate in a process of evolution that begins with the first conversations about the new building but that does not end when it is first occupied. The activity recognized by quantum physicists as one of *becoming* applies to buildings as well. What can the surrounding place become with the creation of a new building? What can the building itself become over time?

Over shorter periods of time, choices of use that do not require physical modifications can be built in. In apartments, a "swing" room may be included adjacent to the living room, with sliding doors that open on to it. This can be used as a den, an alcove, an additional bedroom, a play space or a guest room. In public buildings, facilities with independent entrances and circulation allow for independent scheduling so, for instance, when the museum is closed, the theater and café can be open for evening performances at the Kiasma Museum in Helsinki. Other choices will require physical modifications that have been anticipated in advance. In three single-family houses in San Diego, Ted Smith designed a large loftlike space with a bathroom which, with partitions, can be adapted as two small bedrooms and a play space, two bedrooms or one large bedroom. The future expansion of a public building or complex of buildings can be accommodated with design choices made early on. The separate small buildings, the multiple centers and shifting axes of the Indian Institute of Management designed by Balkrishna Doshi in Bangalore create a flexible site plan that will allow for future changes while retaining the institute's identity (Kazi and Belluardo 1998, p150).

Modifications are made to buildings over and over again, sometimes over hundreds of years. How we intervene today with contemporary materials and design attitudes in buildings completed during a very different period poses tricky problems. It makes little sense to imitate the old, to create a kind of false stasis and suggest that no change has occurred. At the same time what is new should also be sympathetic to what is old.

The new Dipartimento Materno Infantile (Community Center for Pre- and Postnatal Care) was to be located close to the existing S. Donato hospital in Arezzo, within one of the empty buildings of a historic nineteenth-century hospital for the mentally ill. After studying several of the villas and service buildings of the former mental hospital, all located in a lush park setting, Bianca recommended the conversion of three separate but adjacent buildings. One of them, U-shaped, salmon-colored with a generous courtyard, had been built to house male patients in 1890. The two others, built in the 1940s, were a dark yellow garage and a yellow and terracotta striped storage building for garden tools, mysteriously including a tower. These three structures could be connected to make the Dipartimento Materno Infantile while still being independent of each other, with separate entrances, and thereby giving autonomy to the different services to be housed: a birthing center, a health center for pre- and postnatal care, pediatric screening, youth counseling, and a fertility clinic.

While very close to each other, the buildings were on different levels and of different heights even though each of them was only single-story. The courtyard building was almost one complete floor above the other two and its central part, between the two arms, was 8 meters tall, allowing a second floor to be installed. The garage was also tall enough to accommodate an upper floor, which ended up only a foot above the ground floor of the courtyard building, thus expanding the floor area of that level. Together with the addition of these two floors, two glazed galleries were added to the courtyard building, one on the inner side and one on the outer side of each wing, providing waiting areas as well as horizontal connections. To provide the vertical connection between the ground floor of the U-shaped building and the garage a glazed tower was added containing a stair and an elevator. These also connect the Dipartimento to the main hospital via a tunnel located below street level.

A third glass structure connects the garage section to the former storage building. This creates the alignment between the two and the space for the birthing center with its own access from the street and its own private garden on the opposite side. Transparent glazed panels open the gallery of the birthing center to views of the garden while translucent glass block protects it from the street. Glass block is also used to integrate the entrance to the birthing center within the garage facade and to anticipate the glazed connection to the former storage building. Glass block is used in the tower element as well to protect pregnant women from being observed when they are in the garden. Screens of trees will protect them from other views.

The original proposal was to build the galleries completely in glass, walls as well as roofs, in order to interfere as little as possible with the existing buildings of plastered brick. The final accepted proposal, however, is for glazed galleries with green patinated copper roofs because the client felt uncertain about the use of glazed roofs in Italy. The green-turquoise shade of the roofs, with the other colors of the buildings, will add to the center the joyfulness appropriate to its function.

No matter how much potential for change is incorporated into design or anticipated in construction or how much we consider the building as a process extending over time, it is also, still, a physical, largely static object. Ideas of future change and transformation depend upon seeing through the materiality of this eminently hard object to the softness and mutability of the human activities and relationships it houses. How do the hard walls and softer openings shape and constrain those activities and relationships? What patterns of separations and connections, enclosure and exposure, stasis and movement, are encouraged?

Hanging carpets remained the true walls, the visible boundaries of space. The often solid mass behind them was necessary for reasons that had nothing to do with the creation of space; they were needed for security, for supporting a

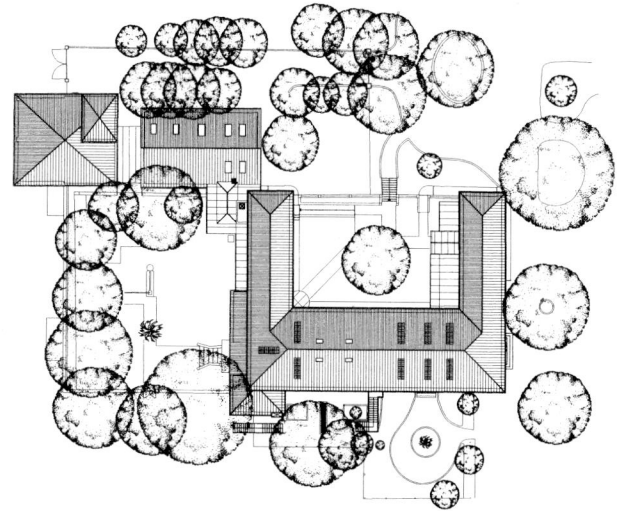
a

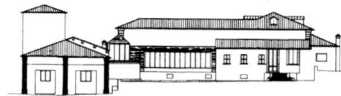

b

Dipartimento Materno Infantile, Arezzo (R. Bianca Lepori)
a. Roof plan
b. Elevations

load, for their permanence and so on. Wherever the need for these secondary functions did not arise, the carpets remained the original means of separating space (Semper 1989, p104).

Can we still sense those carpets? Can we see through the hardness and solidity of the wall to recognize its ancestor in the soft, movable carpet? The building is not fixed, the body is not fixed and the future is not fixed. They are not determined in advance; they are open to change, to evolution.

More than One

A perspective drawing is created from a single pair of eyes at a fixed location that confronts the space portrayed. All lines creating the perspective extend from that one person in that single location outward.

A desire for a single view, for the best answer, permeates contemporary professional and daily life. We enact this desire in the search for a single truth in science and religion, for a single solution in architecture and planning and for the elevation of singular sources of knowledge emanating from those deemed to be experts. The elevation of only one viewpoint forgets that the one view so cherished as singular was shaped by myriad unacknowledged assumptions. It is continuously shaped by conditions and circumstances particular to the time, the place, and the community of persons who hold it.

A single, certain and unvarying answer was one of the hallmarks of Modernism in its promotion of a universal architecture. Modern architecture was the built form of the monotheism of Enlightenment science – only one truth, anywhere, any time. With Modernism, as with objectified knowledge, architects sought to *transcend* the particularities of specific locations, specific bodies, and specific programs. Substantial differences in climate, culture, and program were often largely ignored in the interests of creating "universal space" and an "International Style." Nearly identical box-like buildings of glass, concrete, and steel originally designed in the West were, and still are, built anywhere with the assumption that those materials will be available, that mechanical systems of heating and cooling will counteract differences in climate and that people will learn to live and work in spaces that are not responsive to program or culture.

The idealization of a single view over multiple, differing views presumes that there *is* a single truth or condition that can be known. One provocative challenge to this belief comes from quantum physics which shows that multiple, contradictory conditions exist simultaneously. In a quantum system a particle has wave aspects *and* particle aspects simultaneously: which aspects are apparent depends upon the observer. Even though these quanta of energy are not apparent in the manifest world, the presence of simultaneously existing, contradictory qualities suggests that there can be no single truth – no single, cohesive and dependable answer. Instead what we call "reality" is shifting and responsive and what appears to be reality at any one place or time is shaped by our manner of looking and living, by our embodied locations in culture and history.

Alternative ways of knowing and designing are not infinite in number. Nor are they only portable costumes that authors, or architects, can easily adopt and discard from project to project. Limited in number, they arise from particular personal and social histories in particular locations and contexts and they have consequences. Increasingly, architects and planners recognize that there is no single, universal answer; nor should there be one. Contextualism, regionalism, historic preservation, and sustainable architecture all reflect the acceptance of multiplicity and the rediscovery of the connections between geographical and cultural location and design. Around the world architects are pursuing alternatives to the universalism of modern architecture,

OPPOSITE: "Transit" (Pier Augusto Breccia, oil on canvas)

using materials and design to adapt to local climatic conditions, drawing upon local culture, history, religion, and tradition.

The 35-year-long career of the Indian architect Balkrishna Doshi reflects an increasing attentiveness to climate, culture, and history in a manner that does not reject Modernism but adapts and modifies it. Doshi was an apprentice to Le Corbusier, working primarily on the High Court Building in Chandigarh. After designing several of his own buildings, in the 1960s, Doshi invited Louis Kahn to design the Indian Institute of Management in Ahmedabad and grew to know him as well. In the 1970s, after a phase of designing mass housing projects of up to 3,000 dwellings, Doshi began to travel extensively in India, studying traditional architecture and religion and questioning some of his earlier premises. "I observed a character and quality that my Functionalist outlook could not fully comprehend. I was convinced that in these places much more than physical issues were at work. The experiences touched something deeper than the skin – it was as if all the living forces were at work. Life itself was celebrated in that architecture" (Doshi 1992, p33). As Doshi noticed dimensions of architecture pertaining to ritual, to psychic and spiritual experience, he began incorporating them into his own work.

For the campus and buildings of the Indian Institute of Management in Bangalore, which he designed in collaboration with Joseph Allen Stein, Jai Rattan Bhalla, and Achyut Kanvinde, Doshi studied the internal courtyards and covered passageways of the sixteenth-century capital of Fatehpur Sikri near Agra and the southern temple cities like Madurai. He located the academic areas (library, lecture halls, classrooms, administrative and faculty spaces) in relatively small buildings around several courts and terraces of different dimensions and qualities and linked them with covered and uncovered walkways, sometimes three-stories high. The dormitories, also set around courts, are located at an angle to the academic areas. In this complex of buildings, open spaces and partly open spaces, there is no single axis; instead one's path is guided by views and vistas (Curtis 1983, p29).

The construction is a simple, standardized system of poured-in-place concrete for posts, frames and trellises and a wall system of blocks of local granite. Plantings, the patterns of light and shadow thrown up by the lattices and the changing views make for a richness of experience. The rich variety of indoor and outdoor spaces for walking and for pausing are a generous invitation to spontaneous activity and the sense of ambi-

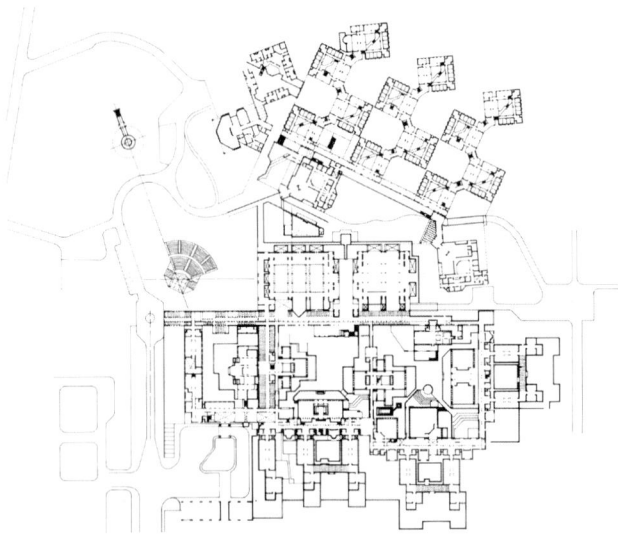

Ground floor plan, Indian Institute of Management, Bangalore, India (Balkrishna Doshi)

Courtyard and gallery

guity of what is indoors and what is outdoors adds further variety to the experience.

The absence of a dominant axis allows easily for future building. Doshi's openness to serendipity and to unforeseen opportunities and his rejection of architecture as an isolated, pristine object are well illustrated by the School of Architecture at Ahmedabad. There he intended the appearance of incompleteness to be an invitation to grow and, after construction was complete, he left the small site office in place, thinking it might be useful. It came to be used as a canteen.

Acceptance of multiplicity and an open-ended approach make the process of design and planning one of discovery, not imposition. Various possible designs for a particular project, which respond to different needs and desires, are not expected to be immediately apparent or to be imposed from on high. They require *uncovering*. What seems so obvious as a circumstance or an answer is only one of several possible descriptions. These other descriptions or answers become apparent as we adopt other view points or as we uncover, beneath the "obvious," other circumstances. This process has been described in a similar fashion by the physicist David Bohm and the architect Hugo Häring. Bohm referred to the "implicate" order, within or beneath the "explicate" order, which requires discovery. In his confrontations with Le Corbusier at CIAM in the 1920s Häring also described a process of discovery while Corbusier insisted, at that time and successfully, on a single set of "rules" or principles for modern architecture to follow.

Openness and multiplicity in the practice of architecture become ways of acting and interacting. Material is drawn from the different locations and different insights of those who participate in the process by inviting the contributions of clients and users in a forum that acknowledges the significance of their experiences and ideas. In this collaborative work among professionals and non-professionals, there is no longer one kind of knowledge or one answer generated by the professionals. Instead different forms of knowledge, all located in particular individuals and generated by their particular experiences, are contributed (Schneekloth and Shibley 1995). This is what took place in the design of the surgery by Penoyre and Prasad, the Lambeth Community Care Centre and the rebuilding of St. Mary's by Cullinan Architects. It continues to take place every few weeks in the storefront design workshops held in the Bronx by Nos Quedamos.

The absence of a foundation or a source of certainty can be troubling in a culture so accustomed to believing in an ultimate truth. ". . . we have not been able to disentangle ourselves from the extremes of absolutism and nihilism and to take seriously the possibilities inherent in a mindful, open-ended stance toward human experience" (Varela et al 1991, p235). This open-ended attitude is needed among participants when the design solution is not known in advance but is to be discovered collaboratively, sometimes working through a high degree of uncertainty. Differences of opinion, outright conflict and struggles to come to decisions will be common, requiring tolerance and patience from all participants. A certain degree of humility on the part of the architect is needed, s/he is no longer all knowing but draws knowledge and *in*sight from listening to others. Listening suggests a process whose outcome, at the beginning, is uncertain, whose identity at first may be illusive.

The future is not fully determined in advance; it is open. Insofar as it can be modelled mathematically, it has to be modelled in terms of chaotic dynamics. And this chaos, openness, spontaneity and freedom of nature provide the matrix for evolutionary creativity. (Rupert Sheldrake 1990, p71)

Note

1 Now virtual reality appears to offer the ultimate dematerialization of buildings and bodies: there they do not exist at all physically but as moving images that we *think* we are occupying. For some architects cyberspace holds the potential to allow us finally to transcend the physical world (Franck 1995; Spiller 1998). Michael Benedikt (1991) refers to this desire as "architecture's self-dematerialization."

References

Ahrentzen, Sherry and Linda Groat. Rethinking architectural education: Patriarchal conventions and alternative visions from the perspectives of women faculty. *Journal of Architecture and Planning Research*. 9:2, Summer 1992:1-17.

Benedikt, Michael. Introduction. In Michael Benedikt (ed) *Cyberspace: First Steps*. Cambridge, Mass.: MIT Press, 1991.

Bohm, David J. *Wholeness and the Implicate Order*. London: Routledge & Kegan Paul, 1980.

Bohm, David J. A new theory of the relationship of mind and matter. *Journal of the American Society for Psychical Research*. 80:2, 1986.

Bordo, Susan R. *The Flight to Objectivity: Essays on Cartesianism and Culture*. Albany: State University of New York Press, 1987.

Brand, Stewart. *How Buildings Learn: What Happens After They're Built*. New York: Viking, 1994.

Brodribb, Somer. *Nothing Mat(t)ers: A Feminist Critique of Postmodernism*. Melbourne, Australia: Spinfex Press, 1992.

Capra, Fritjof and David Steindl-Rast. *Belonging to the Universe: Explorations on the Frontiers of Science and Spirituality*. New York: HarperCollins, 1992.

Curtis, William. *Balkrishna Doshi: An Architecture for India*. New York: Rizzoli, 1988.

Doshi, Balkrishna V. Brahmand: Between the built and the unbuilt. In Maija Karkkainen (ed) *Functionalism: Utopia or the Way Forward*. Jyvaskyla, Sweden: Alvar Aalto Symposium, 1992.

Edelman, Gerald M. *Bright Mind, Brilliant Fire: On the Matter of the Mind*. New York: Basic Books, 1992.

Franck, Karen A. Questioning the American dream. In Rose Gilroy and Roberta Woods (eds) *Housing Women*. London: Routledge, 1994a.

Franck, Karen A. Types are us. In Karen A. Franck and Lynda H. Schneekloth (eds) *Ordering Space: Types in Architecture and Design*. New York: Van Nostrand Reinhold, 1994b.

Franck, Karen A. When I enter virtual reality, what body will I leave behind? *Architectural Design*, Profile 119, 1995.

Franck, Karen A. and Sherry Ahrentzen. *New Households, New Housing*. New York: Van Nostrand Reinhold, 1989.

Futagawa, Yukio. *Steven Holl: GA Document Extra 06*. Tokyo: A.D.A Edita, 1996.

Griffin, Susan. *The Eros of Everyday Life*. New York: Doubleday, 1995.

Holl, Steven. Pre-theoretical ground. In Michel Jacques and Anette Neve (eds) *Steven Holl*. Zurich: Artemis Press, 1993.

Holl, Steven. *Intertwining*. New York: Princeton Architectural Press, 1996.

Jones, Tom, William Petus and Michael Pyatok. *Good Neighbors: Affordable Family Housing*. New York: McGraw Hill, 1997.

Kazi, Ashraf and James Belluardo. *An Architecture of Independence: The Making of Modern South Asia*. New York: The Architectural League of New York, 1998.

Kurokawa, Kisho. *Each One a Hero: The Philosophy of Symbiosis*. Tokyo: Kodansha International, 1998.

Levin, David Michael. *The Listening Self: Personal Growth, Social Change and the Closure of Metaphysics*. London: Routledge, 1989.

Merleau-Ponty, Maurice. *The Visible and the Invisible*, trans. Alphonso Lingis. Evanston, Ill.: Northwestern University Press, 1968.

Pérez-Gómez, Alberto. *Architecture and the Crisis of Modern Science*. Cambridge, Mass.: MIT Press, 1983.

Pérez-Gómez, Alberto. Introduction. In Steven Holl, *Intertwining*. New York: Princeton Architectural Press, 1996.

Powell, Kenneth. *Edward Cullinan Architects*. London: Academy Editions, 1995.

Schneekloth, Lynda and Robert Shibley. *Placemaking: The Art and Practice of Building Communities*. New York: John Wiley, 1995.

Searle, John. *The Mystery of Consciousness*. New York: The New York Review of Books, 1997.

Semper, Gottfried. *The Four Elements of Architecture and Other Writings*, trans. Harry Francis Mallgrave and Wolfgang Herrmann. Cambridge: Cambridge University Press, 1989.

Sheldrake, Rupert. *The Presence of the Past: Morphic Resonance and the Habits of Nature*. London: Collins, 1988.

Sheldrake, Rupert. *The Rebirth of Nature: New Science and the Revival of Animism*. London: Rider, 1990.

Spiller, Neil. *Digital Dreams*. Zurich: Artemis Press, 1998.

Stoner, Jill. The party wall as the architecture of sharing. In Karen A. Franck and Sherry Ahrentzen (eds) *New Households, New Housing*. New York: Van Nostrand Reinhold, 1989.

Tuan, Yi Fu. *Segmented Worlds and Self: Group Life and Individual Consciousness*. Minneapolis, Minn.: University of Minnesota Press, 1982.

Varela, Francisco J., Evan Thompson and Eleanor Rosch. *The Embodied Mind: Cognitive Science and Human Experience*. Cambridge, Mass.: MIT Press, 1991.

Wright, Gwendolyn. Spaces for worship, places for community. *New York Times*, January 17, 1999.

Zohar, Danah and Ian Marshal. *The Quantum Society: Mind, Physics and a New Social Vision*. London: Flamingo, 1993.

Credits

Photographs were taken by the authors unless otherwise noted.

Preface p4 Storefront for Art and Architecture, Steven Holl and Vito Aconci (Paul Warchol); p8 Screen, Eileen Gray (courtesy of The Museum of Modern Art, New York, Guimard Fund)

Chapter 1. Inside, Outside and Inside Out p11 "House", Rachel Whiteread (John Davies); p14 "Architectural Outlooks," Nils Ole-Lund (courtesy of the artist, from *Nils-Ole Lund: Collage Architecture*, Ernst & Sohn, 1990); p15 "Icon #1" and p16 "Lost City", Nancy Wolf (courtesy of the artist, from *Nancy Wolf: Hidden Cities, Hidden Longings*, Academy Editions, 1996); p18 "Piazza", Giacometti (David Heald, courtesy of Solomon R. Guggenheim Foundation, New York); Alcove off living room, E.1027, Eileen Gray (courtesy of The Museum of Modern Art, New York); p19 "The Pleasures of the Door," from *Frances Ponge: Selected Poems*, courtesy of Wake Forest University Press; p23 "Grandmother's Kitchen," Frances Downing and Tom Hubka (courtesy of the artists, from *Remembrance and the Making of Places*, Texas A&M University Press, forthcoming)

Chapter 2. From the Body p40 Cowshed at Gut Garkau farm, Hugo Haring (courtesy of Peter Blundell Jones, prepared for *Hans Scharoun*, Phaidon Press, 1997); p41 Reading area, Exeter Academy Library, Louis Kahn (David Elwell); NSCAP Head Start and Lexington Play Care, Gail Sullivan Associates (Greig Cranna); p42 Rethinking waiting and working, proposals by Galen Cranz (courtesy of David Robinson, from *The Chair: Rethinking Body, Culture and Design*, Norton, 1998); p45 Birthing pool, Lugo di Romagna, R. Bianca Lepori (Enzo Esposito); p48 E.1027 plans, Eileen Gray (courtesy of Stefan Hecker and Christian F. Muller, from *Eileen Gray*, Editorial Gustavo Gili, 1996; p48 Apartment, rue de Chateaubriand, Eileen Gray (drawing and photograph courtesy of Eileen Gray Archive); p49 Tea table, E. 1027, (courtesy of Eileen Gray Archive); p50 Shiranui Psychiatric Hospital and Stress Care Center, Itsuko Hasegawa, View from the waterfront (Hideaki Arizumi) Patients' room (Tonio Ohashi); p51 Shiranui Psychiatric Hospital and Stress Care Center, Itsuko Hasegawa, Balconies facing (photograph by Glynis Berry)

Chapter 3. The Animism of Architecture p54 Shonandai Cultural Centre, Fujisawa City, Japan, Itsuko Hasegawa (Glynis Berry); p58 Traditional roof, Japan (Andrea Ricci); p60 Kasai Rinkai Koen, Yoshio Taniguchi (Andrea Ricci); p62 Shells in a concrete floor, Cona Village, Itsuko Hasegawa (Glynis Berry); p63 Kresge Auditorium, Eero Saarinen (Cinzia Abbate); Yale Center for Breitish Art Studies, Loius Kahn (David Elwell); p64 Entrance to the Louvre, I.M. Pei (David Elwell); p65 "The Fashion of Architecture" (courtesy of Nils-Ole Lund, from *Nils-Ole Lund: Collage Architecture*, Ernst & Sohn, 1990); Asajigahar Rest Area, Itsuko Hasegawa (Tomio Ohashi); p66 Shonandai Cultural Center, Itsuko Hasegawa (Glynis Berry); Makuhari Housing, Steven Holl (Paul Warchol); Con Village, Itsuko Hasegawa (Glynis Berry); p67 Paley Park, Zion & Breen (David Elwell); Fountain at Centre Pompidou, Niki de Sainte Phalle and Jean Tinguely (David Elwell); p69 Willowbrook Green Apartments, Ena Dubnoff (Jim Simmons, ADZ Photography); p75 Indian Institute of Management, trellises, Balkrishna Doshi (John Panikar); p77 Beacon High School ceramica studio, Gail Sullivan Associates (Greig Cranna)

Chapter 4. Space Therapy p80 This passage and all other excerpts from Paul Valery, *Eupalinos or the Architect*, courtesy of the Oxford University Press; p85 and 86 Walworth Road Surgery, Penoyre & Prasad (photographs by Dennis Gilbert) p101 Turtle Creek House, Antoine Predock, View from the garden (Timothy Hursley), View from the street (Robert Reck)

Chapter 5. Product and Process p105 "First the Building and Then the Site", Nile-Ole Lund (courtesy of the artist, from *Nils-Ole Lund: Collage Architecture*, Ernst & Sohn, 1990)

Chapter 6. Balancing Opposites p125 "Implosion," Nancy Wolf (courtesy of the artist, from *Nancy Wolf: Hidden Cities, Hidden Longings*, Academy Editions, 1996); p128 Battery Park City (Tony Holmes); p134 St. Mary's, Barnes, Edward Cullinan Architects (photographs by Teresa Howard); p139 "Transit," Pier Augusto Breccia (courtesy of the artist, from *Il linguaggio sospeso dell'autocoscienza*, Di Renzo Editore, 1999); p140 Indian Institute of Management, Balkrishna Doshi (photograph by the architect)

Karen A. Franck is a professor in the School of Architecture and the Department of Humanities and Social Science at the New Jersey Institute of Technology. She received her PhD in environmental psychology from the City University of New York in 1978. In teaching and writing Karen finds opportunities to explore the many connections between human experience and the built environment. Her other books include *New Households, New Housing* edited with Sherry Ahrentzen, *Types and the Ordering of Space* edited with Lynda Schneekloth and *Nancy Wolf: Hidden Cities, Hidden Longings.*

R. Bianca Lepori is a registered architect practicing in Rome. She received her architecture degree from the University of Genoa in 1975. Bianca sees her role as one of space therapist and has chosen to work on small scale projects with the people who will use them. So far she has concentrated on home environments and institutional structures for natural childbirth. Her book *La nascita e i suoi luoghi* outlines innovative proposals for the design and furnishing of birth places. The pool she designed for relaxation, labor and delivery is now used in several hospitals in Italy.